Foundations of F#

Robert Pickering

apress®

Foundations of F#

Copyright © 2007 by Robert Pickering

ISBN-13: 978-1-4842-2036-8

ISBN-10: 1-59059-757-5

9 8 7 6 5 4 3 2 1

Lead Editors: James Huddleston, Ewan Buckingham
Technical Reviewer: Don Syme
Editorial Board: Steve Anglin, Ewan Buckingham, Gary Cornell, Jason Gilmore, Jonathan Gennick,
    Jonathan Hassell, Chris Mills, Matthew Moodie, Jeffrey Pepper, Dominic Shakeshaft, Matt Wade
Project Manager: Elizabeth Seymour
Copy Edit Manager: Nicole Flores
Copy Editor: Kim Wimpsett
Assistant Production Director: Kari Brooks-Copony
Production Editor: Laura Cheu
Compositor: Lynn L'Heureux
Proofreader: Elizabeth Berry
Indexer: Broccoli Information Management
Artist: April Milne
Cover Designer: Kurt Krames
Manufacturing Director: Tom Debolski

Distributed to the book trade worldwide by Springer-Verlag New York, Inc., 233 Spring Street, 6th Floor, New York, NY 10013. Phone 1-800-SPRINGER, fax 201-348-4505, e-mail orders-ny@springer-sbm.com, or visit http://www.springeronline.com.

For information on translations, please contact Apress directly at 2855 Telegraph Avenue, Suite 600, Berkeley, CA 94705. Phone 510-549-5930, fax 510-549-5939, e-mail info@apress.com, or visit http://www.apress.com.

The source code for this book is available to readers at http://www.apress.com in the Source Code/ Download section.

For Susan and for Jim

Contents at a Glance

Contents

Foreword

A new language needs a simple and clear introductory book that makes it accessible to a broad range of programmers. In *Foundations of F#*, Robert Pickering has captured the essential elements that the professional programmer needs to master in order to get started with F# and .NET. As the designer of F#, I am thrilled to see Robert take up the challenge of presenting F# in a way that is accessible to a wide audience.

F# combines the simplicity and elegance of typed functional programming with the strengths of the .NET platform. Although typed functional programming is relatively new to many programmers and thus requires some learning, in many ways it makes programming simpler. This is mainly because F# programs tend to be built from compositional, correct foundational elements, and type inference makes programs shorter and clearer. Robert first introduces the three foundational paradigms of F#: functional programming, imperative programming, and object-oriented programming, and he shows how F# lets you use them in concert. He then shows how this multiparadigm approach can be used in conjunction with the .NET libraries to perform practical programming tasks such as GUI implementation, data access, and distributed programming. He then introduces some of the particular strengths of F# in the area of "language-oriented" programming.

F# is a practical language, and Robert has ensured that the reader is well equipped with information needed to use the current generation of F# tools well. Many computer professionals first encounter functional programming through a short section of the undergraduate curriculum and often leave these courses uncertain about the real-world applicability of the techniques they have been taught. Similarly, some people encounter functional programming only in its purest forms and are uncertain whether it is possible to combine the elements of the paradigm with other approaches to programming and software engineering. Robert has helped remove this uncertainty: typed functional programming is practical, easy to learn, and a powerful addition to the .NET programming landscape.

F# is also a research language, used in part to deliver recent advances in language design, particularly those that work well with .NET. It combines a stable and dependable base language with more recent extensions. Robert's book describes F# 2.0, the latest release of the language at the time of writing. The rest of the F# team and I are very grateful to Robert's many suggestions, and the language has been greatly improved through this. I hope you enjoy reading this book as much as I enjoyed being its technical reviewer.

Don Syme
Cambridge, UK

About the Author

ROBERT PICKERING was born in Sheffield, in the north of England, but a fascination with computers and the "madchester" indie music scene led him to cross the Pennines and study computer science at the University of Manchester.

After finishing his degree, he moved to London to catch the tail end of the dot-com boom working at marchFirst; then he moved to Avanade to do some more serious work. At Avanade, he specialized in creating enterprise applications using the .NET Framework, and he got the chance to work on projects in Denmark, Holland, and Belgium; he finally settled in Paris, France, where he lives now with his wife and their two cats. He has been writing about F# almost since it began, and the F# wiki on his `http://www.strangelights.com` web site is among the most popular F# web sites.

He currently works for LexiFi, which is an innovative ISV that specializes in software for analyzing and processing complex financial derivatives—products such as swaps and options. LexiFi has pioneered the use of functional programming in finance in order to develop a rigorous formalism for representing financial instruments.

About the Technical Reviewer

DON SYME is a researcher at Microsoft Research, Cambridge. Born in Toowoomba, Australia, his love for programming was sparked by family and teachers at age 10. He studied at the Australian National University and the University of Cambridge, becoming an expert in the application of automated proof to real-world problems, participating in the team that formally verified the correctness of aspects of the Intel Pentium IV floating-point circuits. Joining Microsoft in 1998, he saw the opportunity to enhance and transform the design of the .NET Framework by including elements of functional programming, beginning with the addition of generics to C# 2.0 and the .NET common language runtime, a project he saw through to completion in Visual Studio 2005. In 2003 he began the design and implementation of F#, which has now become the premier functional programming language for the .NET Framework. He continues to be a driving force in the design, implementation, and enhancement of the language.

Acknowledgments

If there is one person I feel I should be acknowledging, it is Jim Huddleston, the book's editor. Jim was there from the book's beginning. He helped me get it commissioned, he aided me in working out the contents, he gave me much encouragement and constructive criticism, and he showed great skill as an editor. Sadly, Jim died on February 25, 2007, just as the book was entering its final stages of production. Even though I never met Jim in person, never even talked to him on the telephone, I feel a real sense of loss knowing he is gone. My thoughts are with his family at this very sad time, and I'm very disappointed that I never got to meet him in person and that he never saw the finished book.

Sadly, Jim's was not the only death that coincided with the closing stages of writing this book. On March 28, 2007, my uncle Gordon lost his battle with cancer. He was a great lover of life, with many interests. He was a maths teacher who was an avid *New Scientist* reader with a deep interest in maths and science and a passion for music; he was a talented musician who played many gigs across Orkney and the north of Scotland. He will be greatly missed by me and all my family.

I feel very lucky to have worked on the project with my technical reviewer, Don Syme, who went above and beyond the cause by contributing many ideas to the book, helping improve the implementations of many of the samples, and giving me much encouragement. I'd also like to thank all the Apress staff who took part in creating this book, especially Elizabeth Seymour, Kim Wimpsett, and Laura Cheu.

I'd also like to thank Don in another capacity, as the creator and developer of F#, along with James Margetson and all the others at Microsoft Research, Cambridge, who worked on F#. Specifically, I'd like to thank them for their hard work on the compiler, and I'd like to let them know that their quick response times to bugs and queries have been very much appreciated. I'd also like to thank all the F# community, in particular Christopher J. Barwick (a.k.a. optionsScalper), who did so much to boost the F# community when he created the hubFS (http://cs.hubfs.net).

I'd like to thank all the people who had to put up with me while I wrote this book. My family: Mum, Dad, and Sister had to put up with me sneaking off to write whenever I went to visit them. Also, my work colleagues often suffered grumpy mornings after late nights of F# hacking and writing: Arnaud, Aurélie, Baptiste, Buuloc, Daniel, Dennis, Emmanuel, Fabrice, François, Frederik, Guillaume, Ibrahima, Jean-Marc, Laurent, Lionel, Oussama, Patrice, Philippe, Regis, Sebastien J., Sebastien P., Stefaan, Stefany, and Stephane—I thank you all. Last but by no means least, I'd like to thank my wife, Susan, for all the help and support she has given; without her understanding, this book could never have happened.

Preface: The Story of the Book

In 2003 I was looking for a way to process IL, the intermediate language into which all .NET languages are compiled. At the time, .NET was fairly new, and there weren't a lot of options for doing this. I quickly realized that the best option at the time, and probably still today, was an API called Abstract IL (AbsIL). AbsIL was written in a language called F#, and I decided to use this language to write a small wrapper around AbsIL so I could extract the information I needed from a DLL in a form more usable from C#. But a funny thing happened while writing the wrapper: even though in those days writing F# was a little hard going because the compiler was far from polished, I found that I actually enjoyed programming in F# so much that when I had finished the wrapper, I didn't want to go back to C#. In short, I was hooked.

At the time I was working as a consultant, so I needed to regularly check out new technologies and their APIs; therefore, I got to do all my experimentation using F#. At the same time, people were talking about a new way to communicate on the Web, and a new word was about to enter the English language: *blog*. I decided I should have a blog because anyone who was anyone in technology seemed to have one, so I created http://www.strangelights.com (where my blog can still be found to this today). This was later followed by a wiki about F#, which can also be found at http://www.strangelights.com and which continues to be very popular.

My job meant I had to do a lot of traveling, so this meant quite a lot of time in hotel rooms or on trains and planes, and I came to view this time as time to try out stuff in F#. So, I ended up exchanging quite a lot emails with Don Syme, and then eventually we met. We went for a beer in the pub where Watson and Crick went after they first pieced together the structure of DNA. Will people talk about the pub were Syme and Pickering first met years from now? Errrm, perhaps not. Anyway, all this led me to the point where I was wondering what I should do with my newfound knowledge of F# and functional programming. About this time a guy called Jim Huddleston mailed the F# mailing list and asked whether anyone would like to write a book about F#. Well, I just couldn't help myself—it sounded like the job for me.

So, with much help and encouragement from Jim, I started writing the book. Some of it was written in Paris where I was living on the weekends, some of it was written in Brussels were I was working during the week, and much of it was written while I was traveling between the two on the Thalys (the high-speed train between France and Belgium). A little of it was written as far north as the Orkney Islands in Scotland while visiting my aunt and uncle, and a little of the reviewing was done while meeting my in-laws in New Zealand. Finally, thanks to the contacts I made while writing the book, I got a new job working for the prestigious ISV LexiFi.

It has been great fun watching the language evolve over time and turn from the beginnings of a language into the fully fledged and highly usable language you see today. I hope reading this book changes your life as much as writing it has changed mine.

■ ■ ■

CHAPTER 1

Introduction

This introductory chapter will address some of the major questions you may have about F# and functional programming.

What Is Functional Programming?

Functional programming (FP) is the oldest of the three major programming paradigms. The first FP language, IPL, was invented in 1955, about a year before Fortran. The second, Lisp, was invented in 1958, a year before Cobol. Both Fortran and Cobol are imperative (or procedural) languages, and their immediate success in scientific and business computing made imperative programming the dominant paradigm for more than 30 years. The rise of the object-oriented (OO) paradigm in the 1970s and the gradual maturing of OO languages ever since have made OO programming the most popular paradigm today.

Despite the vigorous and continuous development of powerful FP languages (SML, OCaml, Haskell, and Clean, among others) and FP-like languages (APL and Lisp being the most successful for real-world applications) since the 1950s, FP remained a primarily academic pursuit until recently. The early commercial success of imperative languages made it the dominant paradigm for decades. Object-oriented languages gained broad acceptance only when enterprises recognized the need for more sophisticated computing solutions. Today, the promise of FP is finally being realized to solve even more complex problems—as well as the simpler ones.

Pure functional programming views all programs as collections of functions that accept arguments and return values. Unlike imperative and object-oriented programming, it allows no side effects and uses recursion instead of loops for iteration. The functions in a functional program are very much like mathematical functions because they do not change the state of the program. In the simplest terms, once a value is assigned to an identifier, it never changes, functions do not alter parameter values, and the results that functions return are completely new values. In typical underlying implementations, once a value is assigned to an area in memory, it does not change. To create results, functions copy values and then change the copies, leaving the original values free to be used by other functions and eventually be thrown away when no longer needed. (This is where the idea of garbage collection originated.)

The mathematical basis for pure functional programming is elegant, and FP therefore provides beautiful, succinct solutions for many computing problems, but its stateless and recursive nature makes the other paradigms convenient for handling many common programming tasks. However, one of F#'s great strengths is that you can use multiple paradigms and mix them to solve problems in the way you find most convenient.

Why Is Functional Programming Important?

When people think of functional programming, they often view its statelessness as a fatal flaw, without considering its advantages. One could argue that since an imperative program is often 90 percent assignment and since a functional program has no assignment, a functional program could be 90 percent shorter. However, not many people are convinced by such arguments or attracted to the ascetic world of stateless recursive programming, as John Hughes pointed out in his classic paper "Why Functional Programming Matters":

> *The functional programmer sounds rather like a medieval monk, denying himself the pleasures of life in the hope that it will make him virtuous.*

John Hughes, Chalmers University of Technology
(http://www.math.chalmers.se/~rjmh/Papers/whyfp.html)

To see the advantages of functional programming, you must look at what FP permits, rather than what it prohibits. For example, functional programming allows you to treat functions themselves as values and pass them to other functions. This might not seem all that important at first glance, but its implications are extraordinary. Eliminating the distinction between data and function means that many problems can be more naturally solved. Functional programs can be shorter and more modular than corresponding imperative and object-oriented programs.

In addition to treating functions as values, functional languages offer other features that borrow from mathematics and are not commonly found in imperative languages. For example, functional programming languages often offer *curried functions*, where arguments can be passed to a function one at a time and, if all arguments are not given, the result is a residual function waiting for the rest of its parameters. It's also common for functional languages to offer type systems with much better "power-to-weight ratios," providing more performance and correctness for less effort.

Further, a function might return multiple values, and the calling function is free to consume them as it likes. I'll discuss these ideas, along with many more, in detail and with plenty of examples, in Chapter 3.

What Is F#?

Functional programming is the best approach to solving many thorny computing problems, but pure FP isn't suitable for general-purpose programming. So, FP languages have gradually embraced aspects of the imperative and OO paradigms, remaining true to the FP paradigm but incorporating features needed to easily write any kind of program. F# is a natural successor on this path. It is also much more than just an FP language.

Some of the most popular functional languages, including OCaml, Haskell, Lisp, and Scheme, have traditionally been implemented using custom runtimes, which leads to problems such as lack of interoperability. F# is a general-purpose programming language for .NET, a general-purpose runtime. F# smoothly integrates all three major programming paradigms. With F#, you can choose whichever paradigm works best to solve problems in the most effective way. You can do pure FP, if you're a purist, but you can easily combine functional, imperative, and object-oriented styles in the same program and exploit the strengths of each paradigm. Like other typed functional languages, F# is strongly typed but also uses inferred typing, so programmers don't need to spend time explicitly specifying types unless an ambiguity exists. Further, F# seamlessly integrates with the .NET Framework base class library (BCL). Using the BCL in F# is as simple as using it in C# or Visual Basic (and maybe even simpler).

F# was modeled on Objective Caml (OCaml), a successful object-oriented FP language, and then tweaked and extended to mesh well technically and philosophically with .NET. It fully embraces .NET and enables users to do everything that .NET allows. The F# compiler can compile for all implementations of the Common Language Infrastructure (CLI), it supports .NET generics without changing any code, and it even provides for inline Intermediate Language (IL) code. The F# compiler not only produces executables for any CLI but can also run on any environment that has a CLI, which means F# is not limited to Windows but can run on Linux, Apple Mac OS X, and OpenBSD. (Chapter 2 covers what it's like to run F# on Linux.)

The F# compiler can be integrated into Visual Studio, supporting IntelliSense expression completion and automatic expression checking. It also gives tooltips to show what types have been inferred for expressions. Programmers often comment that this really helps bring the language to life.

F# was invented by Dr. Don Syme and is now the product of a small but highly dedicated team he heads at Microsoft Research (MSR) in Cambridge, England. However, F# is not just a research or academic language. It is used for a wide variety of real-world applications, whose number is growing rapidly.

Although other FP languages run on .NET, F# has established itself as the de facto .NET functional programming language because of the quality of its implementation and its superb integration with .NET and Visual Studio.

No other .NET language is as easy to use and as flexible as F#!

Who Is Using F#?

F# has a strong presence inside Microsoft, both in MSR and throughout the company as a whole. Ralf Herbrich, coleader of MSR's Applied Games Group, which specializes in machine learning techniques, is typical of F#'s growing number of fans:

> *The first application was parsing 110GB of log data spread over 11,000 text files in over 300 directories and importing it into a SQL database. The whole application is 90 lines long (including comments!) and finished the task of parsing the source files and import- ing the data in under 18 hours; that works out to a staggering 10,000 log lines processed per second! Note that I have not optimized the code at all but written the application in the most obvious way. I was truly astonished as I had planned at least a week of work for both coding and running the application.*

> *The second application was an analysis of millions of feedbacks. We had developed the model equations and I literally just typed them in as an F# program; together with the reading-data-from-SQL-database and writing-results-to-MATLAB-data-file the F# source code is 100 lines long (including comments). Again, I was astonished by the run- ning time; the whole processing of the millions of data items takes 10 minutes on a*

standard desktop machine. My C# reference application (from some earlier tasks) is almost 1,000 lines long and is no faster. The whole job from developing the model equations to having first real world data results took 2 days.

Ralf Herbrich, Microsoft Research
(http://blogs.msdn.com/dsyme/archive/2006/04/01/566301.aspx)

F# usage outside Microsoft is also rapidly growing. I asked Chris Barwick, who runs hubFS (http://cs.hubFS.net), a popular web site dedicated to F#, about why F# was now his language of choice, and he said this:

I've been in scientific and mathematics computing for more than 14 years. During that time, I have waited and hoped for a platform that would be robust in every manner. That platform has to provide effective tools that allow for the easy construction and usage of collateral and that makes a scientific computing environment effective. .NET represents a platform where IL gives rise to consistency across products. F# is the language that provides for competent scientific and mathematical computing on that platform. With these tools and other server products, I have a wide range of options with which to build complex systems at a very low cost of development and with very low ongoing costs to operate and to improve. F# is the cornerstone needed for advanced scientific computing.

Christopher J. Barwick, JJB Research (private email)

Finally, I talked to Jude O'Kelly, a software architect at Derivatives One, a company that sells financial modeling software, about why Derivatives One used F# in its products:

We tested our financial models in both C# and F#; the performance was about the same, but we liked the F# versions because of the succinct mathematical syntax. One of our problems with F# was the lack of information; we think this book improves this situation enormously.

Jude O'Kelly, Derivatives One (private email)

Who Is This Book For?

This book is aimed primarily at IT professionals who want to get up to speed quickly on F#. A working knowledge of the .NET Framework and some knowledge of either C# or Visual Basic would be nice, but it's not necessary. All you really need is some experience programming in any language to be comfortable learning F#.

Even complete beginners, who've never programmed before and are learning F# as their first computer language, should find this book very readable. Though it doesn't attempt to teach introductory programming per se, it does carefully present all the important details of F#.

What's Next?

This book teaches F#, by example, as a compiled language rather than a scripting language. By this I mean most examples are designed to be compiled with the `fsc.exe` compiler, either in Visual Studio or on a command line, rather than executed interactively with `fsi.exe`, the F# interactive environment. In reality, most examples will run fine either way.

Chapter 2 gives you just enough knowledge about setting up an F# development environment to get you going.

Chapters 3, 4, 5, and 6 cover the core F# syntax. I deliberately keep the code simple, because this will give you a better introduction to how the syntax works.

Chapter 7 looks at the core libraries distributed with F# to introduce you to their flavor and power, rather than to describe each function in detail. The F# online documentation (`http://research.microsoft.com/fsharp/manual/namespaces.html`) is the place to get the details.

Then you'll dive into how to use F# for the bread-and-butter problems of the working programmer. Chapter 8 covers user interface programming, Chapter 9 covers data access, and Chapter 10 covers how applications can take advantage of a network.

The final chapters take you through the topics you really need to know to master F#. Chapter 11 looks at support for creating little languages or domain-specific languages (DSLs), a powerful and very common programming pattern in F#. Chapter 12 covers the tools you can use to debug and optimize F# programs. Finally, Chapter 13 explores advanced interoperation issues.

■ ■ ■

CHAPTER 2

How to Obtain, Install, and Use F#

This chapter is designed to get you up and running with F# as quickly as possible. You'll look at how to obtain F#, how to install it on both Windows and Linux, and how to use the compiler in various ways. I'll also discuss what version of software the examples in this book were tested with and what extra software you might need to install.

Obtaining F#

You can download F# from the Microsoft Research F# Download page at `http://research.microsoft.com/fsharp/release.aspx`. The package includes various versions of the compiler, which are compatible with different versions of the CLR, `fsi.exe` (the F# interactive console), some F#-based parsing tools, the F# base class libraries, the F# documentation, and some F# samples.

Installing F# on Windows

Installing F# on Windows is straightforward. You need to be running as an account with system administrator privileges to install F#. Simply unzip the contents of the F# distribution to a temporary location, and then run the `InstallFSharp.msi` package, which is in the root of the distribution. The `.msi` should work whether or not Visual Studio 2003 or Visual Studio 2005 is installed.

If you'd prefer not to use an `.msi`, you can compile from the command line simply by unzipping to your preferred location and running `alternative-install.bat`, which will install the F# runtime libraries into the global assembly cache (GAC). You can also use this batch file to install F# against the Shared Source Common Language Infrastructure (SSCLI), more commonly known as Rotor, by using the `-sscli` command-line switch.

Note The SSCLI is a compressed archive of the source code for a working implementation of the ECMA CLI and the ECMA C# language specifications. This implementation builds and runs on Windows XP, and you can also compile and run it on other operating systems such as Linux or Mac OS X. This implementation is ideal if you really want to get under the covers and see what's going on; however, you may find it more diffi-cult to use than .NET, so you're probably best off sticking with .NET while reading this book.

If you use the `alternative-install.bat` batch file, Visual Studio integration will not be installed. For installing Visual Studio integration, two further batch files are available, `alternative-install-vs2003.bat` and `alternative-install-vs2005.bat`. Please note that at the time of this writing the free Express Editions of Visual Studio do not support plug-ins, so you cannot use F# integration with them.

Installing F# on Linux

It's difficult to write a simple guide to installing F# on Linux, because there are so many differ-ent distributions of Linux and so many ways you can configure them. The following are the steps that worked well for me running SUSE Linux on a single computer. I performed all these steps as the `root` account.

1. Install Mono using the packages provided with the SUSE Linux distribution; you can find these by searching for *mono* and then *sharp* in the Install Software dialog box available from the Computer menu.

2. Unpack the F# distribution, and copy the resulting files to `/usr/lib/fsharp`.

3. In the `/usr/lib/fsharp` directory, run `chmod +x install-mono.sh`.

4. Run the `dos2unix` tool on the text file `install-mono.sh`.

5. Still in the `/usr/lib/fsharp` directory, run the command `sh install-mono.sh`.

After performing those steps, I was able to use F# from any account from the command line by running `mono /usr/lib/fsharp/bin/fsc.exe`, followed by the command-line options. Obviously, this was inconvenient to run every time, so I created a shell script file in `/usr/bin` and as `fsc`:

```
#!/bin/sh
exec /usr/bin/mono $MONO_OPTIONS /usr/lib/fsharp/bin/fsc.exe "$@"
```

I then ran `chmod +x fsc` to give users permission to execute it. After this, running the F# compiler was as simple as typing `fsc` at the command line. The F# interactive compiler, `fsi.exe`, will also run under Linux, but on the installation I used at the time of this writing, I needed to use the `--no-gui` switch. The shell script for this is as follows:

```
#!/bin/sh
exec /usr/bin/mono $MONO_OPTIONS /usr/lib/fsharp/bin/fsi.exe --no-gui "$@"
```

Note I used SUSE Linux, available from `http://www.novell.com/linux/`, because I found it installed smoothly on real and virtual machines, requiring very little manual setup.

Using F# in Different Ways

F# programs are just text files, so you can use any text editor to create them. Just save your program with the extension `.fs`, and use `fsc.exe` to compile them. For example, if you had the following program in the text file `helloworld.fs`:

```
#light
print_endline "Hello World"
```

you could just run `fsc.exe helloworld.fs` to compile your program into `helloworld.exe`, which would output the following to the console:

```
Hello World
```

In my opinion, the easiest and quickest way to develop F# programs is in Visual Studio in conjunction with the F# interactive compiler (see Figure 2-1). You can type F# programs into the text editor, taking advantage of syntax highlighting and IntelliSense code completion; compile them into executables; and debug them interactively by setting breakpoints and pressing F5. Also, you can execute parts of your code interactively using F# interactive. Just highlight the code you want to execute, and press Alt+Enter; F# interactive will execute the code and show the results. This is great for testing snippets individually.

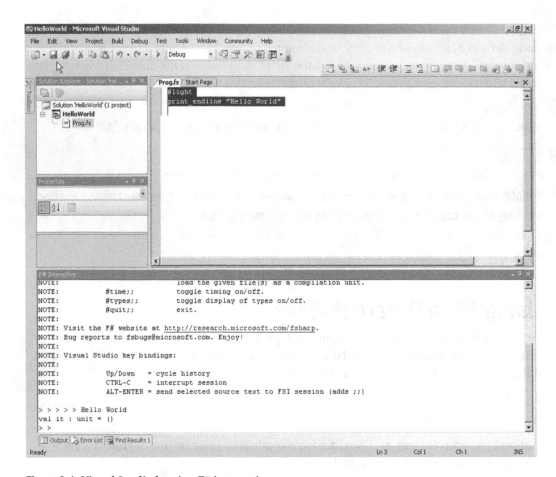

Figure 2-1. *Visual Studio hosting F# interactive*

■**Note** If you are not convinced you want to invest in a copy of Visual Studio, trial versions of this software are available at `https://www.tryvs2005.com`.

If you prefer, you can type your programs into the F# interactive console directly when it's running in stand-alone mode, as shown in Figure 2-2.

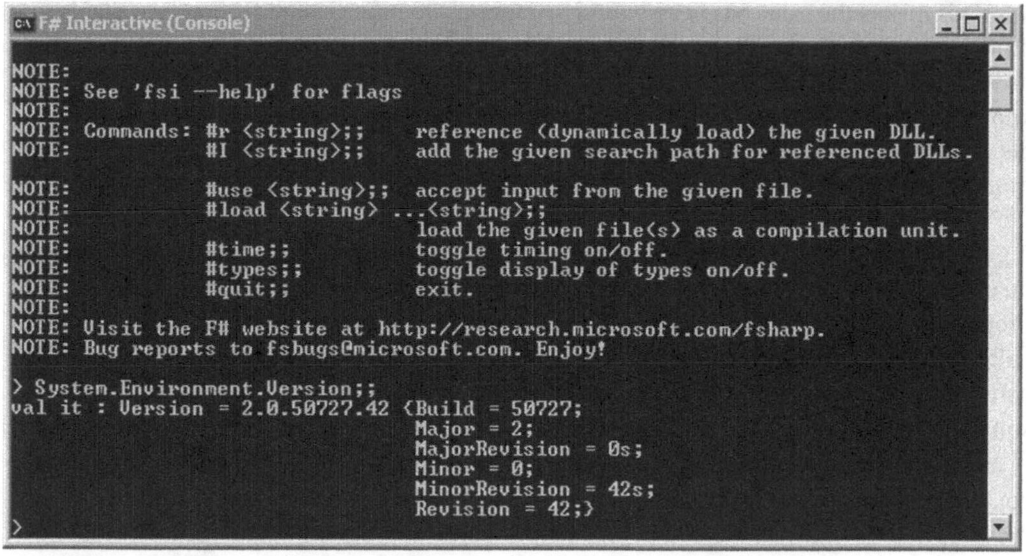

```
F# Interactive (Console)                                                    _ □ ×
NOTE:                                                                           ▲
NOTE: See 'fsi --help' for flags
NOTE:
NOTE: Commands: #r <string>;;      reference (dynamically load) the given DLL.
NOTE:            #I <string>;;      add the given search path for referenced DLLs.
NOTE:
NOTE:            #use <string>;;  accept input from the given file.
NOTE:            #load <string> ...<string>;;
NOTE:                             load the given file(s) as a compilation unit.
NOTE:            #time;;          toggle timing on/off.
NOTE:            #types;;         toggle display of types on/off.
NOTE:            #quit;;          exit.
NOTE:
NOTE: Visit the F# website at http://research.microsoft.com/fsharp.
NOTE: Bug reports to fsbugs@microsoft.com. Enjoy!

> System.Environment.Version;;
val it : Version = 2.0.50727.42 (Build = 50727;
                                 Major = 2;
                                 MajorRevision = 0s;
                                 Minor = 0;
                                 MinorRevision = 42s;
                                 Revision = 42;)
>                                                                               ▼
```

Figure 2-2. *The F# interactive console running in stand-alone mode*

When you use the interactive console, you type the code you want; then when you've completed a section, you use two semicolons (;;) to indicate that the compiler should compile and run it.

F# interactive responds to commands in two ways. If you bind a value to an identifier, it prints the name of the identifier and its type. So, typing the following into F# interactive:

```
> let i = 1 + 2;;
```

gives the following:

```
val i : int
```

However, if you just type a value into F# interactive, it will respond slightly differently. Typing the following into F# interactive:

```
> 1 + 2;;
```

gives the following:

```
val it : int = 3
```

This means the value has been bound to a special identifier, called it, that is available to other code within the F# interactive session. When any expression is evaluated at the top level, its value is also printed, after the equals sign; note the 3 in the previous example. As you get to know fsi.exe and F# in general, using F# interactive will become more and more useful for debugging programs and finding out how they work. (I discuss values, identifiers, and types in more detail in Chapter 3.)

You can get code completions by pressing Tab. I find this mode of working useful in testing short programs by copying and pasting them into the console or for checking properties on existing libraries. For example, in Figure 2-2 I checked the System.Environment.Version property. However, I find this mode inconvenient for creating longer programs since it's difficult to store the programs once they're coded; they have to be copied and pasted from the console. Using Visual Studio, even if you don't intend to just run them interactively, you can still easily execute snippets with Alt+Enter.

If you save your program with the .fsx extension instead of the .fs extension, you can run your programs interactively by right-clicking them and selecting the Run with F# Interactive menu option, as shown in Figure 2-3. This scripting style of programming is great for creating small programs to automate repetitive tasks. This way your program's configuration, such as the file paths it uses, can be stored inside regular strings in the program and can be quickly edited by the programmer using any text editor as needed.

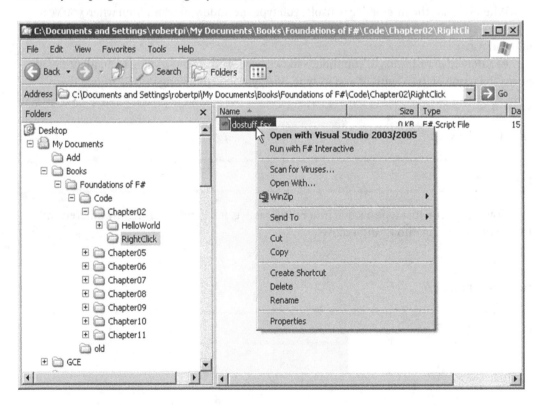

Figure 2-3. *Running an F# script by right-clicking it*

You can find more information about the F# programming tools and general programming tools for .NET in Chapter 11.

Installing the Software Used in This Book

The code in this book will focus on using fsc.exe, rather than fsi.exe. This is because although fsi.exe is great for testing code, running simple scripts, and running experiments, I believe fsc.exe is more useful for producing finished software. Since there's little difference between the syntax and the commands, most examples will work with little or no adaptation in fsi.exe, and I'll warn you when any changes are necessary.

All the samples in this book were created using .NET 2.0 running on Windows XP Professional. If you're using .NET 1.0 or 1.1, you'll experience problems with many of the samples because quite a few of them use classes and methods from the .NET 2.0 base class library (BCL) that aren't available in version 1.0 or 1.1.

The most common problem you will face when working with .NET 1.0 and 1.1 is that I use System.Collections.Generic.List, referred to as ResizeArray in F#, and System.Collections.Generic.Dictionary. You can always work around this by replacing these two classes with System.Collections.ArrayList and System.Collections.Hashtable, respectively. There may be other places where I use methods or classes not available in .NET 1.0 and 1.1, but generally you will be able to work around this with a little extra coding.

At the time of this writing, Mono shipped with its version of Framework 2.0, which the F# compiler targets by default; however, this was still in beta, with a production-quality version due to ship in mid-2007. A small subset of this book's examples has been tested on Mono 2.0, and the examples ran without problems.

A small number of examples use several other software libraries and packages. It's not necessary to immediately download and install all these software packages, but for specific examples, as listed in Table 2-1, you'll need to do this at some point.

Table 2-1. *Additional Software Used Within This Book*

Software	Used In	URL
.NET Framework 3.0	Chapter 8, Chapter 10	http://www.microsoft.com/downloads/details.aspx?FamilyId=10CC340B-F857-4A14-83F5-25634C3BF043&displaylang=en
SDK for .NET Framework 3.0	Chapter 8, Chapter 10	http://www.microsoft.com/downloads/details.aspx?familyid=C2B1E300-F358-4523-B479-F53D234CDCCF&displaylang=en
SQL Server 2005 Express Edition	Chapter 9	http://msdn.microsoft.com/vstudio/express/sql/register/default.aspx
SQL Server 2005 Samples	Chapter 9	http://www.microsoft.com/downloads/details.aspx?familyid=E719ECF7-9F46-4312-AF89-6AD8702E4E6E&displaylang=en
Microsoft .NET LINQ Preview (May 2006)	Chapter 9	http://www.microsoft.com/downloads/details.aspx?familyid=1e902c21-340c-4d13-9f04-70eb5e3dceea&displaylang=en
Windows Server 2003 Resource Kit Tools	Chapter 12	http://www.microsoft.com/downloads/details.aspx?FamilyID=9d467a69-57ff-4ae7-96ee-b18c4790cffd&DisplayLang=en
NUnit	Chapter 12	http://www.nunit.org/index.php?p=download

continued

Table 2-1. *Continued*

Software	Used In	URL
NProf	Chapter 12	http://www.mertner.com/confluence/display/NProf/Home
CLR Profiler for .NET 2.0	Chapter 12	http://www.microsoft.com/downloads/details.aspx?familyid=a362781c-3870-43be-8926-862b40aa0cd0&displaylang=en
Reflector	Chapter 12	http://www.aisto.com/roeder/dotnet/

Obviously, some of these links are a little long to type, so I've summarized them all at http://strangelights.com/FSharp/Foundations/default.aspx/FSharpFoundations.Downloads where I'll keep them updated.

Summary

This chapter described how to install and run F# and the different ways you can work with it. The following chapters will explain how to program with F#, starting in Chapter 3 with functional programming in F#.

CHAPTER 3

■ ■ ■

Functional Programming

You saw in Chapter 1 that pure functional programming treats functions as values, relies on recursion for looping, and does not allow changes to state. In this chapter, you'll survey the major language constructs of F# that support the functional programming paradigm.

Identifiers

Identifiers are the way you give names to values in F# so you can refer to them later in a program. You define an identifier using the keyword let followed by the name of the identifier, an equals sign, and an expression that specifies the value to which the identifier refers. An *expression* is any piece of code that represents a computation that will return a value. The following expression shows a value being assigned to an identifier:

```
let x = 42
```

To most people coming from an imperative programming background, this will look like a variable assignment. There are a lot of similarities, but there are key differences. In pure functional programming, once a value is assigned to an identifier, it never changes. This is why I will refer to them throughout this book as *identifiers* and not *variables*. You will see in the "Scope" section later in this chapter that, under some circumstances, you can redefine identifiers and that in imperative programming in F#, in some circumstances, the value of an identifier can change.

An identifier can refer to either a value or a function, and since F# functions are really values in their own right, this is hardly surprising. (I discuss this relationship in detail in the "Functions and Values" section later in this chapter.) This means F# has no real concept of a function name or parameter name; they are all just identifiers. You write a function definition the same way as a value identifier, except a function has two or more identifiers between the let keyword and the equals sign, as follows:

```
let raisePowerTwo x = x ** 2.0
```

The first identifier is the name of the function, raisePowerTwo, and the identifier that follows it is the name of the function's parameter, x.

Keywords

Most, if not all, programming languages have the concept of keywords. A *keyword* is a language token that the compiler reserves for special use. In F# you cannot use a keyword as an identifier name or a *type* name (I discuss types later in this chapter in "Defining Types"). The following are the F# keywords:

abstract	lsl
and	lsr
as	lxor
assert	match member
asr	mod
begin	module
class	mutable namespace
default	new
delegate	null
do	of
done	open
downcast	or
downto	override
else	rec
end	sig
exception	static
false	struct
finally	then
for	to
fun	true
function	try
if	type
in	val
inherit	when
inline	upcast
interface	while
land	with
lor	

The words listed next are not currently F# keywords but have been reserved for possible future use. It is possible to use them as identifiers or type names now, but the compiler will issue a warning if you do. If you care that your code is compatible with future versions of the compiler, then it is best to avoid using them. I will not use them in the examples in this book.

async	method
atomic	mixin
break	namespace
checked	object
component	process
const	property
constraint	protected
constructor	public
continue	pure
decimal	readonly
eager	return
enum	sealed
event	switch
external	virtual
fixed	void
functor	volatile
include	where

If you really need to use a keyword as an identifier or type name, you can use the double back quote syntax:

```
let ``class`` = "style"
```

The usual reason for doing this is when you need to use a member from a library that was not written in F# and that uses one of F#'s keywords as a name (you'll learn more about using non-F# libraries in Chapter 4). The best practice is to avoid using keywords as identifiers if possible.

Literals

Literals represent constant values and are useful building blocks for computations. F# has a rich set of literals, summarized in Table 3-1.

Table 3-1. *F# Literals*

Example	F# Type	.NET Type	Description
"Hello\t ","World\n"	string	System.String	A string in which a backslash (\) is an escape character
@"c:\dir\fs",@""""	string	System.String	A verbatim string where a backslash (\) is a regular character
"bytesbytesbytes"B	byte array	System.Byte[]	A string that will be stored as a byte array
'c'	char	System.Char	A character
true,false	bool	System.Boolean	A Boolean
0x22	int/int32	System.Int32	An integer as a hexadecimal
0o42	int/int32	System.Int32	An integer as an octal
0b10010	int/ int32	System.Int32	An integer as a binary
34y	sbyte	System.SByte	A signed byte
34uy	byte	System.Byte	An unsigned byte
34s	int16	System.Int16	A 16-bit integer
34us	uint16	System.UInt16	An unsigned 16-bit integer
34l	int/int32	System.Int32	A 32-bit integer
34ul	uint32	System.UInt32	An unsigned 32-bit integer
34n	nativeint	System.IntPtr	A native-sized integer
34un	unativeint	System.UIntPtr	An unsigned native-sized integer
34L	int64	System.Int64	A 32-bit integer
34UL	uint64	System.Int64	An unsigned 32-bit integer
3.0F,3.0f	float32	System.Single	A 32-bit IEEE floating-point number
3.0	float	System.Double	A 64-bit IEEE floating-point number
3474262622571I	bigint	Microsoft.FSharp. Math.BigInt	An arbitrary large integer
474262612536171N	bignum	Microsoft.FSharp. Math.BigNum	An arbitrary large number

In F# string literals can contain newline characters, and regular string literals can contain standard escape codes. Verbatim string literals use a backslash (\) as a regular character, and two double quotes ("") are the escape for a quote. You can define all integer types using hexadecimal and octal by using the appropriate prefix and postfix. The following example shows some of these literals in action, along with how to use the F# printf function with a %A pattern to output them to the console. The printf function interprets the %A format pattern using a combination of F#'s reflection (covered in Chapter 7) and the .NET ToString method, which is available for every type, to output values in a readable way. You can also access this functionality by using the print_any and any_to_string functions from the F# library.

```
#light
let message = "Hello
        World\r\n\t!"
let dir = @"c:\projects"

let bytes = "bytesbytesbytes"B

let xA = 0xFFy
let xB = 0o7777un
let xC = 0b10010UL

let print x = printfn "A%" x

let main() =
    print message;
    print dir;
    print bytes;
    print xA;
    print xB;
    print xC

main()
```

The results of this example, when compiled and executed, are as follows:

```
"Hello\n        World\r\n\t!"
"c:\\projects"
[|98uy; 121uy; 116uy; 101uy; 115uy; 98uy; 121uy; 116uy; 101uy; 115uy; 98uy;
  121uy; 116uy; 101uy; 115uy|]
-1y
4095
18UL
```

Values and Functions

Values and *functions* in F# are indistinguishable because functions *are* values, and F# syntax treats them both similarly. For example, consider the following code. On the first line, the value 10 is assigned to the identifier n; then on the second line, a function, add, which takes two parameters and adds them together, is defined. Notice how similar the syntax is, with the only difference being that a function has parameters that are listed after the function name. Since everything is a value in F#, the literal 10 on the first line is a value, and the result of the expression a + b on the next line is also a value that automatically becomes the result of the add function. Note that there is no need to explicitly return a value from a function as you would in an imperative language.

```
#light
let n = 10

let add a b = a + b

let addFour = add 4

let result = addFour n

printfn "result = %i" result
```

The results of this code, when compiled and executed, are as follows:

```
result = 14
```

F# also supports the idea of the partial application of functions (these are sometimes called *partial* or *curried* functions). This means you don't have to pass all the arguments to a function at once. I did this in the third line in the previous code, where I passed a single argument to the add function, which takes two arguments. This is very much related to the idea that functions are values. Because a function is just a value, if it doesn't receive all its arguments at once, it returns a value that is a new function waiting for the rest of the arguments. So, in the example, passing just the value 4 to the add function results in a new function that I have named addFour because it takes one parameter and adds the value 4 to it. At first glance, this idea can look uninteresting and unhelpful, but it is a powerful part of functional programming that you'll see used throughout the book.

This behavior may not always be appropriate; for example, if the function takes two floating-point parameters that represent a point, it may not be desirable to have these numbers passed to the function separately because they both make up the point they represent. You may alternatively surround a function's parameters with parentheses and separate them with commas, turning them into a *tuple* (rhymes with "couple"). You can see this in the following code, which will not compile because the sub function requires both parameters to be given at once. This is because sub now has only one parameter, the tuple (a, b), instead of two, and although the call to sub in the second line provides only one argument, it's not a tuple. You'll examine tuples properly later in this chapter in "Defining Types."

```
#light
let sub (a, b) = a - b

let subFour = sub 4
```

When attempting to compile this example, you will receive the following error message; this is because the program does not type check as you are trying to pass an integer to a function that takes a tuple.

```
prog.fs(15,19): error: FS0001: This expression has type
    int
but is here used with type
    'a * 'b
```

In general, functions that can be partially applied are preferred over functions that use tuples. This is because functions that can be partially applied are more flexible than tuples, giving users of the function more choice about how to use them. This is especially true when creating a library to be used by other programmers. You may not be able to anticipate all the ways your users will want to use your functions, so it is best to give them the flexibility of functions that can be partially applied.

You never need to explicitly return a value, but how do you compute intermediate values within a function? In F#, this is controlled by whitespace. An indention means that the let binding is an intermediate value in the computation, and the end of the expression is signaled by the end of the indented section.

To demonstrate this, the next example shows a function that computes the point halfway between two integers. The third and fourth lines show intermediate values being calculated. First the difference between the two numbers is calculated, and this is assigned to the identifier dif using the let keyword. To show that this is an intermediate value within the function, it is indented by four spaces. The choice of the number of spaces is left to the programmer, but the convention is four. Note that you cannot use tabs because these can look different in different text editors, which causes problems when whitespace is significant. After that, the example calculates the midpoint, assigning it to the identifier mid using the same indentation. Finally, you want the result of the function to be the midpoint plus a, so you can simply say mid + a, and this becomes the function's result.

```
#light
let halfWay a b =
    let dif =  b - a
    let mid = dif / 2
    mid + a

printfn "(halfWay 5 11) = %i" (halfWay 5 11)
printfn "(halfWay 11 5) = %i" (halfWay 11 5)
```

The results of this example are as follows:

```
(halfWay 5 11) = 8
(halfWay 11 5) = 8
```

Note It's the #light declaration, which should be placed at the top of each F# source file, that makes whitespace significant in F#, allowing you to omit certain keywords and symbols such as in, ;, begin, and end. I believe that significant whitespace is a much more intuitive way of programming, because it helps the programmer decide how the code should be laid out; therefore, in this book, I'll cover the F# syntax only when #light is declared.

Scope

The *scope* of an identifier defines where you can use an identifier (or a type; see "Defining Types" later in this chapter) within a program. Scope is a fairly simple concept, but it is important to have a good understanding because if you try to use an identifier that's not in scope, you will get a compile error.

All identifiers, whether they relate to functions or values, are scoped from the end of their definitions until the end of the sections in which they appear. So, for identifiers that are at the top level (that is, identifiers not local to another function or other value), the scope of the identifier is from the place where it's defined to the end of the source file. Once an identifier at the top level has been assigned a value (or function), this value cannot be changed or redefined. An identifier is available only after its definition has ended, meaning that it is not usually possible to define an identifier in terms of itself.

Identifiers within functions are scoped to the end of the expression that they appear in; ordinarily, this means they're scoped until the end of the function definition in which they appear. So if an identifier is defined inside a function, then it cannot be used outside it. Consider the next example, which will not compile since it attempts to use the identifier message outside the function defineMessage:

```
#light
let defineMessage() =
    let message = "Help me"
    print_endline message

print_endline message
```

When trying to compile this code, you'll get the following error message:

```
Prog.fs(34,17): error: FS0039: The value or constructor 'message' is not defined.
```

Identifiers within functions behave a little differently from identifiers at the top level, because they can be redefined using the let keyword. This is useful; it means that the F# programmer does not have to keep inventing names to hold intermediate values. To demonstrate, the next example shows a mathematical puzzle implemented as an F# function. Here you need to calculate lots of intermediate values that you don't particularly care about; inventing names for each one these would be an unnecessary burden on the programmer.

```
#light
let mathsPuzzle() =
    print_string "Enter day of the month on which you were born: "
    let input =  read_int ()
    let x = input * 4      // Multiply it by 4
    let x = x + 13         // Add 13
    let x = x * 25         // Multiply the result by 25
    let x = x - 200        // Subtract 200
    print_string "Enter number of the month you were born: "
    let input =  read_int ()
    let x = x + input
```

```
    let x = x * 2        // Multiply by 2
    let x = x - 40       // Subtract 40
    let x = x * 50       // Multiply the result by 50
    print_string "Enter last two digits of the year of your birth: "
    let input = read_int ()
    let x = x + input
    let x = x - 10500     // Finally, subtract 10,500
    printf "Date of birth (ddmmyy): %i" x

mathsPuzzle()
```

The results of this example, when compiled and executed, are as follows:

```
Enter day of the month on which you were born: 23
Enter number of the month you were born: 5
Enter last two digits of the year of your birth: 78
Date of birth (ddmmyy): 230578
```

I should note that this is different from changing the value of an identifier. Because you're redefining the identifier, you're able to change the identifier's type, but you still retain type safety.

Note *Type safety*, sometimes referred to as *strong typing*, basically means that F# will prevent you from performing an inappropriate operation on a value; for example, you can't treat an integer as if it were a floating-point number. I discuss types and how they lead to type safety later in this chapter in the section "Types and Type Inference."

The next example shows code that will not compile, because on the third line you change the value of x from an integer to the string "change me", and then on the fourth line you try to add a string and an integer, which is illegal in F#, so you get a compile error:

```
#light
let changeType () =
    let x = 1            // bind x to an integer
    let x = "change me"  // rebind x to a string
    let x = x + 1        // attempt to rebind to itself plus an integer
    print_string x
```

This program will give the following error message because it does not type check:

```
prog.fs(55,13): error: FS0001: This expression has type
    int
but is here used with type
    string
stopped due to error
```

If an identifier is redefined, its old value is available while the definition of the identifier is in progress but after it is defined; that is, after the new line at the end of the expression, the old value is hidden. If the identifier is redefined inside a new scope, the identifier will revert to its old value when the new scope is finished.

The next example defines a message and prints it to the console. It then redefines this message inside an *inner function* called innerFun that also prints the message. Then, it calls the function innerFun and after that prints the message a third time.

```
#light
let printMessages() =
    // define message and print it
    let message = "Important"
    printfn "%s" message;

    // define an inner function that redefines value of message
    let innerFun () =
        let message = "Very Important"
        printfn "%s" message

    // define message and print it
    innerFun ()

    // finally print message again
    printfn "%s" message

printMessages()
```

The results of this example, when compiled and executed, are as follows:

```
Important
Very Important
Important
```

A programmer from the imperative world might have expected that message when printed out for the final time would be bound to the value Very Important, rather than Important. It holds the value Important because the identifier message is rebound, rather than assigned, to the value Very Important inside the function innerFun, and this binding is valid only inside the scope of the function innerFun, so once this function has finished, the identifier message reverts to holding its original value.

Note Using inner functions is a common and excellent way of breaking up a lot of functionality into manageable portions, and you will see their usage throughout the book. They are sometimes referred to as *closures* or *lambdas*, although these two terms have more specific meanings. A *closure* means that the function uses a value that is not defined at the top level, and a *lambda* is an anonymous function. The section "Anonymous Functions" later in the chapter discusses these concepts in more detail.

Recursion

Recursion means defining a function in terms of itself; in other words, the function calls itself within its definition. Recursion is often used in functional programming where you would use a loop in imperative programming. Many believe that algorithms are much easier to understand when expressed in terms of recursion rather than loops.

To use recursion in F#, use the rec keyword after the let keyword to make the identifier available within the function definition. The following example shows recursion in action. Notice how on the fifth line the function makes two calls to itself as part of its own definition.

```
#light
let rec fib x =
    match x with
    | 1 -> 1
    | 2 -> 1
    | x -> fib (x - 1) + fib (x - 2)

printfn "(fib 2) = %i" (fib 2)
printfn "(fib 6) = %i" (fib 6)
printfn "(fib 11) = %i" (fib 11)
```

The results of this example, when compiled and executed, are as follows:

```
(fib 2) = 1
(fib 6) = 8
(fib 11) = 89
```

This function calculates the *n*th term in the Fibonacci sequence. The Fibonacci sequence is generated by adding the previous two numbers in the sequence, and it progresses as follows: 1, 1, 2, 3, 5, 8, 13, …. Recursion is most appropriate for calculating the Fibonacci sequence, because the definition of any number in the sequence, other than the first two, depends on being able to calculate the previous two numbers, so the Fibonacci sequence is defined in terms of itself.

Although recursion is a powerful tool, you should always be careful when using it. It is easy to inadvertently write a recursive function that never terminates. Although intentionally writing a program that does not terminate is sometimes useful, it is rarely the goal when trying to perform calculations. To ensure that recursive functions terminate, it is often useful to think of recursion in terms of a base case and the recursive case. The *recursive case* is the value for which the function is defined in terms of itself; for the function fib, this is any value other than 1 and 2. The *base case* is the nonrecursive case; that is, there must be some value where the function is not defined in terms of itself. In the fib function, 1 and 2 are the base cases. Having a base case is not enough in itself to ensure termination. The recursive case must tend toward the base case. In the fib example, if x is greater than or equal to 3, then the recursive case will tend toward the base case because x will always become smaller and at some point reach 2. However, if x is less than 1, then x will grow continually more negative, and the function will recurse until the limits of the machine are reached, resulting in a stack overflow error (System.StackOverflowException).

The previous code also uses F# pattern matching, which I discuss in the "Pattern Matching" section later in this chapter.

Anonymous Functions

F# provides an alternative way to define functions using the keyword fun; you can see this in the following example. Ordinarily, you would use this notation when it is not necessary to give a name to a function, so these are referred to as *anonymous functions* and sometimes called *lambda functions* or even just *lambdas*. The idea that a function does not need a name may seem a little strange, but if a function is to be passed as an argument to another function, then often you don't need to give it a name of its own. I demonstrate this idea in the section "Lists" later in this chapter when you look at operations on lists. The arguments defined for this style of function can follow the same rules as when defining a function with a name, meaning that you can define the arguments so they can be partially applied or defined in the form of a tuple (see the section "Defining Types" later in this chapter for an explanation of tuples). The following example shows two functions that are created and then immediately applied to arguments so that the identifier x holds the result of the function rather than the function itself:

```
#light
let x = (fun x y -> x + y) 1 2
```

You can create an anonymous function with the keyword function. Creating functions this way differs from using the keyword fun since you can use pattern matching when using the keyword function (see the section "Pattern Matching" later in this chapter). Consequently, it can be passed only one argument, but you can do a couple of things if the function needs to have multiple parameters. The first line of the following example shows a function using the function keyword written so the function can be partially applied, meaning the arguments can be passed one at a time if needed. The second line shows a function defined using the function keyword that takes a tuple argument.

```
let x1 = (function x -> function y -> x + y) 1 2
let x2 = (function (x, y) -> x + y) (1, 2)
```

The keyword fun is generally preferred when defining anonymous functions because it is more compact; you can see this is the case when browsing the source for the libraries and examples distributed with F#.

Operators

In F#, you can think of *operators* as a more aesthetically pleasing way to call functions.

F# has two different kinds of operators, prefix and infix; a *prefix* operator is an operator that takes one operand, and an *infix* operator takes two or more. Prefix operators appear before their operand, whereas infix operators appear between the first two operands.

F# provides a rich and diverse set of operators that you can use with numeric, Boolean, string, and collection types. The operators defined in F# and its libraries are too numerous to be covered in this section, so instead you'll look at the way you use and define operators in F# rather than looking at individual operators.

Like in C#, F# operators are overloaded, meaning you can use more than one type with an operator; however, unlike in C#, both operands must be the same type, or the compiler will generate an error. F# also allows users to define and redefine operators; I discuss how to do that at the end of this section.

Operators follow a set of rules similar to C#'s for operator overloading resolution; therefore, any class in the BCL, or any .NET library, that was written to support operator overloading in C# will support it in F#. For example, you can use the + operator to concatenate stings (you can also use ^ for this) as well as to add a System.TimeSpan to a System.DataTime because these types support an overload of the + operator. The following example illustrates this:

```
#light
let ryhm = "Jack " + "and " + "Jill"
let anotherRyhm = "Wee " ^ "Willy " ^ "Winky"

open System
let oneYearLater =
    DateTime.Now + new TimeSpan(365, 0, 0, 0, 0)
```

Users can define their own operators or redefine any of the existing ones if they want (although this is not always advisable, because the operators then no longer support overloading). Consider the following perverse example that redefines + to perform subtraction:

```
#light
let (+) a b = a - b
print_int (1 + 1)
```

User-defined (*custom*) operators must be nonalphanumeric and can be a single character or a group of characters. You can use the following characters in custom operators:

```
!$%&*+-./<=>?@^|~
:
```

Custom operators can start with any of the characters on the first line and after that can use any of these characters and also the colon (:), listed on the second line. The syntax for defining an operator is the same as using the let keyword to define a function, except the operator replaces the function name and is surrounded by parentheses so the compiler knows that the symbols are used as a name of an operator rather than as the operator itself. The following example shows defining a custom operator, +:*, that adds its operands and then multiplies them:

```
#light
let ( +:* ) a b = (a + b) * a * b

printfn "(1 +:* 2) = %i" (1 +:* 2)
```

The results of this example, when compiled and executed, are as follows:

```
(1 +:* 2) = 6
```

Unary operators always come before the operand; binary operators are always infix.

Lists

F# *lists* are simple collection types that are built into F#. An F# list can be an *empty list*, represented by square brackets ([ ]), or it can be another list with a value concatenated to it. You concatenate values to the front of an F# list using a built-in operator that consists of two colons (::), pronounced "cons." The next example shows some lists being defined, starting with an empty list on the first line, followed by two lists where strings are placed at the front by concatenation:

```
#light
let emptyList = []
let oneItem = "one " :: []
let twoItem = "one " :: "two " :: []
```

The syntax to add items to a list by concatenation is a little verbose, so if you just want to define a list, you can use shorthand. In this shorthand notation, you place the list items between square brackets and separate them with a semicolon (;), as follows:

```
#light
let shortHand = ["apples "; "pairs "]
```

F# has a second operator that works on lists; this is the at (@) symbol, which you can use to concatenate two lists together, as follows:

```
let twoLists = ["one, "; "two, "] @ ["buckle "; "my "; "shoe "]
```

All items in an F# list must be of the same type, and if you try to place items of different types in a list—for example, you try to concatenate a string to a list of integers—you will get a compile error. If you need a list of mixed types, you can create a list of type obj (the F# equivalent of System.Object), as in the following code. I discuss types in F# in more detail in "Types and Type Inference" and "Defining Types" later in this chapter.

```
#light
let emptyList = []
let oneItem = "one " :: []
let twoItem = "one " :: "two " :: []

let shortHand = ["apples "; "pairs "]

let twoLists = ["one, "; "two, "] @ ["buckle "; "my "; "shoe "]

let objList = [box 1; box 2.0; box "three"]

let printList l =
    List.iter print_string l
    print_newline()
```

```
let main() =
    printList emptyList
    printList oneItem
    printList twoItem
    printList shortHand
    printList twoLists

    for x in objList do
        print_any x
        print_char ' '
    print_newline()

main()
```

The results of these examples, when compiled and executed, are as follows:

```
one
one two
apples pairs
one, two, buckle my shoe
1 2.000000 "three"
```

F# lists are *immutable*; in other words, once a list is created, it cannot be altered. The functions and operators that act on lists do not alter them, but they create a new, altered version of the list, leaving the old list available for later use if needed. The next example shows this. An F# list containing a single string is created, and then two more lists are created, each using the previous one as a base. Finally, the List.rev function is applied to the last list to create a new reversed list. When you print these lists, it is easy to see that all the original lists remain unaltered.

```
#light
let one = ["one "]
let two = "two " :: one
let three = "three " :: two

let rightWayRound = List.rev three

let printList l =
    List.iter print_string l
    print_newline()

let main() =
    printList one
    printList two
    printList three
    printList rightWayRound
main()
```

The results of this example, when compiled and executed, are as follows:

```
one
two one
three two one
one two three
```

The regular way to work with F# lists is to use recursion. The empty list is the base case, and when a function working on a list receives the empty list, the function terminates; when the function receives a nonempty list, it processes the first item in the list (the *head*) and then recursively processes the remainder of the list (the *tail*). The next example demonstrates processing a list recursively:

```
#light
let listOfList = [[2; 3; 5]; [7; 11; 13]; [17; 19; 23; 29]]

let rec concatList l =
    if List.nonempty l then
        let head = List.hd l in
        let tail = List.tl l in
        head @ (concatList tail)
    else
        []

let primes = concatList listOfList

print_any primes
```

First, you define an F# list composed of three other lists. Then, you define a recursive function, concatList, which is designed to merge a list of lists into one list. The function uses an F# library function, List.nonempty, to check whether the F# list is empty. If it is not empty, the function takes the head and tail of the list, passes the tail to a call to itself, and then concatenates the head of the list to the result. If the tail is empty, the function must still return something, so it simply returns the empty list, [ ], because concatenating the empty list with another list has no effect on the contents of the list.

The results of this example, when compiled and executed, are as follows:

```
[2; 3; 5; 7; 11; 13; 17; 19; 23; 29]
```

The concatList function is fairly verbose for what this example is trying to achieve. Fortunately, F# includes some pattern matching syntax for lists that can really help tidy this up. I cover this syntax later in this chapter in "Pattern Matching."

All the examples in this section demonstrate another nice feature of F# lists, the set of library functions provided for lists. The List.iter function is a library function that takes two arguments. The first argument is a function that will be applied to each item in the list, and the second is the list to which that function will be applied. You can think of the List.iter function as just a nice shorthand way to write a for loop over a list, and the library contains many other functions for transforming and manipulating lists, including a `List.concat` function that has a similar effect to the `concatList` function defined earlier. For more information about these functions, see Chapter 7, which covers the F# ML compatibility library.

List Comprehensions

List comprehensions make creating and converting collections easy. You can create F# lists, sequences, and arrays directly using comprehension syntax. (I cover arrays in more detail in the next chapter, and *sequences* are collections of type seq, which is F#'s name for the .NET BCL's IEnumerable type; I describe them in the section "Lazy Evaluation.")

The simplest comprehensions specify ranges, where you write the first item you want, either a number or a letter, followed by two periods (`..`) and then the last item you want, all within square brackets (to create a list) or braces (to create a sequence). The compiler then does the work of calculating all the items in the collection, taking the first number and incrementing it by 1, or similarly with characters, until it reaches the last item specified. The following example demonstrates how to create a list of numbers from 0 through 9 and a sequence of the characters from A through Z:

```
#light
let numericList = [ 0 .. 9 ]
let alpherSeq = { 'A' .. 'Z' }
printfn "%A" numericList
printfn "%A" alpherSeq
```

The results of this example are as follows:

```
[0; 1; 2; 3; 4; 5; 6; 7; 8; 9]
seq ['A'; 'B'; 'C'; 'D'; ...]
```

To create more interesting collections, you can also specify a step size for incrementing numbers—note that characters do not support this type of list comprehension. You place the step size between the first and last items separated by an extra pair of periods (`..`). The next example shows a list containing multiples of 3, followed by a list that counts backward from 9 to 0:

```
#light
let multiplesOfThree = [ 0 .. 3 .. 30 ]
let revNumericSeq = [ 9 .. -1 .. 0 ]
printfn "%A" multiplesOfThree
printfn "%A" revNumericSeq
```

The results of this example are as follows:

```
[0; 3; 6; 9; 12; 15; 18; 21; 24; 27; 30]
[9; 8; 7; 6; 5; 4; 3; 2; 1; 0]
```

List comprehensions also allow loops to create a collection from another collection. The idea is that you enumerate the old collection, transform each of its items, and place any generated items in the new collection. To specify such a loop, use the keyword for, followed by an identifier, followed by the keyword in, at the beginning of the list comprehension. In the next example, you create a sequence of the squares of the first ten positive integers. You use for to enumerate the collection 1 .. 10, assigning each item in turn to the identifier x. You then use the identifier x to calculate the new item, in this case multiplying x by itself to square it.

```
#light
let squares =
    { for x in 1 .. 10 -> x * x }
print_any squares
```

The results of this example are as follows:

```
seq [1; 4; 9; 16; ...]
```

You can also add a when guard to suppress items you don't want in the collection. A *when guard* is the keyword when followed by a Boolean expression. Only when the when guard evaluates to true will an item be placed in the collection. The next example demonstrates how to use a when guard, checking whether the modulus of x is zero. This is an easy way to check whether a number is even, and only if the number is even is it placed in the collection. The example also demonstrates how to create a function that returns a sequence based on a list comprehension. In the function evens, the parameter n specifies the size of the collection to be generated.

```
#light
let evens n =
    { for x in 1 .. n when x % 2 = 0 -> x }
print_any (evens 10)
```

The results of this example are as follows:

```
seq [2; 4; 6; 8; ...]
```

It's also possible to use list comprehensions to iterate in two or more dimensions by using a separate loop for each dimension. In the next example, you define a function, squarePoints, that creates a sequence of points forming a square grid, each point represented by a tuple of two integers.

```
#light
let squarePoints n =
    { for x in 1 .. n
        for y in 1 .. n  -> x,y }
print_any (squarePoints 3)
```

The results of this example are as follows:

```
[(1, 1); (1, 2); (1, 3); (2, 1); ...]
```

You'll look at using comprehensions with arrays and collections from the .NET Framework BCL in Chapter 4.

Control Flow

F# has a strong notion of *control flow*. In this way it differs from many pure functional languages, where the notion of control flow is very loose, because expressions can be evaluated in essentially any order. You can see the strong notion of control flow in the following if ... then ... else ... expression.

In F# the if ... then ... else ... construct is an expression, meaning it returns a value. One of two different values will be returned, depending on the value of the Boolean expression between the if and then keywords. The next example illustrates this. The if ... then ... else ... expression is evaluated to return either "heads" or "tails" depending on whether the program is run on an even second or an odd second.

```
#light
let result =
    if System.DateTime.Now.Second % 2 = 0 then
        "heads"
    else
        "tails"
print_string result
```

The if ... then ... else ... expression has some implications that you might not expect if you are more familiar with imperative-style programming. F#'s type system requires that the values being returned by the if ... then ... else ... expression must be the same type, or the compiler will generate an error. So, if in the previous example you were to replace the string "tails" with an integer or Boolean value, you would get a compile error. If you really require the values to be of different types, you can create an if ... then ... else ... expression of type obj (F#'s version of System.Object); the next example shows how to do this. It prints either "heads" or false to the console.

```
#light
let result =
    if System.DateTime.Now.Second % 2 = 0 then
        box "heads"
    else
        box false
print_any result
```

Imperative programmers may be surprised that an if ... then ... else ... expression must have an else if the expression returns a value. This is pretty logical when you think about it and if you consider the examples you've just seen. If the else were removed from the code, the identifier result could not be assigned a value when the if evaluated to false, and having uninitialized identifiers is something that F#, and functional programming in general, aims to avoid. There is a way for a program to contain an if ... then expression without the else, but this is very much in the style of imperative programming, so I discuss it in Chapter 4.

Types and Type Inference

F# is a *strongly typed* language, which means you cannot use a function with a value that is inappropriate. You cannot call a function that has a string as a parameter with an integer argument; you must explicitly convert between the two. The way the language treats the type of its values is referred to as its *type system*. F# has a type system that does not get in the way of routine programming. In F#, all values have a type, and this includes values that are functions.

Ordinarily, you don't need to explicitly declare types; the compiler will work out the type of a value from the types of the literals in the function and the resulting types of other functions it calls. If everything is OK, the compiler will keep the types to itself; only if there is a type mismatch will the compiler inform you by reporting a compile error. This process is generally referred to as *type inference*. If you want to know more about the types in a program, you can make the compiler display all inferred types with the –i switch. Visual Studio users get tooltips that show types when they hover the mouse pointer over an identifier.

The way type inference works in F# is fairly easy to understand. The compiler works through the program assigning types to identifiers as they are defined, starting with the top leftmost identifier and working its way down to the bottom rightmost. It assigns types based on the types it already knows, that is, the types of literals and (more commonly) the types of functions defined in other source files or assemblies.

The next example defines two F# identifiers and then shows their inferred types displayed on the console with the F# compiler's –i switch. The types of these two identifiers are unsurprising, string and int, respectively, and the syntax used by the compiler to describe them is fairly straightforward: the keyword val (meaning "value") and then the identifier, a colon, and finally the type.

```
#light
let aString = "Spring time in Paris"

let anInt = 42
```

```
val aString : string
val anInt : int
```

The definition of the function makeMessage in the next example is a little more interesting. You should note two things about makeMessage. First, its definition is prefixed with the keyword val, just like the two values you saw before, since even though it is a function, the F# compiler still considers it to be a value. Second, the type itself uses the notation int -> string, meaning a function that takes an integer and returns a string. The -> between the type names (an *ASCII arrow*, or just *arrow*) represents the transformation of the function being applied. It is worth noting that the arrow represents a transformation of the value but not necessarily the type, because it can represent a function that transforms a value into a value of the same type, as shown in the half function on the second line.

```
#light
let makeMessage x = (string_of_int x) + " days to spring time"
let half x = x / 2
```

```
val makeMessage : int -> string
val half : int -> int
```

The types of functions that can be partially applied and functions that take tuples differ. See the section "Values and Functions" earlier in the chapter for an explanation of the difference between these types of functions. The functions div1 and div2 are designed to illustrate this. The function div1 can be partially applied, and its type is int -> int -> int, representing that the arguments can be passed in separately. You can compare this to the function div2 that has the type int * int -> int, meaning a function that takes a pair of integers, a tuple of integers, and turns them into a single integer. You can see this in the function div_remainder, which performs integer division and also returns the remainder at the same time. Its type is int -> int -> int * int, meaning a curried function that returns an integer tuple.

```
let div1 x y = x / y
let div2 (x, y) = x / y

let divRemainder  x y = x / y, x % y
```

```
val div1 : int -> int -> int
val div2 : int * int -> int
val divRemainder : int -> int -> int * int
```

The next function, doNothing, looks inconspicuous enough, but it is quite interesting from a typing point of view. It has the type 'a -> 'a, meaning a function that takes a value of one type and returns a value of the same type. Any type that begins with a single quotation mark (') means a *variable* type. F# has a type, obj, that maps to System.Object and that represents a value of any type, a concept that you will probably be familiar with from other common language runtime (CLR)–based programming languages (and indeed many languages that do not target the CLR). However, a variable type is not the same. Notice how the type has an 'a on both sides of the arrow. This means the compiler knows that even though it does not yet know the type, it knows that the type of the return value will be the same as the type of the argument. This feature of the type system, sometimes referred to as *type parameterization*, allows the compiler to find more type errors at compile time and can help avoid casting.

```
let doNothing x = x
```

```
val doNothing : 'a -> 'a
```

Note The concept of a variable type, or type parameterization, is closely related to the concept of *generics* that were introduced in the CLR version 2.0 and have now become part of the EMCA specification for the CLI version 2.0. When F# targets a CLI that has generics enabled, it takes full advantage of them by using them anywhere it finds an undetermined type. It is also worth noting that Don Syme, the creator of F#, designed and implemented generics in the .NET CLR before he started working on F#. One might be temped to infer that he did this so he could create F#!

The function doNothingToAnInt, shown next, is an example of a value being constrained, a *type constraint*; in this case, the function parameter x is constrained to be an int. The syntax for constraining a value to be of a certain type is straightforward. Within parentheses, the identifier name is followed by a colon (:) followed by the type name; this is also sometimes called a *type annotation*. Constraining values is not usually necessary when writing pure F#, though it can occasionally be useful. It's most useful when using .NET libraries written in languages other than F# and for interoperation with unmanaged libraries. In both these cases, the compiler has less type information, so it is often necessary to give it enough information to disambiguate things. It is possible to constrain any identifier, not just function parameters, to be of a certain type, though it is more typical to have to constrain parameters. The list stringList here shows how to constrain an identifier that's not a function parameter:

```
let doNothingToAnInt (x : int) = x

let intList = [1; 2; 3]
let (stringList : list<string>) = ["one"; "two"; "three"]
```

```
val doNothingToAnInt _int : int -> int
val intList : int list
val stringList : string list
```

The intList value is a list of integers, and the identifier's type is int list. This indicates that the compiler has recognized that the list contains only integers and that in this case the type of its items is not undetermined but is int. Any attempt to add anything other than values of type int to the list will result in a compile error. The identifier stringList has a type annotation. Although this is unnecessary, since the compiler can resolve the type from the value, it is used to show an alternative syntax for working with undermined types. You can place the type between angle brackets after the type that it is associated with instead of just writing it before the type name. Note that even though the type of stringList is constrained to be list<string> (a list of strings), the compiler still reports its type as string list when displaying the type, and they mean exactly the same thing. This syntax is supported to make F# types with a type parameter look like generic types from other .NET libraries.

Pattern Matching

Pattern matching allows you to look at the value of an identifier and then make different computations depending on its value. It is a bit like a chain of if … then … else … expressions and also might be compared to the switch statement in C++ and C#, but it is much more powerful and flexible than either.

The pattern matching construct in F# allows you to pattern match over a variety of types and values. It also has several different forms and crops up in several places in the language including its exception handling syntax, which I discuss in "Exceptions and Exception Handling" later in this chapter. The simplest form of pattern matching is matching over a value, and you have already seen this earlier in this chapter in the section "Values and Functions," where you used it to implement a function that generated numbers in the Fibonacci sequence. To illustrate the syntax, the next example shows an implementation of a function that will produce the Lucas numbers, a sequence of numbers as follows: 1, 3, 4, 7, 11, 18, 29, 47, 76, …. The Lucas sequence has the same definition as the Fibonacci sequence; only the starting points are different.

```
#light
let rec luc x =
    match x with
    | x when x <= 0 -> failwith "value must be greater than 0"
    | 1 -> 1
    | 2 -> 3
    | x -> luc (x - 1) + luc (--x - 2)

printfn "(luc 2) = %i" (luc 2)
printfn "(luc 6) = %i" (luc 6)
printfn "(luc 11) = %i" (luc 11)
printfn "(luc 12) = %i" (luc 12)
```

The results of this example, when compiled and executed, are as follows:

```
(luc 2) = 3
(luc 6) = 18
(luc 11) = 199
(luc 12) = 322
```

This syntax for pattern matching is the keyword match followed by the identifier that will be matched and then the keyword with. This is followed by all the possible matching *rules* separated by vertical bars (|). In the simplest case, a rule consists of either a constant or an identifier, followed by an arrow (->) and then by the expression to be used when the value matches the rule. In this definition of the function luc, you can see that the second two cases are literals, the values 1 and 2, and these will just be replaced with the values 1 and 3, respectively. The fourth case will match any value of x greater than 2, and this will cause two further calls to the luc function.

The rules are matched in the order in which they are defined, and the compiler will issue an error if pattern matching is incomplete, that is, if there is some possible input value that will not match any rule. This would be the case in the luc function if you had omitted the final rule, because any values of x greater than 2 would not match any rule. The compiler will also issue a warning if there are any rules that will never be matched, typically because there is another rule in front of them that is more general. This would be the case in the luc function if the fourth rule were moved ahead of the first rule. In this case, none of the other rules would ever be matched because the first rule would match any value of x.

You can add a when guard (as in the first rule of the example) to give exact control about when a rule fires. A when guard is composed of the keyword when followed by a Boolean expression. Once the rule is matched, the when clause is evaluated, and the rule will fire only if the expression evaluates to true. If the expression evaluates to false, the remaining rules will be searched for another match. The first rule is designed to be the function's error handler. The first part of the rule is an identifier that will match any integer, but the when guard means the rule will match only those integers that are less than or equal to zero.

If you want, you can omit the first |. This can be useful when the pattern match is small and you want to fit it on one line. You can see this in the next example, which also demonstrates the use of the underscore (_) as a *wildcard*. The _ will match any value and is a way of telling the compiler that you're not interested in using this value. For example, in this booleanToString function, you do not need to use the constant true in the second rule, because if the first rule is matched, you know that the value of x will be true. Moreover, you do not need to use x to derive the string "True", so you can ignore the value and just use _ as a wildcard.

```
#light
let booleanToString x =
    match x with false -> "False" | _ -> "True"
```

Another useful feature of pattern matching is that you can combine two patterns into one rule through the use of the vertical bar (|). The next example, stringToBoolean, demonstrates this. In the first two rules, you have two strings that you would like to have evaluate to the same value, so rather than having two separate rules, you can just use | between the two patterns.

```
#light
let stringToBoolean x =
    match x with
    | "True" | "true" -> false
    | "False" | "false" -> true
    | _ -> failwith "unexpected input"

printfn "(booleanToString true) = %s"
    (booleanToString true)
printfn "(booleanToString false) = %s"
    (booleanToString false)

printfn "(stringToBoolean \"True\") = %b"
    (stringToBoolean "True")
printfn "(stringToBoolean \"false\") = %b"
    (stringToBoolean "false")
printfn "(stringToBoolean \"Hello\") = %b"
    (stringToBoolean "Hello")
```

The results of these examples, when compiled and executed, are as follows:

```
(booleanToString true) = True
(booleanToString false) = False
(stringToBoolean "True") = false
(stringToBoolean "false") = true
(stringToBoolean "Hello") = Microsoft.FSharp.FailureException: unexpected input
    at Prog.stringToBoolean(String x)
    at Prog._main()
```

It is also possible to pattern match over most of the types defined by F#. The next two examples demonstrate pattern matching over tuples, with two functions that implement a Boolean "and" and "or" using pattern matching. Each takes a slightly different approach.

```
#light
let myOr b1 b2 =
    match b1, b2 with
    | true, _ -> true
    | _, true -> true
    | _ -> false

let myAnd p =
    match p with
    | true, true -> true
    | _ -> false
```

The myOr function has two Boolean parameters, and they are placed between the match and with keywords and separated by commas to form a tuple. The myAnd function has one parameter, which is itself a tuple. Either way, the syntax for creating pattern matches for tuples is the same and similar to the syntax for creating tuples.

If it's necessary to match values within the tuple, the constants or identifiers are separated by commas, and the position of the identifier or constant defines what it matches within the tuple. This is shown in the first and second rules of the myOr function and in the first rule of the myAnd function. In these rules, you match parts of the tuples with constants, but you could have used identifiers if you wanted to work with the separate parts of the tuple later in the rule definition. Just because you're working with tuples doesn't mean you always have to look at the various parts that make up the tuple. The third rule of myOr and the second rule of myAnd show the whole tuple matched with a single _ wildcard character. This too could have been replaced with an identifier if you wanted to work with the value in the second half of the rule definition.

```
printfn "(myOr true false) = %b" (myOr true false)
printfn "(myOr false false) = %b" (myOr false false)

printfn "(myAnd (true, false)) = %b" (myAnd (true, false))
printfn "(myAnd (true, true)) = %b" (myAnd (true, true))
```

The results of these examples, when compiled and executed, are as follows:

```
(myOr true false) = true
(myOr false false) = false
(myAnd (true, false)) = false
(myAnd (true, true)) = true
```

A common use of a pattern matching in F# is pattern matching over a list; in fact, this is the preferred way to deal with lists. The next example is a reworking of an example given in earlier in this chapter in the "Lists" section, but this one uses pattern matching instead of if … then … else …. For convenience, the original function definition is shown, renamed to concatListOrg. Comparing the two, it is easy to see that the version that uses pattern matching is about half the number of lines, a much preferable implementation. The pattern syntax for pulling the head item off a list is the same as the syntax for concatenating an item to a list. The pattern is formed by the identifier representing the head, followed by :: and then the identifier for the rest of the list. You can see this in the first rule of concatList. You can also pattern match against list constants; you can see this in the second rule of concatList, where you have an empty list.

```
#light
let listOfList = [[2; 3; 5]; [7; 11; 13];  [17; 19; 23; 29]]

let rec concatList l =
    match l with
    | head :: tail -> head @ (concatList tail)
    | [] -> []

let rec concatListOrg l =
    if List.nonempty l then
        let head = List.hd l in
        let tail = List.tl l in
        head @ (concatListOrg tail)
    else
        []

let primes = concatList listOfList

print_any primes
```

The results of this example, when compiled and executed, are as follows:

```
[2; 3; 5; 7; 11; 13; 17; 19; 23; 29]
```

Taking the head from a list, processing it, and then recursively processing the tail of the list is the most common way of dealing with lists via pattern matching, but it certainly isn't the only thing you can do with pattern matching and lists. The following example shows a few other uses of this combination of features. The first rule demonstrates how to match a list of a fixed length, in this case a list of three items, and here you use identifiers to grab the values of these items so they can be printed to the console. The second rule looks at the first three items in the list to see whether they are the sequence of integers 1, 2, 3, and if they are, it prints a message to the console. The final two rules are the standard head/tail treatment of a list, designed to work their way through the list doing nothing, if there is no match with the first two rules.

```
#light
let rec findSequence l =
    match l with
    | [x; y; z] ->
        printfn "Last 3 numbers in the list were %i %i %i"
                x y z
    | 1 :: 2 :: 3 :: tail ->
        printfn "Found sequence 1, 2, 3 within the list"
        findSequence tail
    | head :: tail -> findSequence tail
    | [] -> ()

let testSequence = [1; 2; 3; 4; 5; 6; 7; 8; 9; 8; 7; 6; 5; 4; 3; 2; 1]

findSequence testSequence
```

The results of this example, when compiled and executed, are as follows:

```
Found sequence 1, 2, 3 within the list
Last 3 numbers in the list were 3 2 1
```

Because pattern matching is such a common task in F#, the language provides an alternative shorthand syntax. If the sole purpose of a function is to pattern match over something, then it may be worth using this syntax. In this version of the pattern matching syntax, you use the keyword function, place the pattern where the function's parameters would usually go, and then separate all the alternative rules with |. The next example shows this syntax in action in a simple function that recursively processes a list of strings and concatenates them into a single string.

```
#light
let rec conactStringList  =
    function head :: tail -> head + conactStringList tail
           | [] -> ""

let jabber = ["'Twas "; "brillig, "; "and "; "the "; "slithy "; "toves "; "..."]

let completJabber = conactStringList jabber
print_endline completJabber
```

The results of this example, when compiled and executed, are as follows:

```
'Twas brillig, and the slithy toves ...
```

Pattern matching has a couple of other uses within F#, but I have not yet covered in detail the types on which these other kinds of pattern matching are based. You can find further details on pattern matching with record types and union types in the next section, "Defining Types." You can find details of pattern matching and exception handling in the section "Exceptions and Exception Handling," and you can find details of how to pattern match over types from non-F# libraries in Chapter 3.

Defining Types

The type system in F# provides a number of features for defining custom types. All of F#'s type definitions fall into two categories. The first category is types that are *tuples* or *records*. These are a set of types composed to form a composite type (similar to structs in C or classes in C#). The second category is *sum* types, sometimes referred to as *union* types.

Tuples are a way of quickly and conveniently composing values into a group of values. Values are separated by commas and can then be referred to by one identifier, as shown in the first line of the next example. You can then retrieve the values by doing the reverse, as shown in the second and third lines, where identifiers separated by commas appear on the left side of the equals sign, with each identifier receiving a single value from the tuple. If you want to ignore a value in the tuple, you can use _ to tell the compiler you are not interested in the value, as in the second and third lines.

```
#light
let pair = true, false
let b1, _ = pair
let _, b2 = pair
```

Tuples are different from most user-defined types in F# because you do not have to explicitly declare them using the type keyword. To define a type, you use the type keyword followed by the type name, an equals sign, and then the type you are defining. In its simplest form, you can use this to give an alias to any existing type, including tuples. Giving aliases to single types is not often useful, but giving aliases to tuples can be very useful, especially when you want to use a tuple as a type constraint. The next example shows how to give an alias to a single type and a tuple and also how to use an alias as a type constraint:

```
#light
type Name = string
type Fullname = string * string

let fullNameToSting (x : Fullname) =
    let first, second = x in
    first + " " + second
```

Record types are similar to tuples in that they compose multiple types into a single type. The difference is that in record types each *field* is named. The next example illustrates the syntax for defining record types. You place field definitions between braces and separate them with semicolons. A field definition is composed of the field name followed by a colon and the field's type. The type definition Organization1 is a record type where the field names are unique. This means you can use a simple syntax to create an instance of this type where there is no need to mention the type name when it is created. To create a record, you place the field names followed by equals signs and the field values between braces ({}), as shown in the Rainbow identifier:

```
#light
type Organization1 = { boss : string ; lackeys : string list }

let rainbow =
    { boss  = "Jeffrey" ;
      lackeys = ["Zippy"; "George"; "Bungle"] }

type Organization2 = { chief : string ; underlings : string list }
type Organization3 = { chief : string ; indians : string list }

let thePlayers =
    { new Organization2
         with chief = "Peter Quince"
         and  underlings = ["Francis Flute"; "Robin Starveling";
                               "Tom Snout"; "Snug"; "Nick Bottom"] }
let wayneManor =
    { new Organization3
         with chief = "Batman"
         and  indians = ["Robin"; "Alfred"] }
```

F# does not force field names to be unique, so sometimes the compiler cannot infer the type of a field from the field names alone. In this case, you must use the syntax that specifies the type. Again, you place the record definition between braces, but the new keyword, the type name, and the keyword with precede the field definitions. The field definitions themselves remain the same but are separated with the keyword and instead of semicolons. This is illustrated by the types Organization2 and Organization3 and their instances thePlayers and wayneManor. (This syntax is similar to that used for object expressions, which are a way of creating .NET objects in F# and are discussed in Chapter 5.)

Ordinarily the scope of a type definition is from where it is declared forward to the end of the source file in which it is declared. If a type needs to reference a type declared after it, it can do so if they are declared together, in the same *block*. Types declared in the same block must be declared next to each other, that is, no value definitions in between, and the keyword type is replaced by the keyword and for every type definition after the first one. Types declared in this way are not any different from types declared the regular way. They can reference any other type in the block, and they can even be *mutually referential*. The next example shows two types, recipe and ingredient, declared in the same block. If they were declared separately, recipe would not be able to reference ingredient because recipe is declared before ingredient; because their declarations are joined with the keyword and, recipe can have a field of type ingredient.

```
#light
type recipe =
    { recipeName ; string ;
      ingredients : ingredient list ;
      instructions : string }
```

```
and ingredient =
    { ingredientName : string ;
      quantity : int }

let greenBeansPineNuts =
    { recipeName = "Green Beans & Pine Nuts" ;
      ingredients =
            [{ ingredientName = "Green beans" ; quantity = 250 };
             { ingredientName = "Pine nuts" ; quantity = 250 };
             { ingredientName = "Feta cheese" ; quantity = 250 };
             { ingredientName = "Olive oil" ; quantity = 10 };
             { ingredientName = "Lemon" ; quantity = 1 }] ;
      instructions = "Parboil the green beans for about 7 minutes. Roast the pine
nuts carefully in a frying pan. Drain the beans and place in a salad bowl
with the roasted pine nuts and feta cheese. Coat with the olive oil
and lemon juice and mix well. Serve ASAP." }

let name = greenBeansPineNuts.recipeName
let toBuy =
    List.fold_left
        (fun acc x ->
            acc +
            (Printf.sprintf "\t%s - %i\r\n" x.ingredientName x.quantity) )
        "" greenBeansPineNuts.ingredients
let instructions = greenBeansPineNuts.instructions

printf "%s\r\n%s\r\n\r\n\t%s" name toBuy instructions
```

The results of this example, when compiled and executed, are as follows:

```
Green Beans & Pine Nuts

        Green beans - 250
        Pine nuts - 250
        Feta cheese - 250
        Olive oil - 10
        Lemon - 1

        Parboil the green beans for about 7 minutes. Roast the pine
nuts carefully in a frying pan. Drain the beans and place in a salad bowl
with the roasted pine nuts and feta cheese. Coat with the olive oil
and lemon juice and mix well. Serve ASAP.
```

As well as demonstrating two types being declared together, this example also demonstrates how you access fields in records. One advantage that records have over tuples is that accessing their contents is easier. The construct is simply an identifier dot (.) field name, as shown when associating values with the identifiers name, toBuy, and instructions.

Record types can also be pattern matched; that is, you can use pattern matching to match fields within the record type. The findDavid function in the next example does this. As you would expect, the syntax for examining a record using pattern matching is similar to the syntax used to construct it.

You can compare a field to a constant with *field* = *constant*. You can assign the values of fields with identifiers with *field* = *identifier*. Or, you can ignore a field with *field* = _. The first rule in the find_david function is the one that does the real work, where you check the her field of the record to see whether it is "Posh", David's wife. The him field is associated with the identifier x so it can be used in the second half of the rule.

```
#light
type couple = { him : string ; her : string }

let couples =
    [ { him = "Brad" ; her = "Angelina" };
      { him = "Becks" ; her = "Posh" };
      { him = "Chris" ; her = "Gwyneth" };
      { him = "Michael" ; her = "Catherine" } ]

let rec findDavid l =
    match l with
    | { him = x ; her = "Posh" } :: tail -> x
    | _ :: tail -> findDavid tail
    | [] -> failwith "Couldn't find David"

print_string (findDavid couples)
```

The results of this example, when compiled and executed, are as follows:

```
Becks
```

Field values can also be functions. Since this technique is mainly used in conjunction with mutable state to form values similar to objects, I won't discuss this here but in its own section in Chapter 4.

Union types, sometimes called *sum types* or *discriminated unions*, are a way of bringing together data that may have a different meaning or structure. The next example defines a type volume whose values can have three different meanings—liter, U.S. pint, or imperial pint. Although the structure of the data is the same and is represented by a float, the meanings are quite different. Mixing up the meaning of data in an algorithm is a common cause of bugs in programs, and the volume type is in part an attempt to avoid this.

You define a union type using the type keyword, followed by the type name, followed by an equals sign—just as all type definitions. Then comes the definition of the different *constructors*, separated by vertical bars. The first vertical bar is optional. A constructor is composed of a name that must start with a capital letter; this is to stop the common bug of getting constructor names mixed up with identifier names. The name can optionally be followed by the keyword of and then the types that make up that constructor. Multiple types that make up a constructor are separated by asterisks. The names of constructors within a type must be unique. If several union types are defined, then the names of their constructors can overlap; however, you should be careful when doing this, because it can be that further type annotations are required when constructing and consuming union types.

The following Volume type is a union type with three constructors, each composed of a single item of type float. The syntax for constructing a new instance of a union type is the constructor name followed by the values for the types, with multiple values separated by commas. Optionally, you can place the values in parentheses. You use the three different Volume constructors to construct three different identifiers, vol1, vol2, and vol3.

```
#light
type Volume =
| Liter of float
| UsPint of float
| ImperialPint of float

let vol1 = Liter 2.5
let vol2 = UsPint 2.5
let vol3 = ImperialPint (2.5)
```

To deconstruct the values of union types into their basic parts, you always use pattern matching. When pattern matching over a union type, the constructors make up the first half of the pattern matching rules. You don't need a complete list of rules, but if you don't, there must be a default rule, using either an identifier or a wildcard to match all remaining rules. The first part of a rule for a constructor consists of the constructor name followed by identifiers or wildcards to match the various values within it. The following functions, convertVolumeToLiter, convertVolumeUsPint, and convertVolumeImperialPint, demonstrate this syntax:

```
let convertVolumeToLiter x =
    match x with
    | Liter x -> x
    | UsPint x -> x * 0.473
    | ImperialPint x -> x * 0.568

let convertVolumeUsPint x =
    match x with
    | Liter x -> x * 2.113
    | UsPint x -> x
    | ImperialPint x -> x * 1.201

let convertVolumeImperialPint x =
    match x with
    | Liter x -> x * 1.760
    | UsPint x -> x * 0.833
    | ImperialPint x -> x
```

```
let printVolumes x =
    printfn "Volume in liters = %f,
in us pints = %f,
in imperial pints = %f"
        (convertVolumeToLiter x)
        (convertVolumeUsPint x)
        (convertVolumeImperialPint x)

printVolumes vol1
printVolumes vol2
printVolumes vol3
```

The results of these examples, when compiled and executed, are as follows:

```
Volume in liters = 2.500000,
in us pints = 5.282500,
in imperial pints = 4.400000
Volume in liters = 1.182500,
in us pints = 2.500000,
in imperial pints = 2.082500
Volume in liters = 1.420000,
in us pints = 3.002500,
in imperial pints = 2.500000
```

Both union and record types can be *parameterized*. Parameterizing a type means leaving one or more of the types within the type being defined to be determined later by the consumer of the types. This is a similar concept to the variable types discussed earlier in this chapter. When defining types, you must be a little bit more explicit about which types are variable.

F# supports two syntaxes for type parameterization. In the first, you place the type being parameterized between the keyword type and the name of the type, as follows:

```
#light
type 'a BinaryTree =
| BinaryNode of 'a BinaryTree * 'a BinaryTree
| BinaryValue of 'a

let tree1 =
    BinaryNode(
        BinaryNode ( BinaryValue 1, BinaryValue 2),
        BinaryNode ( BinaryValue 3, BinaryValue 4) )
```

In the second syntax, you place the types being parameterized in angle brackets after the type name, as follows:

```
#light
type Tree<'a> =
| Node of Tree<'a> list
| Value of 'a

let tree2 =
    Node( [ Node( [Value "one"; Value "two"] ) ;
            Node( [Value "three"; Value "four"] ) ]  )
```

Like variable types, the names of type parameters always start with a single quote (') followed by an alphanumeric name for the type. Typically, just a single letter is used. If multiple parameterized types are required, you separate them with commas. You can then use the type parameters throughout the type definition. The previous examples defined two parameterized types, using the two different syntaxes that F# offers. The BinaryTree type used OCaml-style syntax, where the type parameters are placed before the name of the type. The tree type used .NET-style syntax, with the type parameters in angle brackets after the type name.

The syntax for creating and consuming an instance of a parameterized type does not change from that of creating and consuming a nonparameterized type. This is because the compiler will automatically infer the type parameters of the parameterized type. You can see this in the following construction of tree1 and tree2 and their consumption by the functions printBinaryTreeValues and printTreeValues:

```
let rec printBinaryTreeValues x =
    match x with
    | BinaryNode (node1, node2) ->
        printBinaryTreeValues node1;
        printBinaryTreeValues node2
    | BinaryValue x -> print_any x; print_string ", "

let rec printTreeValues x =
    match x with
    | Node l -> List.iter printTreeValues l
    | Value x ->
        print_any x
        print_string ", "

printBinaryTreeValues tree1
print_newline()
printTreeValues tree2
```

The results of this example, when compiled and executed, are as follows:

```
1, 2, 3, 4,
"one", "two", "three", "four",
```

You may have noticed that although I've discussed defining types, creating instances of them, and examining these instances, I haven't discussed updating them. This is because it is not possible to update these kinds of types because the idea of a value that changes over time goes against the idea of functional programming. However, F# does have some types that are updatable, and I discuss them in Chapter 4.

Exceptions and Exception Handling

Exception definitions in F# are similar to defining a constructor of a union type, and the syntax for handling exceptions is similar to pattern matching.

You define exceptions using the exception keyword followed by the name of the exception and then optionally the keyword of and the types of any values the exception should contain, with multiple types separated by asterisks. The next example shows the definition of an exception, WrongSecond, which contains one integer value:

```
exception WrongSecond of int
```

You can raise exceptions with the raise keyword, as shown in the else clause in the following testSecond function. F# also has an alterative to the raise keyword, the failwith function, as shown in the following if clause. If, as is commonly the case, you just want to raise an exception with a text description of what went wrong, you can use failwith to raise a generic exception that contains the text passed to the function.

```
let primes =
    [ 2; 3; 5; 7; 11; 13; 17; 19; 23; 29; 31; 37; 41; 43; 47; 53; 59 ]

let testSecond() =
    try
        let currentSecond = System.DateTime.Now.Second in
        if List.exists (fun x -> x = currentSecond) primes then
            failwith "A prime second"
        else
            raise (WrongSecond currentSecond)
    with
        WrongSecond x ->
            printf "The current was %i, which is not prime" x

testSecond()
```

As shown in testSecond, the try and with keywords handle exceptions. The expressions that are subject to error handling go between the try and with keywords, and one or more pattern matching rules must follow the with keyword. When trying to match an F# exception, the syntax follows that of trying to match an F# constructor from a union type. The first half of the rule consists of the exception name, followed by identifiers or wildcards to match values that the exception contains. The second half of the rule is an expression that states how the exception should be handled. One major difference between this and the regular pattern matching constructs is that no warning or error is issued if pattern matching is incomplete. This is because any exceptions that are unhandled will propagate until they reach the top level and stop execution. The example handles exception wrongSecond, while leaving the exception raised by failwith to propagate.

F# also supports a finally keyword, which is used with the try keyword. You can use the finally keyword in conjunction with the with keyword as well as some rules for error handling or no rules. Always place the finally expression after the with block, if it exists; the finally expression will be executed whether an exception is thrown. The next example shows a finally block being used to ensure a file is closed and disposed of after it is written to:

```
#light
let writeToFile() =
    let file = System.IO.File.CreateText("test.txt") in
    try
        file.WriteLine("Hello F# users")
    finally
        file.Dispose()


writeToFile()
```

■Caution Programmers coming from an OCaml background should be careful when using exceptions in F#. Because of the architecture of the CLR, throwing an exception is pretty expensive—quite a bit more expensive than in OCaml. If you throw lots of exceptions, profile your code carefully to decide whether the performance costs are worth it. If the costs are too high, revise the code appropriately. I discuss tools for profiling F# applications in Chapter 12.

Lazy Evaluation

Lazy evaluation is something that goes hand in hand with functional programming. The theory is that if there are no side effects in the language, the compiler or runtime is free to choose the evaluation order of expressions. As you know, F# allows functions to have side effects, so it's not possible for the compiler or runtime to have a free hand in function evaluation; therefore, F# is said to have a *strict evaluation order* or be a *strict language*. You can still take advantage of lazy evaluation but must be explicit about which computations can be delayed, that is, evaluated in a lazy manner. You use the keyword lazy to delay a computation, that is, invoke lazy evaluation. The computation within the lazy expression remains unevaluated until evaluation; it is explicitly forced with the force function from the Lazy module. When the force function is applied to a particular lazy expression, the value is computed; then the result is cached, and subsequent calls to the force function return the cached value, whatever it is, even if this means raising an exception. The following code shows a simple use of lazy evaluation:

```
#light
let lazyValue = lazy ( 2 + 2 )
```

```
let actualValue = Lazy.force lazyValue

print_int actualValue
print_newline()
```

On the first line, you delay a simple expression for evaluation later. The next line forces evaluation. Then you print the value. The value has been cached, so any side effects that take place when the value is computed will occur only the first time the lazy value is forced. This is fairly easy to demonstrate. In the next example, you create a lazy value that has a side effect when it is calculated: it writes to the console. To show that this side effect takes place only once, you force the value twice, and it is plain to see from the result that writing to the console takes place only once.

```
#light
let lazySideEffect =
    lazy
        ( let temp = 2 + 2
            print_int temp
            print_newline()
            temp )

print_endline "Force value the first time: "
let actualValue1 = Lazy.force lazySideEffect

print_endline "Force value the second time: "
let actualValue2 = Lazy.force lazySideEffect
```

The results of this example are as follows:

```
Force value the first time:
4
Force value the second time:
```

Laziness can also be useful when working with collections. The idea of a lazy collection is that elements in the collection are calculated on demand. Some collection types also cache the results of these calculations, so there is no need to recalculate elements. F# provides the LazyList collection type, which caches computed results and is useful for functional programming and search. The second lazy collection is the seq type, a shorthand for the BCL's IEnumerable type. This plays a similar role to LazyList but does not cache computed results. LazyList and seq values are created and manipulated using functions in the LazyList and Seq modules, respectively. Many other values are also compatible with the type seq; for example, all F# lists and arrays are compatible with this type, as are most other collection types.

The next example shows how to use the LazyList module. Possibly its most important function, and probably the most difficult to understand, is unfold. This function allows you to create a lazy list. What makes it complicated is that you must provide a function that will be repeatedly evaluated to provide the elements of the list. The function passed to LazyList. unfold can take any type of parameter and must return an option type. An option type is a union type that can be either None or Some(x), where x is a value of any type. None is used to represent the end of a list. The Some constructor must contain a tuple. The first item in the tuple represents the value that will become the first value in the list. The second value in the tuple is the value that will be passed into the function the next time it is called. You can think of this value as an accumulator.

The next example shows how this works. The identifier lazyList will contain three values. If the value passed into the function is less than 13, you append the list using this value to form the list element and then add 1 to the value passed to the list. This will be value passed to the function the next time it is called. If the value is greater than or equal to 13, you terminate the list by returning None. To display the list, you use the function display, a simple recursive function that processes the head of the list and then recursively processes the tail.

```
#light
let lazyList =
    LazyList.unfold
        (fun x ->
            if x < 13 then
                Some(x, x + 1)
            else
                None)
        10

let rec display l =
    match  l with
    | LazyList.Cons(h,t) ->
        print_int h
        print_newline ()
        display t
    | LazyList.Nil ->
        ()

display lazyList
```

The results of this example, when compiled and executed, are as follows:

```
10
11
12
```

Lazy lists are also useful to represent lists that don't terminate. A nonterminating list can't be represented by a classic list, which is constrained by the amount of memory available. The next example demonstrates this by creating fibs, an infinite list of all the Fibonacci numbers; it uses the Seq module, although it could just as well have used the LazyList module because the unfold function works in the same way in both. To display the results conveniently, you use the function Seq.take to turn the first 20 items into an F# list, but you carry on calculating many more Fibonacci numbers as you use F# bigint integers, so you are limited by the size of a 32-bit integer.

```
#light
let fibs =
    Seq.unfold
      (fun (n0, n1)  ->
          Some(n0, (n1, n0 + n1)))
      (1I,1I)

let first20 = Seq.take 20 fibs

print_any first20
```

The results of this example are as follows:

```
[1I; 1I; 2I; 3I; 5I; 8I; 13I; 21I; 34I; 55I; 89I; 144I; 233I; 377I; 610I; 987I;
 1597I; 2584I; 4181I; 6765I]
```

These examples are too simple to really demonstrate the power of lazy evaluation. You'll look at lazy evaluation again in several places in this book, notably in Chapter 7, where you'll see how to use lazy evaluation in user-interface programming to make user interfaces more responsive by ensuring computations do not happen until really needed.

Summary

In this chapter, you looked at the major functional programming constructs in F#. This is the core of the language, and I hope you've developed a good feel for how to approach writing algorithms and handling data in F#. The next chapter will cover imperative programming, and you'll see how to mix functional and imperative programming techniques to handle tasks such as input/output (I/O).

CHAPTER 4

■ ■ ■

Imperative Programming

As you saw in Chapter 3, you can use F# for pure functional programming. However, some issues, most notably I/O, are almost impossible to address without some kind of state change. F# does not require that you program in a stateless fashion. It allows you to use *mutable* identifiers whose values can change over time. F# also has other constructs that support imperative programming. You've already seen some in Chapter 3. Any example that wrote to the console included a few lines of imperative code alongside functional code. In this chapter, you'll explore these constructs, and many others, in much more detail.

First, you'll look at F#'s unit type, a special type that means "no value," which enables some aspects of imperative programming. Next, you'll look at some of the ways F# can handle *mutable state*, that is, types whose values can change over time. These are the ref type, mutable record types, and arrays. Finally, you'll look at using .NET libraries. The topics will include calling static methods, creating objects and working with their members, using special members such as indexers and events, and using the F# |> operator, which is handy when dealing with .NET libraries.

The unit Type

Any function that does not accept or return values is of type unit, which is similar to the type void in C# and System.Void in the CLR. To a functional programmer, a function that doesn't accept or return a value might not seem interesting, since if it doesn't accept or return a value, it does nothing. In the imperative paradigm, you know that side effects exist, so even if a function accepts or returns nothing, you know it can still have its uses. The unit type is represented as a literal value, a pair of parentheses (()). This means that whenever you want a function that doesn't take or return a value, you just put () in the code:

```
#light
let main() =
    ()
```

In this example, main is a function because you placed parentheses after the identifier, where its parameters would go. If you didn't this, it would mean main is not a function and instead just a value that is not a function. As you know, all functions are values, but here the difference between a function and a nonfunction value is important. If main were a nonfunction value, the expressions within it would be evaluated only once. Since it is a function, the expressions will be evaluated each time it is called.

■ **Caution** Just because a function is named main doesn't mean it is the entry point of the program and is executed automatically. If you wanted your main function to be executed, then you would need to add a call to main() at the end of the source file. Chapter 6 details exactly how the entry point is determined for an F# program.

Similarly, by placing () after the equals sign, you tell the compiler you are going to return nothing. Ordinarily, you need to put something between the equals sign and the empty parentheses, or the function is pointless; however, for the sake of keeping things simple, I'll leave this function pointless. Now you'll see the type of main by using the fsc -i switch; the results of this are as follows. (I explained the notation used by the compiler's -i switch in Chapter 3's "Types and Type Inference.") As you can see, the type of main is a function that accepts unit and transforms it into a value of type unit:

```
val main : unit -> unit
```

Because the compiler now knows the function doesn't return anything, you can now use it with some special imperative constructs. To call the function, you can use the let keyword followed by a pair of parentheses and the equals sign. This is a special use of the let keyword, which means "call a function that does not return a value." Alternatively, you can simply call the function without any extra keywords at all:

```
#light
let () = main()
// -- or --
main()
```

Similarly, you can chain functions that return unit together within a function—simply make sure they all share the same indentation. The next example shows several print_endline functions chained together to print text to the console:

```
#light
let poem() =
    print_endline "I wandered lonely as a cloud"
    print_endline "That floats on high o'er vales and hills,"
    print_endline "When all at once I saw a crowd,"
    print_endline "A host, of golden daffodils"
poem()
```

It's not quite true that the only functions that return unit type can be used in this manner; however, using them with a type other than unit will generate a warning, which is something most programmers want to avoid. So, to avoid this, it's sometimes useful to turn a function that does return a value into a function of type unit, typically because it has a side effect. The need to do this is fairly rare when just using F# libraries written in F# (although situations where it is useful do exist), but it is more common when using .NET libraries that were not written in F#.

CHAPTER 4 ■ IMPERATIVE PROGRAMMING

The next example shows how to turn a function that returns a value into a function that returns unit:

```
#light
let getShorty() = "shorty"

let _ = getShorty()
// -- or --
ignore(getShorty())
// -- or --
getShorty() |> ignore
```

First you define the function getShorty, which returns a string. Now imagine, for whatever reason, you want to call this function and ignore its result. The next two lines demonstrate different ways to do this. First, you can use a let expression with an underscore (_) character in place of the identifier. The underscore tells the compiler this is a value in which you aren't interested. Second, this is such a common thing to do that it has been wrapped into a function, ignore, which is available in the F# base libraries and is demonstrated on the third line. The final line shows an alternative way of calling ignore using the pass-forward operator to pass the result of getShorty() to the ignore function. I explain the pass-forward operator in the "The |> Operator" section.

The mutable Keyword

In Chapter 3 I talked about how you could bind identifiers to values using the keyword let and noted how under some circumstances you could redefine and rebound, but not modify, these identifiers. If you want to define an identifier whose value can change over time, you can do this using the mutable keyword. A special operator, the *left ASCII arrow* (or just *left arrow*), is composed of a less-than sign and a dash (<-) and is used to update these identifiers. An update operation using the left arrow has type unit, so you can chain these operations together as discussed in the previous section. The next example demonstrates defining a mutable identifier of type string and then changing the changing the value it holds:

```
#light
let mutable phrase = "How can I be sure, "
print_endline phrase
phrase <- "In a world that's constantly changing"
print_endline phrase
```

The results are as follows:

```
How can I be sure,
In a world that's constantly changing
```

At first glance this doesn't look too different from redefining an identifier, but it has a couple of key differences. When you use the left arrow to update a mutable identifier, you can change its value but not its type—when you redefine an identifier, you can do both. A compile error is produced if you try to change the type; the next example demonstrates this:

```
#light
let mutable number = "one"
phrase <- 1
```

When attempting to compile this code, you'll get the following error message:

```
Prog.fs(9,10): error: FS0001: This expression has type
    int
but is here used with type
    string
```

The other major difference is where these changes are visible. When you redefine an identifier, the change is visible only within the scope of the new identifier. When it passes out of scope, it reverts to its old value. This is not the case with mutable identifiers. Any changes are permanent, whatever the scope. The next example demonstrates this:

```
#light
let redefineX() =
    let x = "One"
    printfn "Redefining:\r\nx = %s" x
    if true then
        let x = "Two"
        printfn "x = %s" x
    else ()
    printfn "x = %s" x

let mutableX() =
    let mutable x = "One"
    printfn "Mutating:\r\nx = %s" x
    if true then
        x <- "Two"
        printfn "x = %s" x
    else ()
    printfn "x = %s" x

redefineX()
mutableX()
```

The results are as follows:

```
Redefining:
x = One
x = Two
x = One
Mutating:
x = One
x = Two
x = Two
```

Identifiers defined as mutable are somewhat limited because they can't be used within a subfunction. You can see this in the next example:

```
#light
let mutableY() =
    let mutable y = "One"
    printfn "Mutating:\r\nx = %s" y
    let f() =
        y <- "Two"
        printfn "x = %s" y
    f()
    printfn "x = %s" y
```

The results of this example, when compiled and executed, are as follows:

```
Prog.fs(35,16): error: The mutable variable 'y' has escaped its scope.  Mutable
variables may not be used within an inner subroutine.  You may need to use a heap-
allocated mutable reference cell instead, see 'ref' and '!'.
```

As the error messages says, this is why the ref type, a special type of mutable record, has been made available—to handle mutable variables that need to be shared among several functions. I discuss mutable records in the next section and the ref type in the section after that.

Defining Mutable Record Types

In Chapter 3, when you first met record types, I did not discuss how to update their fields. This is because record types are immutable by default. F# provides special syntax to allow the fields in record types to be updated. You do this by using the keyword mutable before the field in a record type. I should emphasize that this operation changes the contents of the record's field rather than changing the record itself.

```
#light
type Couple = { her : string ; mutable him : string }

let theCouple = { her = "Elizabeth Taylor " ; him = "Nicky Hilton" }

let print o = printf "%A\r\n" o

let changeCouple() =
    print theCouple;
    theCouple.him <- "Michael Wilding";
    print theCouple;
    theCouple.him <- "Michael Todd";
    print theCouple;
    theCouple.him <- "Eddie Fisher";
    print theCouple;
```

```
theCouple.him <- "Richard Burton";
print theCouple;
theCouple.him <- "Richard Burton";
print theCouple;
theCouple.him <- "John Warner";
print theCouple;
theCouple.him <- "Larry Fortensky";
print theCouple
```

```
changeCouple()
```

The results are as follows:

```
{her = "Elizabeth Taylor "; him = "Nicky Hilton"}
{her = "Elizabeth Taylor "; him = "Michael Wilding"}
{her = "Elizabeth Taylor "; him = "Michael Todd"}
{her = "Elizabeth Taylor "; him = "Eddie Fisher"}
{her = "Elizabeth Taylor "; him = "Richard Burton"}
{her = "Elizabeth Taylor "; him = "Richard Burton"}
{her = "Elizabeth Taylor "; him = "John Warner"}
{her = "Elizabeth Taylor "; him = "Larry Fortensky"}
```

This example shows a mutable record in action. A type, couple, is defined where the field him is mutable but the field her is not. Next, an instance of couple is initialized, and then you change the value of him many times, each time displaying the results. I should note that the mutable keyword applies per field, so any attempt to update a field that is not mutable will result in a compile error; for example, the next example will fail on the second line:

```
#light
theCouple.her <- "Sybil Williams";
print_any theCouple
```

When attempting to compile this program, you'll get the following error message:

```
prog.fs(2,4): error: FS0005: This field is not mutable
```

The ref Type

The ref type is a simple way for a program to use mutable state, that is, values that change over time. The ref type is just a record type with a single mutable field that is defined in the F# libraries. Some operators are defined to make accessing and updating the field as straightforward as possible. F#'s definition of the ref type uses *type parameterization*, a concept introduced in the previous chapter, so although the value of the ref type can be of any type, you cannot change the type of the value once you have created an instance of the value.

Creating a new instance of the ref type is easy; you use the keyword ref followed by whatever item represents the value of ref. The next example is the compiler's output (using the -i option, which shows that the type of phrase is string ref, meaning a reference type that can contain only strings):

```
let phrase = ref "Inconsistency"
```

```
val phrase : string ref
```

This syntax is similar to defining a union type's constructors, also shown in the previous chapter. The ref type has two built-in operators to access it; the exclamation point (!) provides access to the value of the reference type, and an operator composed of a colon followed by an equals sign (:=) provides for updating it. The ! operator always returns a value of the type of the contents of the ref type, known to the compiler thanks to type parameterization. The := operator has type unit, because it doesn't return anything.

The next example shows how to use a ref type to total the contents of an array. On the third line of totalArray, you see the creation of the ref type. In this case, it is initialized to hold the value 0. On the fifth line, you see the ref type being both accessed and updated. First, ! is used to access the value with the ref type; then, after it has been added to the current value held in the array, the value of the ref type is updated through the use of the := operator. Now the code will correctly print 6 to the console.

```
#light
let totalArray () =
    let a = [| 1; 2; 3 |]
    let x = ref 0
    for n in a do
        x := !x + n
    print_int !x
    print_newline()

totalArray()
```

The result is as follows:

```
6
```

Caution If you are used to programming in one of the C family of programming languages, you should be careful here. When reading F# code, it is quite easy to misinterpret the ref type's ! operator as a Boolean "not" operator. F# uses a function called not for Boolean "not" operations.

The ref type is a useful way to share mutable values between several functions. An identifier can be bound to a ref type defined in scope that is common to all functions that want to use the value; then the functions can use the value of the identifier as they like, changing it or merely reading it. Because in F# functions can be passed around as if they were values, everywhere the function goes, the value follows it. This process is known as *capturing a local* or *creating a closure*. The next example demonstrates this by defining three functions, inc, dec, and show, which all share a common ref type holding an integer. The functions inc, dec, and show are all defined in their own private scopes and then returned to the top level as a tuple so they are visible everywhere. Note how n is not returned; it remains private, but inc, dec, and show are all still able to access n. This is a useful technique for controlling what operations can take place on mutable data.

```
#light
let inc, dec, show =
    let n = ref 0
    let inc () =
        n := !n + 1
    let dec () =
        n := !n - 1
    let show () =
        print_int !n
    inc, dec, show

inc()
inc()
dec()
show()
```

The result is as follows:

1

Arrays

Arrays are a concept that most programmers are familiar with, since almost all programming languages have some sort of array type. The F# array type is based on the BCL System.Array type, so anyone who has used in arrays in C# or Visual Basic will find that the underlying concepts are the same.

Arrays are a mutable collection type in F#. Arrays are the opposite of lists, discussed in Chapter 3. The values within arrays are updatable, whereas lists are not, and lists can grow dynamically, whereas arrays cannot. One-dimensional arrays are sometimes referred to as *vectors*, and multidimensional arrays are sometimes called *matrices*. Arrays are defined by a sequence of items separated by semicolons (;) and delimited by an opening square bracket and a vertical bar ([|) and a closing bar and square bracket (|]). The syntax for referencing an array element is the name of the identifier of the array followed by period (.) and then the index of the element in square brackets ([ ]). The syntax for retrieving the value of an element stops there. The syntax for setting the value of an element is the left arrow (<-) followed by the value to be assigned to the element.

The next example shows an array being read from and written to. First an array, rhymeArray, is defined, and then you read all the members from it. Then you insert new values into the array, and finally you print out all the values you have.

```
#light
let rhymeArray =
    [| "Went to market" ;
        "Stayed home" ;
        "Had roast beef" ;
        "Had none" |]

let firstPiggy = rhymeArray.[0]
let secondPiggy = rhymeArray.[1]
let thirdPiggy = rhymeArray.[2]
let fourthPiggy = rhymeArray.[3]

rhymeArray.[0] <- "Wee,"
rhymeArray.[1] <- "wee,"
rhymeArray.[2] <- "wee,"
rhymeArray.[3] <- "all the way home"
print_endline firstPiggy
print_endline secondPiggy
print_endline thirdPiggy
print_endline fourthPiggy
print_any rhymeArray
```

The results of this example, when compiled and executed, are as follows:

```
Went to market
Stayed home
Had roast beef
Had none
[|"Wee,"; "wee,"; "wee,"; "all the way home"|]
```

Arrays, like lists, use type parameterization, so the type of the array is the type of its contents followed by the array's type, so rhymeArray has type string array, which may also be written string[].

Multidimensional arrays in F# come in two slightly different flavors, jagged and rectangular. *Jagged* arrays, as the name suggests, are arrays where the second dimension is not a regular shape. They are simply arrays whose contents happen to other arrays, and the length of the inner arrays is not forced to be the same. In *rectangular* arrays, all inner arrays are of the same length; in fact, there is really no concept of an inner array since the whole array is just the same object. The method of getting and setting items in the two different types of arrays differs slightly

For jagged arrays, you use the period followed by the index in parentheses, but you have to use this twice (one time for each dimension), because the first time you get back the inner array and the second time you get the element within it.

The next example demonstrates a simple jagged array, called jagged. The array members are accessed in two different ways. The first inner array (at index 0) is assigned to the identifier singleDim, and then its first element is assigned to itemOne. On the fourth line, the first element of the second inner array is assigned to itemTwo, using one line of code.

```
#light
let jagged = [| [| "one" |] ; [| "two" ; "three" |] |]
let singleDim = jagged.[0]
let itemOne = singleDim.[0]
let itemTwo =  jagged.[1].[0]

printfn "%s %s" itemOne itemTwo
```

The results of this example, when compiled and executed, are as follows:

```
one two
```

To reference elements in rectangular arrays, use a period (.) followed by all the indexes in square brackets, separated by commas. Unlike jagged arrays, which are multidimensional but can be defined using the same ([| |]) syntax as single-dimensional arrays, you must create rectangular arrays with the create function of the Array2 and Array3 modules, which support two- and three-dimensional arrays, respectively. This doesn't mean rectangular arrays are limited to three dimensions, because it's possible to use the System.Array class to create rectangular arrays with more than three dimensions; however, creating such arrays should be considered carefully, because adding extra dimensions can quickly lead to very large objects.

The next example creates a rectangular array, square. Then its elements are populated with the integers 1, 2, 3, and 4.

```
#light
let square = Array2.create 2 2 0
square.[0,0] <- 1
square.[0,1] <- 2
square.[1,0] <- 3
square.[1,1] <- 4
printf "%A\r\n" square
```

Now let's look at the differences between jagged and rectangular arrays. First create a jagged array to represent Pascal's Triangle:

```
#light
let pascalsTriangle = [|
    [|1|];
    [|1; 1|];
    [|1; 2; 1|];
    [|1; 3; 3; 1|];
```

```
[|1; 4; 6; 4; 1|];
[|1; 5; 10; 10; 5; 1|];
[|1; 6; 15; 20; 15; 6; 1|];
[|1; 7; 21; 35; 35; 21; 7; 1|];
[|1; 8; 28; 56; 70; 56; 28; 8; 1|];
|]
```

Then create a rectangular array that contains various number sequences that are hidden within pascalsTriangle:

```
let numbers =
    let length = (Array.length pascalsTriangle) in
    let temp = Array2.create 3 length 0 in
    for index = 0 to length - 1 do
        let naturelIndex = index - 1 in
        if naturelIndex >= 0 then
            temp.[0, index] <- pascalsTriangle.[index].[naturelIndex];
        let triangularIndex = index - 2 in
        if triangularIndex >= 0 then
            temp.[1, index] <- pascalsTriangle.[index].[triangularIndex];
        let tetrahedralIndex = index - 3 in
        if tetrahedralIndex >= 0 then
            temp.[2, index] <- pascalsTriangle.[index].[tetrahedralIndex]
    done
    temp
```

Then display the sequences you've retrieved:

```
print_any numbers
```

The results of this example, when compiled and executed, are as follows:

```
[|[|0; 1; 2; 3; 4; 5; 6; 7; 8|];
[|0; 0; 1; 3; 6; 10; 15; 21; 28|];
[|0; 0; 0; 1; 4; 10; 20; 35; 56|]|]|]
```

The following shows the types displayed when you use the compiler's -i switch:

```
val pascals_triangle : int array array
val numbers : int [,]
```

As you may expect, jagged and rectangular arrays have different types. The type of a jagged array is the same as a single-dimensional array, just with an array per dimension, so the type of pascalsTriangle is int array array. Rectangular arrays use a more C#-style notation. First comes the name of the type of the array's elements, and after that comes square brackets ([]) with one comma for every dimension greater than 1, so the type of the example two-dimensional numbers array is int[,].

Caution To write code that is compatible with both .NET 1.1 and 2.0, you must use the `Microsoft.FSharp.Compatibility` namespace's `CompatArray` and `CompatMatrix` types. This is because of differences in the way that arrays behave in different .NET versions. In .NET 1.1, arrays are pseudogeneric, because you can create arrays of different types as though they were generic; however, they are not really generic, since .NET 1.1 doesn't support generics. In .NET 2.0, arrays became properly generic, and their behavior changed in a number of subtle ways that F# cannot abstract away. The result is that you must explicitly choose whether you want to use arrays that are supported in .NET 1.1.

Array Comprehensions

I introduced compression syntax in Chapter 3 for lists and sequences. You can use a corresponding syntax to create arrays. The only difference between this and the functional-style syntax is the characters that delimit the array. You use vertical bars surrounded by square brackets for arrays:

```
#light
let chars = [| '1' .. '9' |]

let squares =
    [| for x in 1 .. 9
        -> x, x*x |]
printfn "%A" chars
printfn "%A" squares
```

The results are as follows:

```
[|'1'; '2'; '3'; '4'; '5'; '6'; '7'; '8'; '9'|]
[|(1, 1); (2, 4); (3, 9); (4, 16); (5, 25); (6, 36); (7, 49); (8, 64); (9, 81)|]
```

Control Flow

Unlike the pseudo-control-flow syntax described in Chapter 3, F# does have some imperative control-flow constructs. In addition to the imperative use of `if`, there are also `while` and `for` loops.

The major difference from using the `if` expression in the imperative style, that is, using it with a function that returns type `unit`, is that you aren't forced to use an `else`, as the next example demonstrates:

```
#light
if System.DateTime.Now.DayOfWeek = System.DayOfWeek.Sunday then
    print_endline "Sunday Playlist: Lazy On A Sunday Afternoon - Queen"
```

Though it isn't necessary to have an else expression if the if expression has type unit, you can add one if necessary. This too must have type unit, or the compiler will issue an error. The next example demonstrates this:

```
#light
if System.DateTime.Now.DayOfWeek = System.DayOfWeek.Monday then
    print_endline "Monday Playlist: Blue Monday - New Order"
else
    print_endline "Alt Playlist: Fell In Love With A Girl - White Stripes"
```

You can use whitespace to detect where an if expression ends. The code that belongs to the if expression is indented, and the if expression ends when it goes back to its original indentation. So, in the next example, the string "Tuesday Playlist: Ruby Tuesday - Rolling Stones" will be printed on a Tuesday, and "Everyday Playlist: Eight Days A Week - Beatles" will be printed every day of the week.

```
#light
if System.DateTime.Now.DayOfWeek = System.DayOfWeek.Tuesday then
    print_endline "Tuesday Playlist: Ruby Tuesday - Rolling Stones"
print_endline "Everyday Playlist: Eight Days A Week - Beatles"
```

If you want multiple statements to be part of the if statement, then you would simply give them the same indention, as shown in the next example where both strings will be printed only on a Friday:

```
#light
if System.DateTime.Now.DayOfWeek = System.DayOfWeek.Friday then
    print_endline "Friday Playlist: Friday I'm In Love - The Cure"
    print_endline "Friday Playlist: View From The Afternoon - Arctic Monkeys"
```

Most programmers are familiar with for loops because they are commonly found in imperative programming languages. The idea of a for loop is to declare an identifier, whose scope is the for loop, that increases its value by 1 after each iteration of the loop and provides the condition for loop termination. F# follows this syntax. It starts with the keyword for followed by the identifier that will hold the counter value; then comes an equals sign, followed by an expression for the initial counter value, then the keyword to, and then an expression for the terminal value. The code that forms the body of the for loop comes after this, sandwiched between the keywords do and done. The for loop has type unit, so the code that forms the body of the loop should have type unit; otherwise, the compiler will issue a warning.

The next example demonstrates a common usage of a for loop—to enumerate all the values in an array. The identifier index will take on values starting at 0 and ending at 1 less than the length of the array. You can use this identifier as the index for the array.

```
#light
let ryunosukeAkutagawa = [| "Green "; "frog, ";
    "Is "; "your "; "body "; "also ";
    "freshly "; "painted?" |]

for index = 0 to Array.length ryunosukeAkutagawa - 1 do
    print_string ryunosukeAkutagawa.[index]
```

The results of this example, when compiled and executed, are as follows:

```
Green frog, Is your body also freshly painted?
```

In a regular for loop, the initial value of the counter must always be *less* than the final value, and the value of the counter will increase as the loop continues. There is a variation on this, where to is replaced by downto. In this case, the initial counter value must always be *greater* than the final value, and the counter will decrease as the loop continues. An example of how to use downto is as follows:

```
#light
let shusonKato = [| "watching."; "been "; "have ";
    "children "; "three "; "my "; "realize "; "and ";
    "ant "; "an "; "kill "; "I ";
      |]

for index = Array.length shusonKato - 1 downto 0 do
    print_string shusonKato.[index]
```

The results of this example, when compiled and executed, are as follows:

```
I kill an ant and realize my three children have been watching.
```

The while loop is another familiar imperative language construct. It is an expression that creates a loop over a section of code until a Boolean expression changes to false. To create a while loop in F#, you use the keyword while followed by a Boolean expression that determines whether the loop should continue. As with for loops, you place the body of the loop between the keywords do and done, and the body should have type unit; otherwise, the compiler will issue a warning. Here's an example of a while loop:

```
#light
let matsuoBasho = ref [ "An "; "old "; "pond! ";
    "A "; "frog "; "jumps "; "in- ";
    "The "; "sound "; "of "; "water" ]

while (List.nonempty !matsuoBasho) do
    print_string (List.hd !matsuoBasho);
    matsuoBasho := List.tl !matsuoBasho
```

You enumerate over a list, and the Boolean expression to terminate the loop is based on whether the list is empty. Within the body of the loop, you print the head of the list and then remove it, shortening the list on each iteration.

The results of this example, when compiled and executed, are as follows:

```
An old pond! A frog jumps in- The sound of water
```

Loops over Comprehensions

You can use loops using `for` to enumerate collections, performing an imperative action, one that returns `unit`, on each element. This is similar to the `foreach` loop available in many programming languages. The syntax for using a comprehension to enumerate a collection is the `for` keyword followed by the identifier that will be bound to each item in the collection, then the collection, and then the keyword `do`. The code for processing each item in the collection comes next—indented to show it belongs to the `for` loop. The following example demonstrates this, enumerating an array of strings and printing each one:

```
#light
let words = [| "Red"; "Lorry"; "Yellow"; "Lorry" |]

for word in words do
    print_endline word
```

The results are as follows:

```
Red
Lorry
Yellow
Lorry
```

As you'll see later in this chapter, and in many examples throughout the book, this can be a convenient way to work with collections returned by .NET BCL methods.

Calling Static Methods and Properties from .NET Libraries

One extremely useful feature of imperative programming in F# is being able to use just about any library written in a .NET programming language, including the many methods and classes available as part of the BCL itself. I consider this to be imperative programming, because libraries written in other languages make no guarantees about how state works inside them, so you can't know whether a method you call has side effects.

A distinction should be made between calling libraries written in F# and libraries written in any other language. This is because libraries written in F# have metadata that describes extra details about the library, such as whether a method takes a tuple or whether its parameters can be curried. This metadata is specific to F# and in a binary form understood by the F# compiler. This is largely why the `Microsoft.FSharp.Reflection` API is provided—to bridge the gap between F# and .NET metadata.

The basic syntax when calling static or instance properties or methods is the same. Method calls to a non-F# library must have their arguments separated by commas and surrounded by parentheses. (Remember, F# function calls usually use whitespace to separate arguments, and parentheses are needed only to impose precedence.) Method calls to a non-F# library cannot be curried, and the methods themselves are not equivalent to values, so they cannot be passed as arguments. Despite this difference, calling a method from a non-F# library is pretty straightforward. You'll start off by using static properties and methods:

```
#light
open System.IO

if File.Exists("test.txt") then
    print_endline "Text file \"test.txt\" is present"
else
    print_endline "Text file \"test.txt\" does not exist"
```

This example calls a static method from the .NET Framework BCL. Calling a static method is almost identical to calling an F# function. First comes the class name followed by a period (.) and then the name of the method; the only real difference is in the syntax for passing the arguments, which are surrounded by parentheses and separated by commas. You make a call to the System.IO.File class's Exists method to test whether a file exists and print an appropriate message depending on the result.

Often, you'll want to use the functionality of an existing .NET method but also want to use it in a functional manner. A common pattern in F# to achieve this is to *import* the function by writing a thin .NET wrapper. The next example demonstrates this:

```
#light
open System.IO
let exists filePath = File.Exists(filePath)

let files = ["test1.txt"; "test2.txt"; "test3.txt"]

let results = List.map exists files

print_any results
```

Unless you've created these specific text files in the directory where it runs, your result will be [false; false; false]. You have used the BCL Exists method to test whether a list of files exists. On the first line, you create a function that wraps the Exists method call, so you can use it in a functional manner and pass it to the map function.

When using .NET methods with lots of arguments, it can sometimes be helpful to know the names of the arguments to help you keep track of what each argument is doing. F# lets you use named arguments, where you give the name of the argument, then an equals sign, and then the value of the argument. The following example demonstrates this with an overload of File.Open() that takes four arguments:

```
#light
open System.IO

let file = File.Open(path = "test.txt",
                     mode = FileMode.Append,
                     access = FileAccess.Write,
                     share = FileShare.None)

file.Close()
```

Using Objects and Instance Members from .NET Libraries

Using classes from non-F# libraries is also straightforward. The syntax for instantiating an object consists of the keyword new, then the name of the class to be instantiated, and then constructor arguments separated by commas within parentheses. You can use the let keyword to bind an instance of a class to an identifier. Once associated with an identifier, the object behaves a lot like a record type; the object referred to cannot be changed, but its contents can. Also, if the identifier is not at the top level, then it can be redefined or hidden by an identifier of the same name in another scope. Accessing fields, properties, events, and methods should be pretty intuitive to both C# and Visual Basic programmers because the syntax is similar. To access any member, you use the identifier of the object followed by a period (.) and then the name of the member. Arguments to instance methods follow the same convention as for static methods, and they must be within parentheses and separated by commas. To retrieve the value of a property or field, only the name of member is needed, and to set it, you use the left arrow (<-).

The next example demonstrates how to create a System.IO.FileInfo object and then use various members of the class to manipulate it in different ways. On the first line, you make the System.IO namespace available to F#; then on the second, you create the FileInfo object, passing it the name of the file in which you're interested. Then you check whether the file exists using the Exists instance property. If it doesn't exist, you create a new file using the CreateText() instance method and then set it to be read-only using the Attributes instance property. The next example uses the using function to clean up resources. I explain this fully in the section "Microsoft.FSharp.Core.Operators" in Chapter 7.

```
#light
open System.IO
let file = new FileInfo("test.txt")

if not file.Exists then
    using (file.CreateText()) (fun stream ->
        stream.WriteLine("hello world"))
file.Attributes <- FileAttributes.ReadOnly

print_endline file.FullName
```

F# also lets you to set properties when you're constructing the object. It's quite common to set object properties as part of the process of initially configuring the object, especially in Win-Forms programming (see Chapter 8 for more information about WinForms). To set a property at construction time, place the property name inside the constructor followed by an equals sign and then by the value for the property. Separate multiple properties with commas. The following is a variation on the previous example; it sets the ReadOnly attribute when the object is the constructor:

```
#light
open System.IO
let filename = "test.txt"
let file =
    if File.Exists(filename) then
        Some(new FileInfo(filename, Attributes = FileAttributes.ReadOnly))
    else
        None
```

Note that you need to test for the file's existence to avoid a runtime exception when trying to set the Attributes property. F# allows you to set type parameters when calling a constructor, because it is not always possible to infer the type parameter of when making a constructor call. The type parameters are surrounded by angle brackets (<>) and separated by commas. The next example demonstrates how to set a type parameter when calling a constructor. You can create an instance of System.Collections.Generic.List, which can be used only with integers by setting its type parameter when it is created. In F# System.Collections.Generic.List is called ResizeArray to avoid confusion with F# lists.

```
#light
open System

let intList =
    let temp = new ResizeArray<int>() in
    temp.AddRange([| 1 ; 2 ; 3 |]);
    temp

intList.ForEach( fun i -> Console.WriteLine(i) )
```

The results are as follows:

```
1
2
3
```

The previous example also demonstrates another nice feature of F# when interoperating with non-F# libraries. .NET APIs often use a .NET construct called *delegates*, which are conceptually a kind of function value. F# functions will automatically be converted to .NET delegate objects if their signatures match. You can see this on the last line, where an F# function is passed directly to a method that takes a .NET delegate type.

To keep methods as flexible as possible, you may prefer not to specify a type parameter when importing methods that take generic delegates or perhaps when you're creating a wrapper F# function around constructors for a non-F# library. You achieve this by using the underscore (_) in place of the type parameter, as in the first line of the next example. (The following example uses the forward operator, |>, which I explain in the "The |> Operator" section.)

```
#light
open System
```

```
let findIndex f arr = Array.FindIndex(arr, new Predicate<_>(f))

let rhyme = [|"The"; "cat"; "sat"; "on"; "the"; "mat" |]

printfn "First word ending in 'at' in the array: %i"
    (rhyme |> findIndex (fun w -> w.EndsWith("at")))
```

The results of this example, when compiled and executed, are as follows:

```
First word ending in 'at' in the array: 1
```

Here you import the FindIndex method from the System.Array class, so you can use it in a curried style. If you had not explicitly created a delegate, the identifier f would have represented a predicate delegate rather than a function, meaning all calls to findIndex would need to explicitly create a delegate object, which is not ideal. However, if you had specified a type when creating the Predicate delegate in the definition of findIndex, then you would have limited the use of the findIndex function to arrays of a specific type. Occasionally, this may be what you want to do, but it is not usually the case. By using the underscore, you avoid having to specify a type for the findIndex function, keeping it nice and flexible.

Using Indexers from .NET Libraries

Indexers are a .NET concept that are designed to make a collection class look more like an array. Under the hood an indexer is a special property that is always called Item and has one or more parameters. It is important you have easy access to an indexer property, because many classes within the BCL have indexers.

In respect to syntax, F# offers two ways of using an indexer. You can explicitly use the Item property, or you can use an array-like syntax, with brackets instead of parentheses around the index.

```
open System.Collections.Generic

let stringList =
    let temp = new ResizeArray<string>() in
    temp.AddRange([| "one" ; "two" ; "three" |]);
    temp

let itemOne = stringList.Item(0)
let itemTwo = stringList.[1]

printfn "%s %s" itemOne itemTwo
```

This example associates the strings "one" and "two" with the identifiers itemOne and itemTwo, respectively. The association of "one" with itemOne demonstrates explicitly using the Item property. The association of "two" with itemTwo uses the bracket syntax.

■**Note** This example also demonstrates a common pattern in F#. Note how you want to create the identifier stringList as an object from a non-F# library and at the same time initialize it to a certain state. To do this you assign the object to a temporary identifier and then call an instance member on the object to manipulate its state. Finally, you return the temporary identifier so it becomes the value of stringList. In this way, you keep the object creation and initialization logic close together.

Working with Events from .NET Libraries

Events are special properties of objects that allow functions to be attached to them. The functions that are attached to events are sometimes referred to as *handlers*. When the event occurs, it executes all the functions that have been attached to it. An example of this might be that a Button object exposes a Click event, which occurs when a user clicks the button. This would mean that any functions that have been attached to the button's Click event would execute when the button is clicked. This is extremely useful, since it's common to need notifications of what the user has done when creating user interfaces.

Adding a hander to an event is fairly straightforward. Each event exposes a method called Add, and the handling event is passed to this method. Events come from non-F# libraries, so the Add method follows the convention that its arguments must be surrounded by parentheses. In F# it is common to place the handler function inside the Add method itself using F#'s anonymous function feature. The type of the handler function must match the type of the Add method's parameter, and this parameter has type 'a -> unit. This means that for events exposed by objects in the BCL, the parameter of the Add method will have a type similar to EventArgs -> Unit.

The next example shows the creation of a Timer object and a function being added to the timer's Elapsed event. A Timer object is an object that will fire its Elapsed event at regular intervals. In this case, the handler will show a message box displaying a notice to the user. Notice how you do not care about the argument that will be passed to the handler function, so you ignore it using the underscore.

```
#light
open System.Timers
module WF = System.Windows.Forms

let timer =
    let temp = new Timer()
    temp.Interval <- 3000.0
    temp.Enabled <- true
    let messageNo = ref 0
    temp.Elapsed.Add(fun _ ->
        let messages = ["bet"; "this"; "gets";
        "really"; "annoying"; "very"; "quickly";]
        WF.MessageBox.Show(List.nth messages !messageNo) |> ignore
        messageNo := (!messageNo + 1) % (List.length messages))
    temp
```

```
print_endline "Whack the return to finish!"
read_line() |> ignore
timer.Enabled <- false
```

It is also possible to remove handlers from events. To do this, you must keep the function you are going to add to the event in scope; you can pass it to the event's RemoveHandler method. The RemoveHandler method accepts a delegate, which is an object that wraps a regular .NET method to allow it to be passed around like a value. This means the handler function must be given to the event already wrapped in a delegate and must therefore use the event's AddHandler (or Removehandler) method instead of its Add (or Remove) method. Creating a delegate in F# is straightforward. You simply call the delegate's constructor, the same way you call any constructor for an object from any non-F# library, passing it the function that delegate should wrap.

```
#light
open System
open System.Windows.Forms

let form =
    let temp = new Form()
    let stuff _ _ = ignore(MessageBox.Show("This is \"Doing Stuff\""))
    let stuffHandler = new EventHandler(stuff)
    let event = new Button(Text = "Do Stuff", Left = 8, Top = 40, Width = 80)
    event.Click.AddHandler(stuffHandler)
    let eventAdded = ref true
    let label = new Label(Top = 8, Left = 96)
    let setText b = label.Text <- (Printf.sprintf "Event is on: %b" !b)
    setText eventAdded
    let toggle = new Button(Text = "Toggle Event", Left = 8, Top = 8, Width = 80)
    toggle.Click.Add(fun _ ->
            if !eventAdded then
                event.Click.RemoveHandler(stuffHandler)
            else
                event.Click.AddHandler(stuffHandler)
            eventAdded := not !eventAdded
            setText eventAdded)
    let dc c = (c :> Control)
    temp.Controls.AddRange([| dc toggle;  dc event;  dc label; |]);
    temp

do Application.Run(form)
```

This example shows the creation of a simple WinForm in F#. Events are synonymous with user interface programming, so I thought it would be good to show an example event of events being used in this context. Near the beginning of the example, you create a delegate, stuffHandler, which is then added to the Click event on the button event. Later you add a handler directly to the toggle button's Click event, which adds or removes the handler from the button's event.

Caution The previous sample will not work in the F# interactive console, fsi, because of the call to Application.Run. Users of fsi should replace this with form.Visible <- true;;.

Pattern Matching over .NET Types

As you saw in Chapter 3, pattern matching is a powerful feature of F#. Pattern matching allows a programmer to specify that different computations are executed depending on some value. F# has a construct that allows pattern matching over .NET types. The rule to match a .NET type is formed from a colon and question mark operator (:?) followed by the name of the .NET type to be matched. Because it is impossible have an exhaustive list of .NET types, you must always provide a default rule when pattern matching over .NET types.

```
#light
let simpleList = [ box 1; box 2.0; box "three" ]

let recognizeType (item : obj) =
    match item with
    | :? System.Int32 -> print_endline "An integer"
    | :? System.Double -> print_endline "A double"
    | :? System.String -> print_endline "A string"
    | _ -> print_endline "Unknown type"

List.iter recognizeType simpleList
```

The results are as follows:

```
An integer
A double
A string
```

This example shows a function, recognizeType, that is designed to recognize three of the .NET basic types via pattern matching. This function is then applied to a list. A couple of details about this function are noteworthy. First, the function takes an argument of type obj, and you need to use a type annotation to make sure it does. If you didn't use the type annotation, the compiler would infer that the function can take any type and would use type 'a. This would be a problem, because you cannot use pattern matching of this kind over F#'s types, but only over .NET types. Second, the function's default case uses the underscore to ignore the value.

Once you've recognized that a value is of a certain type, it's common to want to be able to do something with that value. To be able to use the value on the right side of a rule, you can use the as keyword followed by an identifier. You can see this in the next example, where you rewrite recognizeType to include the value in the message that is printed when a type is recognized:

```
#light
let anotherList = [ box "one"; box 2; box 3.0 ]

let recognizeAndPrintType (item : obj) =
    match item with
    | :? System.Int32 as x -> printfn "An integer: %i" x
    | :? System.Double as x -> printfn "A double: %f" x
    | :? System.String as x -> printfn "A string: %s" x
    | x -> printfn "An object: %A" x

List.iter recognizeAndPrintType anotherList
```

The results of this example, when compiled and executed, are as follows:

```
A string: one
An integer: 2
A double: 3.000000
```

Notice how for a final default rule you just use an identifier. You don't need to match it to a type since you already know it will be of type obj, since the value being matched over is already of type obj. In fact, if you try to create a rule where you match with type obj, you will get a compile error since this rule will always match. You can see this in the next example, where the previous example is reworked to generate the compile error I'm talking about:

```
#light
let thirdList = [ ("one" :> obj); (2 :> obj); (3.0 :> obj) ]

let reconizeTypeWrongly (item : obj) =
    match item with
    | :? System.Int32 -> print_endline "An integer"
    | :? System.Double -> print_endline "A double"
    | :? System.String -> print_endline "A string"
    | :? System.Object -> print_endline "Unknown type"

List.iter reconizeTypeWrongly thirdList
```

Pattern matching over .NET types is also useful for handling exceptions thrown by .NET methods. The pattern match rules are formed in the same way except they are used with the try … with construct instead of the try … match construct. The next example shows two .NET exceptions being thrown and then caught. The exceptions thrown are pattern matched over, and a different message is printed to the console depending on the type of exception thrown.

```
#light
try
    if System.DateTime.Now.Second % 3 = 0 then
        raise (new System.Exception())
    else
        raise (new System.ApplicationException())
```

```
with
| :? System.ApplicationException ->
    print_endline "A second that was not a multiple of 3"
| _ ->
    print_endline "A second that was a multiple of 3"
```

The |> Operator

The *pass-forward*, *pipe-forward*, or just *forward* operator (|>) is useful when working with .NET libraries. This is because it helps the compiler infer the correct types for method parameters without the need for explicit type annotations.

To understand why this operator is useful, it is helpful to probe a little deeper into to how right-to-left type inference works. Consider the following simple example, where you define a list of integers, called intList, of type int list and then pass this list as the second argument to the library function List.iter. The first argument to List.iter is a function of type int -> unit:

```
let int_list = [ 1 ; 2 ; 3 ]

List.iter (fun i -> print_int i) int_list
```

Now you need to understand how these expressions in the program were assigned their types. The compiler started at the top of the input file, found the identifier int_list, and inferred its type from the literal that is bound to it. Next, it found the function List.iter and knows that its type is ('a -> unit) -> 'a list -> unit. Since it has a generic or undetermined type 'a within it, the compiler must first examine the anonymous function (fun i -> print_int i). Because the parameter i is passed to the function print_int, the compiler infers that the type of i is int. Similarly, because the return type of print_int is unit, the return type of the anonymous function is unit. Because the parameter of the anonymous function is an integer, the compiler now knows that the parameter of the type of the undetermined type 'a is int, and this means the list passed to the function must be of type int list.

To fully understand the implications of this, it is helpful to look at an example that does not compile. Consider the next example, where you pass an identifier of type string list as the second argument to the library function List.iter whose first argument is a function of type int -> unit. Then you rewrite the code using the forward operator.

```
#light
let stringList = [ "1" ; "2" ; "3" ]

List.iter (fun i -> print_int i) stringList
stringList |> List.iter (fun i -> print_int i)
```

When trying to compile this function, you'll get the following error:

```
Prog.fs(3,36): error: FS0001: Type mismatch. Expecting a
    int list
but given a
    string list.
The type int does not match the type string
```

```
Prog.fs (4,48): error: FS0001: This expression has type
    string
but is here used with type
    int
```

The problem is that in the first case you're expecting an int list but are given a string list, and in the second case you're expecting an int but are given a string. In the first case, the type of the list was inferred from the type of the function, but in the second case the type of the function was inferred from the type of the list.

That you can infer the type of a function that operates on a list from the type of the list it operates on is incredibly useful when working with .NET libraries not written in F#. Consider the following example, where you define a list of type System.DateTime list and pass it to List.iter as the second argument. For the first argument, you try to define a function that will print the Year property of the DateTime type. Then you rewrite this function call using the forward operator.

```
#light
open System
let dateList = [ new DateTime(1999,12,31);
    new DateTime(1999,12,31);
    new DateTime(1999,12,31) ]

List.iter (fun d -> print_int d.Year) dateList
dateList |> List.iter (fun d -> print_int d.Year)
```

When trying to compile this function, you'll get the following error:

```
List.iter (fun d -> print_int d.Year) date_list
-----------------------------^^^^^^^
```

Prog.fs (11,33): error: Lookup on object of indeterminate type. A type annotation may be needed to constrain the type of the object in order for the lookup to be resolved.

Note that you receive only one error, when the List.iter function is written without the forward operator. Written with the forward operator, it compiles successfully. The error you receive means that the compiler has not been able to work out the type of the parameter d, so it cannot verify that it has a property Year. In the second case, by using the forward operator, the compiler is able to infer the type of the function is DateTime -> unit because it has already seen the list dateList and knows it is of type System.DateTime list.

One subtlety to watch out for is that, when working with types defined in F#, the compiler can often infer the type from the way it is used. Consider the next example, where you rewrite the previous example, this time using a date type that you've defined as an F# type, rather than a System.DateTime, which is defined in a library not written in F#.

```
#light
type date = { year : int; month : int; day : int }
```

```
let fsDateList =
    [ { year = 1999 ; month = 12; day = 31 };
      { year = 1999 ; month = 12; day = 31 };
      { year = 1999 ; month = 12; day = 31 } ]

List.iter (fun d -> print_int d.year) fsDateList
fsDateList |> List.iter (fun d -> print_int d.year)
```

Although this code is virtually the same as the previous example, it will compile without error. This is because the compiler can infer that the parameter d is of type date from the use of date's year field. It is important to remember that both cases work here, so although the forward operator isn't quite as useful when working with F#'s record types and its union type, you can still use it. In fact, you should consider using it even when working with F# types, because this will lead to working with both external .NET types and F# types in a consistent manner.

The forward operator > operator > operator is also incredibly useful when trying to chain functions together, that is, when one function operates on the result of another. Consider the next example, where you obtain a list of all the .NET assemblies in memory and then process this list until you end up with a list of all the .NET methods in memory. As each function operates on the result of the previous function, the forward operator is used to show the results being piped or passed forward to the next function. You don't need to declare intermediate variables to hold the results of a function.

```
#light
let methods = System.AppDomain.CurrentDomain.GetAssemblies()
             |> List.of_array
             |> List.map ( fun assm -> assm.GetTypes() )
             |> Array.concat
             |> List.of_array
             |> List.map ( fun t -> t.GetMethods() )
             |> Array.concat

print_any methods
```

You'll use this technique throughout the rest of the book, particularly when you cover data access in Chapter 9.

Summary

In this chapter, you learned about the imperative features of F#. Combined with the functional features in Chapter 3, you now have a full range of techniques to attack any computing problem. F# allows you to choose techniques from the appropriate paradigm and combine them whenever necessary. In the next chapter, you'll see how F# supports the third programming paradigm, object-oriented programming.

CHAPTER 5

■ ■ ■

Object-Oriented Programming

Object-oriented programming is the third major programming paradigm. At its heart, object-oriented programming has a few simple ideas, some of which you've already encountered. Possibly the most important idea is that the implementations and state should be encapsulated, that is, hidden behind well-defined boundaries. This makes the structure of a program easier to manage. In F#, things are hidden by using signatures for modules and type definitions and also by simply defining them locally to an expression or class construction (you'll see examples of both in this chapter).

The second idea is that you can implement abstract entities in multiple ways. In OOP this is known as polymorphism. You've met a number of simple abstract entities already, such as function types. A function type is abstract because a function with specific type can be implemented in many different ways; for example, the function type int -> int can be implemented as a function that increments the given parameter, a function that decrements the parameter, or any one of millions of mathematical sequences. Other abstract entities can be built out of existing abstract components such as the interface types defined in the .NET BCL. More sophisticated abstract entities are modeled using user-defined interface types. Interface types have the advantage that they can be arranged hierarchically; this is called interface inheritance. For example, the .NET BCL includes a hierarchical classification of collection types, available in the System.Collections and System.Collections.Generic namespaces.

In OOP you can sometimes arrange implementation fragments hierarchically. This is called implementation inheritance. This tends to be less important in F# programming because of the flexibility that functional programming provides for defining and sharing implementation fragments. However, it is significant for domains such as graphical user interface (GUI) programming.

Casting

Casting is a way of explicitly altering the static type of a value by either throwing information away, upcasting, or rediscovering it, downcasting. In F#, upcasts and downcasts have their own operators. The type hierarchy starts with obj (or System.Object) at the top and all its descendants below it. An upcast moves a type up the hierarchy, and a downcast moves a type down the hierarchy.

Upcasts change a value's static type to one of its ancestor types. This is a safe operation since the compiler can always tell whether this will work because the compiler always knows all the ancestors of a type so is able to work out through static analysis whether an upcast will be successful. An upcast is represented by a colon followed by the greater-than sign (:>). The following code shows an example of using an upcast to convert a string to an obj:

```
#light
let myObject = ("This is a string" :> obj)
```

Generally, upcasts are required when defining collections that contain disparate types. If an upcast is not used, the compiler will infer that the collection has the type of the first element and give a compile error if elements of other types are placed in the collection. The next example demonstrates how to create an array of controls, a pretty common task when working with WinForms. Notice that all the individual controls are upcast to their common base class, Control.

```
#light
open System.Windows.Forms

let myControls  =
    [| (new Button() :> Control);
       (new TextBox() :> Control);
       (new Label() :> Control) |]
```

An upcast also has the effect of automatically boxing any value type. Value types are held in memory on the program stack, rather than on the managed heap. Boxing means that the value is pushed onto the managed heap, so it can be passed around by reference. The following example demonstrates a value being boxed:

```
#light
let boxedInt = (1 :> obj)
```

A downcast changes a value's static type to one of its descendant types and thus recovers information hidden by an upcast. Downcasting is dangerous since the compiler doesn't have any way to statically determine whether an instance of a type is compatible with one of its derived types. This means you can get it wrong, and this will cause an invalid cast exception (System.InvalidCastException) to be issued at runtime. Because of the inherent danger of downcasting, it is often preferred to replace it with pattern matching over .NET types, as demonstrated in Chapter 3. Nevertheless, a downcast can be useful in some places, so a downcast operator, composed of a colon, question mark, and greater-than sign (:?>), is available. The next example demonstrates downcasting:

```
#light
open System.Windows.Forms

let moreControls  =
    [| (new Button() :> Control);
       (new TextBox() :> Control) |]

let control =
    let temp = moreControls.[0]
    temp.Text <- "Click Me!"
    temp
```

```
let button =
    let temp = (control :?> Button)
    temp.DoubleClick.Add(fun e -> MessageBox.Show("Hello") |> ignore)
    temp
```

It creates an array of two Windows control objects, upcasting them to their base class, Control. Then it binds the first control to the control identifier. It then downcasts this to its specific type, Button, before adding a handler to its DoubleClick event, an event not available on the Control class.

Type Tests

Closely related to casting is the idea of type tests. An identifier can be bound to an object of a derived type, as you did earlier when you bound a string to an identifier of type obj:

```
#light
let anotherObject = ("This is a string" :> obj)
```

Since an identifier can be bound to an object of a derived type, it is often useful to be able to test what this type is. To do this, F# provides a type test operator, which consists of a colon followed by a question mark (:?). To compile, the operator and its operands must be surrounded by parentheses. If the identifier in the type test is of the specified type or a type derived from it, the operator will return true; otherwise, it will return false. The next example shows two type tests, one that will return true and the other false:

```
#light
let anotherObject = ("This is a string" :> obj)

if (anotherObject :? string) then
    print_endline "This object is a string"
else
    print_endline "This object is not a string"
if (anotherObject :? string[]) then
    print_endline "This object is a string array"
else
    print_endline "This object is not a string array"
```

First you create an identifier, anotherObject, of type obj but bind it to a string. Then you test whether the anotherObject is a string, which will return true. Then you test whether it is a string array, which will, of course, return false.

Type Annotations for Subtyping

As shown in Chapter 3, type annotations are a way of constraining an identifier, usually a parameter of a function, to be a certain type. What may seem counterintuitive to an OO programmer is that the form of type annotation introduced in Chapter 3 is rigid; in other words, it does not take into account the inheritance hierarchy. This means that if such a type annotation is applied to an expression, then that expression must have precisely that type statically; a derived type will not fit in its place. To illustrate this point, consider the following example:

```
#light
open System.Windows.Forms

let showForm (form : Form) =
    form.Show()

// PrintPreviewDialog is defined in the BCL and is
// derived directly the Form class
let myForm = new PrintPreviewDialog()

showForm myForm
```

When you try to compile the previous example, you will receive the following error:

```
Prog.fs(11,10): error: FS0001: This expression has type
    PrintPreviewDialog
but is here used with type
    Form
```

One way to call a function with a rigid type annotation on a parameter is to use an explicit upcast at the place where the function is called in order to change the type to be the same as the type of the function's parameter. The following line of code changes the type of myForm to be the same as the type of the parameter of showForm:

```
showForm (myForm :> Form)
```

Although upcasting the argument to showForm is a solution, it's not a very pretty one, because it means littering client code with upcasts. So, F# provides another type annotation, the derived type annotation, in which the type name is prefixed with a hash sign. This has the effect of constraining an identifier to be of a type or any of its derived types. This means you can rewrite the previous example as shown next to remove the need for explicit upcasts in calling code. I think this is a huge benefit to anyone using the functions you define.

```
#light
let showFormRevised (form : #Form) =
    form.Show()

// ThreadExceptionDialog  is define in the BCL and is
// directly derived type of the Form class
let anotherForm = new ThreadExceptionDialog(new Exception())

showFormRevised anotherForm
```

You can use this kind of type annotation to tidy up code that uses a lot of casting. For example, as shown in the "Casting" section earlier in this chapter, a lot of casting is often needed when creating a collection with a common base type, and this can leave code looking a little bulkier than it should. A good way to remove this repeated casting, as with any commonly repeated section of code, is to define a function that does it for you:

```
#light
let myControls =
    [| (new Button() :> Control);
       (new TextBox() :> Control);
       (new Label() :> Control) |]

let uc (c : #Control) = c :> Control

let myConciseControls  =
    [| uc (new Button()); uc (new TextBox()); uc (new Label()) |]
```

This example shows two arrays of controls being defined. The first, myControls, explicitly upcasts every control; the second, myConciseControls, delegates this job to a function. Also, given that the bigger the array, the bigger the savings and that it is quite common for these arrays to get quite big when working with WinForms, this is a good technique to adopt.

Records As Objects

It is possible to use the record types you met in Chapter 3 to simulate object-like behavior. This is because records can have fields that are functions, which you can use to simulate an object's methods. This technique was first invented before functional programming languages had object-oriented constructs as a way of performing tasks that lent themselves well to object-oriented programming. Some programmers still prefer it, because only the function's type (or as some prefer, its signature) is given in the record definition, so the implementation can easily be swapped without having to define a derived class as you would in object-oriented programming. I discuss this in greater detail in "Object Expressions" and again in "Inheritance" later in this chapter.

Let's take a look at a simple example of records as objects. The next example defines a type, Shape, that has two members. The first member, reposition, is a function type that moves the shape, and the second member, draw, draws the shape. You use the function makeShape to create a new instance of the shape type. The makeShape function implements the reposition functionality for you; it does this by accepting the initPos parameter, which is then stored in a mutable ref cell, which is updated when the reposition function is called. This means the position of the shape is encapsulated, accessible only through the reposition member. Hiding values in this way is a common technique in F# programming.

```
#light
open System.Drawing

type Shape =
    { reposition: Point -> unit;
      draw      : unit -> unit  }

let makeShape initPos draw =
    let currPos  = ref initPos in
    { reposition = (fun newPos  -> currPos := newPos);
      draw       = (fun ()      -> draw !currPos); }
```

```
let circle initPos =
    makeShape initPos (fun pos ->
        printfn
            "Circle, with x = %i and y = %i"
            pos.X
            pos.Y)

let square initPos =
    makeShape initPos (fun pos ->
        printfn
            "Square, with x = %i and y = %i"
            pos.X
            pos.Y)

let point (x,y) = new Point(x,y)

let shapes =
    [ circle (point (10,10));
      square (point (30,30)) ]

let moveShapes() =
    shapes |> List.iter (fun s -> s.draw())

let main() =
    moveShapes()
    shapes |> List.iter (fun s -> s.reposition (point (40,40)))
    moveShapes()

main()
```

```
Circle, with x = 10 and y = 10
Square, with x = 30 and y = 30
Circle, with x = 40 and y = 40
Square, with x = 40 and y = 40
```

This example may have seemed trivial, but you can actually go quite a long way with this technique. The next example takes things to their natural conclusion, actually drawing the shapes on a form:

```
#light
open System
open System.Drawing
open System.Windows.Forms
```

```
type Shape =
    { reposition: Point -> unit;
      draw      : Graphics -> unit  }

let movingShape initPos draw =
    let currPos = ref initPos in
    { reposition = (fun newPos  -> currPos := newPos);
      draw       = (fun g        -> draw !currPos g); }

let movingCircle initPos diam =
    movingShape initPos (fun pos g ->
        g.DrawEllipse(Pens.Blue,pos.X,pos.Y,diam,diam))

let movingSquare initPos size =
    movingShape initPos (fun pos g ->
        g.DrawRectangle(Pens.Blue,pos.X,pos.Y,size,size) )

let fixedShape draw =
    { reposition = (fun newPos  -> ());
      draw       = (fun g        -> draw g); }

let fixedCircle (pos:Point) (diam:int) =
    fixedShape (fun g -> g.DrawEllipse(Pens.Blue,pos.X,pos.Y,diam,diam))

let fixedSquare (pos:Point) (size:int) =
    fixedShape (fun g -> g.DrawRectangle(Pens.Blue,pos.X,pos.Y,size,size))

let point (x,y) = new Point(x,y)

let shapes =
    [ movingCircle (point (10,10)) 20;
      movingSquare (point (30,30)) 20;
      fixedCircle (point (20,20)) 20;
      fixedSquare (point (40,40)) 20; ]

let mainForm =
    let form = new Form()
    let rand = new Random()
    form.Paint.Add(fun e ->
        shapes |> List.iter (fun s ->
            s.draw e.Graphics)
    )
```

```
form.Click.Add(fun e ->
    shapes |> List.iter (fun s ->
        s.reposition(new Point(rand.Next(form.Width),
                               rand.Next(form.Height)));
        form.Invalidate())
)
form
```

```
[<STAThread>]
do Application.Run(mainForm)
```

Again, you define a Shape record type that has the members reposition and draw. Then you define the functions makeCircle and makeSquare to create different kinds of shapes and use them to define a list of shape records. Finally, you define the form that will hold your records. Here you must do a bit more work than perhaps you would like. Since you don't use inheritance, the BCL's System.Winows.Forms.Form doesn't know anything about your shape "objects," and you must iterate though the list, explicitly drawing each shape. This is actually quite simple to do and takes just three lines of code where you add an event handler to mainForm's Paint event:

```
temp.Paint.Add(
    fun e ->
        List.iter (fun s -> s.draw e.Graphics) shapes);
```

This example shows how you can quickly create multifunctional records without having to worry about any unwanted features you might also be inheriting. In the next section, you'll look at how you can represent operations on these objects in a more natural way: by adding members to F# types.

F# Types with Members

It is possible to add functions to both F#'s record and union types. A function added to a record or union type can be called using dot notation, just like a member of a class from a library not written in F#. This provides a convenient way of working with records with mutable state. It is also useful when it comes to exposing types you define in F# to other .NET languages. (I discuss this in more detail in Chapter 13.) Some programmers from object-oriented backgrounds just prefer to see function calls made on an instance value, and this provides a nice way of doing it for all F# types.

The syntax for defining an F# record or union type with members is the same as the syntax you learned in Chapter 3, except it includes member definitions that always come at the end, between the with and end keywords. The definition of the members themselves start with the keyword member, followed by an identifier that represents the parameter of the type the member is being attached to, then a dot, then the function name, and then any other parameters the function takes. After this comes an equals sign followed by the function definition, which can be any F# expression.

The following example defines a record type, point. It has two fields, left and top, and a member function, Swap. The function Swap is a simple function that swaps the values of left and top. Note how the x parameter, given before the function name swap, is used within the function definition to get access to the record's other members, its fields:

```
#light
type Point =
    { mutable top : int ;
      mutable left : int }
    with
        member x.Swap() =
            let temp = x.top
            x.top <- x.left
            x.left <- temp
    end

let printAnyNewline x =
    print_any x
    print_newline()

let main() =
    printAnyNewline myPoint
    myPoint.Swap()
    printAnyNewline myPoint

main()
```

The results of this example, when compiled and executed, are as follows:

```
{top = 3;
 left = 7;}
{top = 7;
 left = 3;}
```

You may have noticed the x parameter in the definition of the function Swap:

```
member x.Swap() =
    let temp = x.top
    x.top <- x.left
    x.left <- temp
```

This is the parameter that represents the object on which the function is being called. When a function is called on a value, as follows:

```
myPoint.Swap()
```

the value it is being called on is passed to the function as an argument. This is logical, when you think about it, because the function needs to be able to access the fields and methods of the value on which it is being called. Some OO languages use a specific keyword for this, such as this or Me, but F# lets you choose the name of this parameter by specifying a name for it after the keyword member, in this case x.

Union types can have member functions too. You define them in the same way as for record types. The next example shows a union type, DrinkAmount, that has a function added to it:

```
#light
type DrinkAmount =
    | Coffee of int
    | Tea of int
    | Water of int
    with
        override x.ToString() =
            match x with
            | Coffee x -> Printf.sprintf "Coffee: %i" x
            | Tea x -> Printf.sprintf "Tea: %i" x
            | Water x -> Printf.sprintf "Water: %i" x
    end

let t = Tea 2

print_endline (t.ToString())
```

The results of this example, when compiled and executed, are as follows:

```
Tea: 2
```

Note how this uses the keyword override in place of the keyword member. This has the effect of replacing, or overriding, an existing function of the type. This is not that common a practice with function members associated with F# types because only four methods are available to be overridden (ToString, Equals, GetHashCode, and Finalize) that are inherited from System.Object by every .NET type. Because of the way some of these methods interact with the CLR, the only one I recommend overriding is ToString. Only four methods are available for overriding because record and union types can't act as base or derived classes, so you cannot inherit methods to override (except from System.Object).

Object Expressions

Object expressions are at the heart of succinct object-oriented programming in F#. They provide a concise syntax to create an object that inherits from an existing type. This is useful if you want to provide a short implementation of an abstract class or an interface or want to tweak an existing class definition. An object expression allows you to provide an implementation of a class or interface while at the same time creating a new instance of it.

The syntax is similar to the alterative syntax for creating new instances of record types, with a few small alterations. You surround the definition of an object expression with braces. At the beginning is the name of the class or interfaces, and the name of a class must be followed by a pair of parentheses that can have any values passed to the constructor between them. Interface names need nothing after them, though both class names and interface names can have a type parameter following them, which must be surrounded by angled brackets. This is followed by the keyword with and the definition of the methods of the class or interfaces being implemented. These methods are separated by the keyword and, the name of the method must be the same as the name of a virtual or abstract method in the class or interface definition, and their parameters must be surrounded by parentheses and separated by commas, like .NET methods must be (unless the method has one parameter, when you can get away with excluding the parentheses). Ordinarily you don't need to give type annotations, but if the base class contains several overall for a method, then you might have to give type annotations. After the name of a method and its parameters comes an equals sign and then the implementation of the methods body, which is just an F# expression that must match the return value of the method.

```
#light
open System
open System.Collections.Generic

let comparer =
    { new IComparer<string>
        with
            Compare(s1, s2) =
                let rev (s : String) =
                    new String(Array.rev (s.ToCharArray()))
                let reversed = rev s1
                reversed.CompareTo(rev s2) }

let winners =
    [| "Sandie Shaw" ;
       "Bucks Fizz" ;
       "Dana International" ;
       "Abba";
       "Lordi" |]

print_any winners
print_newline()
Array.Sort(winners, comparer)
print_any winners
```

The results of the previous example, when compiled and executed, are as follows:

```
[|"Sandie Shaw"; "Bucks Fizz"; "Dana International"; "Abba"; "Lordi"|]
[|"Abba"; "Lordi"; "Dana International"; "Sandie Shaw"; "Bucks Fizz"|]
```

The previous shows an example of the IComparer interface being implemented. This is an interface with one method, Compare, which takes two parameters and returns an integer that represents the result of the parameter comparison. It accepts one type parameter; in this case, you pass it a string. You can see this on the second line of the definition of the identifier comparer. After this comes the definition of the method body, which in this case compares reversed versions of the string parameters. Finally, you use the comparer by defining an array and then sorting using the comparer and displaying the "before" and "after" results in the console.

It is possible to implement multiple interfaces or a class and several other interfaces within one object expression. It is not possible to implement more than one class within an object expression. If you are implementing a class and an interface, the class must always come first in the expression. In either case, the implementation of any other interfaces after the first interface or class must come after the definitions of all the methods of the first interface or class. The name of the interface is prefixed by the keyword interface and is followed by the keyword with. The definition of the methods is the same as for the first interface or class.

```
#light
open System
open System.Drawing
open System.Windows.Forms

let makeNumberControl (n : int) =
    { new Control(Tag = n, Width = 32, Height = 16) with
        override x.OnPaint(e) =
            let font = new Font(FontFamily.Families.[1], 12.0F)
            e.Graphics.DrawString(n.ToString(),
                                  font,
                                  Brushes.Black,
                                  new PointF(0.0F, 0.0F))
      interface IComparable with
        CompareTo(other) =
            let otherControl = other :?> Control in
            let n1 = otherControl.Tag :?> int in
            n.CompareTo(n1) }

let numbers =
    let temp = new ResizeArray<Control>()
    let rand = new Random()
    for index = 1 to 10 do
        temp.Add(makeNumberControl (rand.Next(100)))
    temp.Sort()
    let height = ref 0
    temp |> IEnumerable.iter
        (fun c ->
            c.Top <- !height
            height := c.Height + !height)
    temp.ToArray()

let numbersForm =
    let temp = new Form() in
    temp.Controls.AddRange(numbers);
    temp

[<STAThread>]
do Application.Run(numbersForm)
```

The previous example shows the definition of object expression that implements both the class Control and the interface IComparable. IComparable allows objects that implement this interface to be compared, primarily so they can be sorted. In this case, the implementation of IComparable's CompareTo method sorts the controls according to which number they are displaying. After the implementation of the makeNumberControl function, you create an array of controls, numbers. The definition of numbers is a little complicated; first you initialize it to be full of controls in a random order, and then you sort the array. Finally, you ensure each control is displayed at the appropriate height.

Object expressions are a powerful mechanism to quickly and concisely introduce object-oriented functionality from objects from non-F# libraries into your F# code. They have the drawback that they do not allow you to add extra properties or methods to these objects. For example, in the previous example, notice how it was necessary to place the number associated with control in the control's Tag property. This is more of a workaround than a proper solution. However, sometimes you don't need extra properties or methods on a type, and this syntax can be very useful then.

Defining Interfaces

Interfaces can contain only abstract methods and properties. They define a "contract" for all classes that implement them, exposing those components that clients can use while insulating clients from their actual implementation. A class can inherit from only one base class, but it can implement any number of interfaces. Since any class implementing an interface can be treated as being of the interface type, interfaces provide similar benefits but avoid the complexities of multiple-class inheritance.

You define interfaces using the keyword interface; after this, you list all the members of the interface. The types of members that interfaces can have are somewhat limited, interfaces have no constructors, and they can declare only abstract methods and properties.

The following code defines an interface that declares one method, ChangeState.

```
type MyInterface = interface
    abstract ChangeState : myInt : int -> unit
end
```

Implementing Interfaces

To implement an interface, use the keyword interface, followed by the interface name, then keyword with, then the code to affect the interface members, and then the keyword end. Member definitions are prefixed by the keyword member but otherwise are the same as the definition of any method or property. You can implement interfaces by either classes or structs; I cover how to create classes in some detail in the following sections, and I cover structs in the section "Structs" later in this chapter.

The next example defines, implements, and uses an interface. The class Implementation implements the interface MyInterface.

```
#light
type MyInterface = interface
    abstract ChangeState : myInt : int -> unit
end
```

```
type Implementation = class
    val mutable state : int
    new() = {state = 0}
    interface  MyInterface with
        member x.ChangeState y = x.state <- y
    end
end

let imp = new Implementation()
let inter = imp :> MyInterface

let pintIntNewline i =
    print_int i
    print_newline()

let main() =
    inter.ChangeState 1
    pintIntNewline imp.state
    inter.ChangeState 2
    pintIntNewline imp.state
    inter.ChangeState 3
    pintIntNewline imp.state

main()
```

The results are as follows:

```
1
2
3
```

Note near the end of the example you must cast the identifier imp to the interface MyInterface before you can use the method ChangeState:

```
let imp = new Implementation()
let inter = imp :> MyInterface
```

This is because interfaces are explicitly implemented in F#. If you want the methods of the interface to be available directly on the class that implements it, instead of after casting the object to the interface, you can add the interface members to the definition of the class. To revise the example, you simply add ChangeState as a member of the class Implementation. Now it is no longer necessary to cast the identifier imp. I cover adding members to methods in the section "Classes and Methods" later in the chapter.

```
#light
type MyInterface = interface
    abstract ChangeState : int -> unit
end
```

```
type Implementation = class
    val mutable state : int
    new() = {state = 0}
    interface MyInterface with
        member x.ChangeState y = x.state <- y
    member x.ChangeState y = x.state <- y
end

let imp = new Implementation()

let pintIntNewline i =
    print_int i
    print_newline()

let main() =
    imp.ChangeState 1
    pintIntNewline imp.state
    imp.ChangeState 2
    pintIntNewline imp.state

main()
```

The results are as follows:

```
1
2
```

Classes, Fields, and Explicit Constructors

Until now you've relied on classes available in non-F# libraries. In this and the following sections, you'll learn how to define classes of your own. First, you'll learn how to define fields and constructors so you can create instances. Then, in the following sections, you'll learn about inheritance and methods associated with classes.

In F#, classes are essentially just special kinds of types, so you define them using the type keyword followed by an equals sign and then the keyword class. To terminate your class definition, you use the keyword end. The next example shows the simplest class definition possible, of a class with nothing in it, or an empty class. It then attempts to instantiate it.

```
#light
type Empty = class
end

let emptyItem = new Empty()
```

This code will not compile because of the last line. You didn't provide a constructor for our class, so there's no way to create an instance of it. To enable you to create an instance of the class, you must explicitly add a constructor. To do this, you need to add a member, which is always named new and is followed the constructor within parentheses. After this comes an equals sign followed by a block (delimited by braces), which contains expressions to initialize every field in the class. The following example defines a simple constructor for an empty class:

```
#light
type JustConstruct = class
    new() = {}
end

let constructed = new JustConstruct()
```

This may come as a surprise to experienced object-oriented programmers since most object-oriented languages provide a default constructor for any class that doesn't define one. F#'s philosophy is to provide a more powerful construct called implicit class construction that often subsumes the need for explicit constructors altogether. You'll return to implicit class construction in the next section. Furthermore, default constructors can easily leave some fields uninitialized and therefore null and can leave some at risk of causing a NullReferenceException. This is why a constructor in F# must initialize all fields defined by a class.

Fields are defined using the keyword val, followed the name of the field, and then the name of the type separated from the property name by a colon. The next example shows a simple class, file1, that has two fields, path and innerFile, that are initialized in the constructor, which has one parameter, path:

```
#light
open System.IO

type File1 = class
    val path: string
    val innerFile: FileInfo
    new(path) =
        { path = path ;
          innerFile = new FileInfo(path) }
end

let myFile1 = new File1("whatever.txt")
```

It's possible to overload constructors; one simply adds a second constructor with a different number of parameters. If you want to overload with parameters of different types, then you must provide type annotations. The following example shows a class, File2, with two constructors, one with no parameters and one with one parameter:

```
#light
open System.IO

type File2 = class
    val path: string
    val innerFile: FileInfo
```

```
    new() = new File2("default.txt")
    new(path) =
        { path = path ;
          innerFile = new FileInfo(path) }
end

let myFile2 = new File2("whatever2.txt")
```

Note that the only thing you can do in the initialization block of a constructor is to initialize the fields of a class or call another constructor to do that for you. If you want to do other things in a constructor, you must you use the keyword then after the block and follow it by the extra expressions you want in the constructor. This separates the initialization of fields from other code to ensure that nothing can happen to the fields of a class before they are properly initialized. If you want to access the fields in a class outside the initialization block, you must give a name to the instance you're creating by qualifying the constructor; you do this using the keyword as followed by the alias for the instance. The next example shows a constructor with some code following the initialization block. The alias, x, is defined for the instance. This is later used to test whether the file associated with the FileInfo object bound to the field innerFile exists.

```
#light
open System.IO

type File3 = class
    val path: string
    val innerFile: FileInfo
    new(path) as x =
        { path = path ;
          innerFile = new FileInfo(path) }
        then
        if not x.innerFile.Exists then
            let textFile = x.innerFile.CreateText()
            textFile.Dispose()
end

let myFile3 = new File3("whatever.txt")
```

By default, fields in a class are immutable, which means once they have been bound to a value, the value can be rebound to another value. For F# records with mutable fields and .NET objects, this does not mean their internal state cannot change; it simply means you cannot replace the whole value to which the field is bound. You can see this in the previous example; if the file you are creating doesn't exist, the file will be created, changing the value of the Exists flag to true. However, you cannot set the field innerFile to be another instance of the FileInfo object.

From time to time, it can be useful to rebind a field to another value. To allow this to happen, F# provides the keyword mutable; when a field is defined as mutable, it can be rebound whenever the programmer chooses. The following example illustrates its usage. In this example, you see that the mutable keyword is applied to the FileInfo field so that you can change the instance of the object it refers to later. You see that if the file does not exist, it is replaced by the first file available in the directory.

```
#light
open System.IO

type File4 = class
    val path: string
    val mutable innerFile: FileInfo
    new(path) as x =
        { path = path ;
          innerFile = new FileInfo(path) }
        then
        if not x.innerFile.Exists then
          let dir = x.innerFile.Directory in
          let files = dir.GetFiles() in
          if files.Length > 0 then
              x.innerFile <- files.(0)
          else
              failwith "no files exist in that dir"
end

let myFile4 = new File4("whatever2.txt")
```

Implicit Class Construction

So far you've defined classes using the explicit syntax for constructors. A recent enhancement to F# is called implicit class construction or the compact class syntax. This allows a class to implicitly define a construction sequence through a series of let bindings prior to the member definitions of the class. These bindings are private to the class. For example, you can define the File1 example from the previous section simply by using the following:

```
type File1(path) = class
    let innerFile = new FileInfo(path)
    member x.InnerFile = innerFile
end

let myFile1 = new File1("whatever.txt")
```

Classes using implicit class construction have a tuple of arguments such as path after the name of the type constructor. Furthermore, the body of the class may contain let bindings, which are always private to the class. Here you have also added the property member InnerFile to reveal the value of the value of the innerFile. I discuss property members later in this chapter. Here is a second example:

```
type Counter(start, increment, length) = class
    let finish = start + length
    let mutable current = start
```

```
    member obj.Current = current
    member obj.Increment() =
        if current > finish then failwith "finished!";
        current <- current + increment
end
```

Logically speaking, this class is equivalent to the following one that defines fields and a constructor explicitly:

```
// The previous code is equivalent to the following:
type Counter = class
    val start: int
    val increment: int
    val length : int
    val finish : int
    val mutable current : int
    new(start, increment, length) =
        { start=start;
          increment=increment;
          length=length;
          finish = start + length;
          current = start; }
    member obj.Current = current
    member obj.Increment() =
        if obj.current > obj.finish then failwith "finished!";
            obj.current <- obj.current + obj.increme
end
```

However, the F# compiler is free to optimize the fields of the class away where possible. For example, the start value is required only during initialization of the object and thus will not be included as a field of the object.

The first definition of Counter is a third the size of the second, so obviously the syntax has some advantages. I use both implicit and explicit constructors in this book because it is necessary in some circumstances to understand the more explicit syntax, for example, when writing classes with multiple constructors.

Classes and Inheritance

I have already covered inheritance in a limited way in the section "Object Expressions." Inheritance allows you to extend a class that is already defined and to tweak its behavior to add new or replace original functionality. Like most modern object-oriented languages, F# allows single inheritance (from one base class) as well as the implementation of multiple interfaces (see the sections "Defining interfaces" and "Implementing Interfaces" later in this chapter). This section will cover the very basics of inheritance, and then the following section, "Classes and Their Methods," will show how to implement methods to make full use of inheritance.

You specify inheritance with the inherit keyword, which must come directly after the keyword class. Let's kick off by looking at a simple example of inheritance between two F# types. The following example shows an F# class, sub, that derives from a base class, base. The class base has one field, state, and the class sub has another called otherState. The example shows that both fields can be used by the sub derived class, because state is inherited from the base class.

```
#light
type Base = class
    val state: int
    new() = { state = 0 }
end

type Sub = class
    inherit Base
    val otherState: int
    new() = { otherState = 0 }
end

let myObject = new Sub()

printfn
    "myObject.state = %i, myObject.otherState = %i"
    myObject.state
    myObject.otherState
```

The results of this example, when compiled and executed, are as follows:

```
myObject.state = 0, myObject.otherState = 0
```

For this to work properly, the base class must have a parameterless constructor, that is, a constructor that does not take any arguments. If the base class does not have a parameterless constructor, then it cannot be initialized implicitly when the derived class is instantiated. This doesn't mean you can't derive from it; it just means you need to explicitly call the base class's constructor. You do this using the inherit keyword again but this time within the constructor's initializer block. The following example shows how to derive from a class that has no parameterless constructor:

```
#light
type Base1 = class
    val state: int
    new(state) = { state = state }
end

type Sub1 = class
    inherit Base1
    val otherState: int
    new(state) = { inherit Base1(state) ; otherState = 0 }
end

let myOtherObject = new Sub1(1)
```

```
printfn
    "myObject.state = %i, myObject.otherState = %i"
    myOtherObject.state
    myOtherObject.otherState
```

The results of this example, when compiled and executed, are as follows:

```
myOtherObject.state = 1, myOtherObject.otherState = 0
```

When using implicit class construction, the call to the base class constructor is specified as part of the inherits declaration. For example, you can rewrite the previous example as follows, giving the same results:

```
type Base1(state) = class
    member x.State = state
end

type Sub1(state) = class
    inherit Base1(state)
    member x.OtherState = state
end

let myOtherObject = new Sub1(1)

printfn
    "myObject.state = %i, myObject.otherState = %i"
    myOtherObject.State
    myOtherObject.OtherState
```

Classes and Methods

The previous two sections gave you the basics of putting together a class. Now you'll take a look at really getting the most out of object-oriented programming by adding methods to your class. A method is a function that has access to the fields of an object and can change them if they are mutable. A derived class can define new methods and can override methods inherited from its base class.

Methods are defined using four keywords, either member, override, abstract, or default. The simplest way to declare a method is to use the member keyword; this defines a method that cannot be overridden. The override keyword defines a method that overrides an inherited method that has an implementation in a base class. The abstract keyword defines a method that has no implementation and must be overridden in a derived class. The keyword default has a similar meaning to the override keyword, except it is only ever used to override an abstract method.

The member, override, and default definitions have the same syntax. The keyword is followed by the parameter that represents the instance of the object whose class you are in the process of defining. You can use this parameter in the method implementation to get access to all the class's fields and properties. After this special parameter comes a dot and then the name of the method. Next come the parameters of the method. After that comes an equals sign followed by the implementation of the method.

Methods declared using the keyword abstract are a little different, because there is no implementation. Because there is no implementation, you omit the parameter that represents the object itself, so the keyword abstract is followed directly by the method name. Following this is the method's type, which is separated from the method name using a colon, just like any other type annotation.

The next example is designed to illustrate the use of all four kinds of methods:

```
#light
type Base = class
    val mutable state: int
    new() = { state = 0 }
    member x.JiggleState y = x.state <- y
    abstract WiggleState: int -> unit
    default x.WiggleState y = x.state <- y + x.state
end

type Sub = class
    inherit Base
    new() = {}
    default x.WiggleState y = x.state <- y &&& x.state
end

let myBase = new Base()
let mySub = new Sub()

let testBehavior (c : #Base) =
    c.JiggleState 1
    print_int c.state
    print_newline()
    c.WiggleState 3
    print_int c.state
    print_newline()

print_endline "base class: "
testBehavior myBase
print_endline "sub class: "
testBehavior mySub
```

The results of this example, when compiled and executed, are as follows:

```
base class:
1
4
sub class:
1
1
```

You first implement a method, JiggleState, in class Base. The method cannot be overridden, so all derived classes will inherit this implementation. You then define an abstract method, WiggleState, that can be overridden (and, in fact, must be) by derived classes. To define a new method that can be overridden, you always need to use a combination of the abstract and default keywords. This could mean that abstract is used on the base class while the default is used on the derived class, but often you will use them together in the same class, as shown in the previous example. This requires the programmer to explicitly give types to a method they are providing to be overridden. Although the F# philosophy is generally not to require the programmer to give explicit types and to try to let the compiler work them out, the compiler has no way to infer these types, so you must give them explicitly.

As shown in the results when JiggleState is called, the behavior remains the same in both the base class and the derived class, where the behavior of WiggleState changes because it is overridden.

Accessing the Base Class

When accessing methods within a class, they will usually call the version of the method in the most derived class. That means if you try to call a method on the base class and it has been overridden by the derived class, then it will automatically call the version on the derived class. Ordinarily this is used to call the base implementation of a method you are overriding. This isn't always necessary but generally is required by library design guidelines because it can lead to the base class malfunctioning if you do not do this.

To get access to methods on the base class, you give the base class a name. You do this by using the keyword as after the name of the class you are inheriting from, followed by the name you want to give to the base class. This name then acts like the keyword base in C#, giving you access to the base class's methods.

The following example shows an implementation of a class that derives from System.Windows.Form. The identifier base is assigned to base class Form, as shown at the top of the definition of the MySquareForm class. The example uses implicit class construction, indicated by the fact that the type MySquareForm takes a parameter, color.

```
open System.Drawing
open System.Windows.Forms

type MySquareForm(color) = class
    inherit Form() as base
    override x.OnPaint(e) =
        e.Graphics.DrawRectangle(color,
                                 10, 10,
                                 x.Width - 30,
                                 x.Height - 50)
        base.OnPaint(e)
    override x.OnResize(e) =
        x.Invalidate()
        base.OnResize(e)
end
```

```
let form = new MySquareForm(Pens.Blue)
do Application.Run(form)
```

In this form you override two methods, OnPaint and OnResize, and in these methods you use the identifier base, which grants access to the base class, to call the base class's implementation of this method.

Properties and Indexers

Properties are a special form of method that look like a value to the code that calls it. Indexers are a similar concept that makes a method look a bit like a collection to the calling code. Both properties and indexers have accessors, which include a get accessor for reading and a set accessor for writing.

A property definition starts the same way as a method definition, with the keyword member followed by the parameter that represents the object, then a dot, and then the member name. After this, instead of the method parameters, you use the keyword with, followed by either get or set. Then comes the parameters; a get method must take unit, and a set method must take one single parameter. After this is an equals sign and an expression that forms the method body. If a second method is required, you use the keyword and to join them together.

The following sample shows the definition of a class that has a single property, MyProp, which returns a random number. Setting the property resets the seed of the random number generator.

```
#light
type Properties() = class
    let mutable rand = new System.Random()
    member x.MyProp
        with get () = rand.Next()
        and set y = rand <- new System.Random(y)
end
let prop = new Properties()

let print i = printfn "%d" i

prop.MyProp <- 12
print prop.MyProp
print prop.MyProp
print prop.MyProp
```

The results of the previous example, when compiled and executed, are as follows:

```
2137491492
726598452
334746691
```

It is also possible to declare abstract properties. The syntax is similar, the keyword member is replaced by abstract, and the parameter that represents the object is omitted, just like for a method. After the member name comes the name of the type separated from the member name by a colon. Then follows the keyword, followed by either get or set, representing whether the inheritor must implement a get or set method, or both, separated by a comma. Properties look exactly like a field to the calling code.

The following example shows the previous example revised so now it uses a base class, AbstractProperties. You will notice how the derived class ConcreteProperties must implement the get and set methods using the keywords with and then and.

```
#light
type AbstractProperties() = class
    abstract MyProp : int
        with get, set
end

type ConcreteProperties() = class
    inherit AbstractProperties()
    let mutable rand = new System.Random()
    override x.MyProp
        with get() = rand.Next()
        and  set(y) = rand <- new System.Random(y)
end
```

Indexers are properties that take two or more parameters, one to represent the element being placed in the pseudocollection and others to represent the index in it. In C# all indexers are called Item in the underlying implementation, but the programmer never actually uses this name because it is always implicit. In F#, the programmer can choose the name of the indexer property. If the programmer chooses the name Item, then there is special syntax for accessing the property.

The syntax for creating an indexer is the same as a property, except a get method has one or more parameters, and a set method has two or more parameters. To access an element in an indexer, if its name is Item, you can use a special syntax that looks like array access except with the parentheses replaced by square brackets:

```
#light
type Indexers(vals:string[]) = class
    member x.Item
        with get (y) = vals.[y]
        and set (y, z) = vals.[y] <- z
    member x.MyString
        with get (y) = vals.[y]
        and set (y, z) = vals.[y] <- z
end

let index = new Indexers [|"One"; "Two"; "Three"; "Four"|]

index.[0] <- "Five";
index.Item(1) <- "Six";
index.MyString(3) <- "Seven";
print_endline index.[0]
```

```
print_endline (index.Item(1))
print_endline (index.MyString(2))
print_endline (index.MyString(3))
```

The results of the previous example, when compiled and executed, are as follows:

```
Five
Two
Six
Seven
```

Note When working with indexers with a name other than `Item`, remember that it will be difficult for other .NET languages to use your classes.

Classes and Static Methods

Static methods are like instance methods, except they are not specific to any instance of a class so have no access to the class's fields.

To create a static method, you use the keyword `static`, followed by the keyword `member`. Then comes the method name, its parameters, an equals sign, and then the method definition. This is basically the same as declaring an instance method, just with the addition of the keyword `static` and the removal of the parameter that represents the object. Removing the parameter that represents the object is quite logical because the method has no access to the object's properties.

The following example shows the definition of a static method, `rev_string`, associated with a class, `MyClass`:

```
#light
type MyClass = class
    static member revString (s : string) =
        let chars = s.ToCharArray() in
        let reved_chars = Array.rev chars in
        new string(reved_chars)
end

let myString = MyClass.revString "dlrow olleH"

print_string myString
```

The results of the previous example, when compiled and executed, are as follows:

```
Hello world
```

You will notice from the previous example that the static methods called use the name of the type they are associated with, rather than a value of the type with which the method is associated.

Static methods can also be useful for providing operators for your classes to use. The basic syntax for declaring an operator is the same as for declaring any other static method, except the name of the method is replaced by the operator in brackets. The parameters of the operator must be given as a tuple and typically need type annotations to indicate their types.

The following example assumes that for some reason you want to reimplement the int type in a class called MyInt. The MyInt class has a plus operator defined on it.

```
#light
type MyInt(state:int) = class
    member x.State = state
    static member ( + ) (x:MyInt, y:MyInt) : MyInt = new MyInt(x.State + y.State)
    override x.ToString() = string_of_int state
end

let x = new MyInt(1)
let y = new MyInt(1)

printfn "(x + y) = %A" (x + y)
```

The results of the previous example, when compiled and executed, are as follows:

```
(x + y) = 2
```

Overriding Methods from Non-F# Libraries

When overriding methods from non-F# libraries, the method definition must be in the tuple style, that is, surrounded by brackets and separated by commas. If you need to use a method like this as a value, then you will need to create an F# function from the method.

The following sample shows a class that implements the interface System.Net.ICredentials. Its single method, GetCredential, has two parameters. Just after the interface has been implemented, the example demonstrates using it as a value in the method GetCredentialList.

```
#light
type CredentialsFactory() = class
    interface System.Net.ICredentials with
        member x.GetCredential(uri, authType) =
            new System.Net.NetworkCredential("rob", "whatever", "F# credentials")
    member x.GetCredentialList uri authTypes =
        let y = (x :> System.Net.ICredentials)
        let getCredential s = y.GetCredential(uri, s)
        List.map getCredential authTypes
end
```

I discuss the relationship between F# signatures and C# signatures in Chapter 13.

Defining Delegates

Delegates are the mechanism both C# and Visual Basic use to treat their methods as values. A delegate basically acts as a .NET object that wraps the method and provides an invoke method so it can be called. There is rarely a need to define delegates in F# because it can treat a function as a value without the need for any wrapper. However, sometimes they are useful— to define delegates to expose F# functionality to other .NET languages in a friendlier manner and to define callbacks for directly calling C code from F#.

To define a delegate, you use the keyword delegate followed directly by the keyword of and then the type of the delegate's signature, which follows the standard F# type annotation notation.

The next example shows the definition of a delegate, MyDelegate, which takes an int and returns unit. You then create a new instance of this delegate and apply it to a list of integers. As you've already seen in Chapter 3, there are much shorter ways of implementing this functionality in F#.

```
#light
type MyDelegate = delegate of int -> unit

let inst = new MyDelegate (fun i -> print_int i)

let ints = [1 ; 2 ; 3 ]

ints
|> List.iter (fun i -> inst.Invoke(i))
```

The results of this example, when compiled and executed, are as follows:

```
123
```

Structs

You define structs in a similar manner to classes. The keyword class is replaced with struct. The main difference between a class and struct is the area of memory where the object will be allocated. When used as a local variable or parameter, a struct is allocated on the stack, while a class is allocated on the managed heap. Because structs are allocated on the stack, they are not garbage collected but are automatically deallocated when a function exits. It is generally slightly faster accessing their fields and slightly slower passing them to methods, but these differences do tend to be quite small. Because they are allocated on the stack, it is generally best to create structs with a small number of fields to avoid stack overflow. You can't use inheritance when implementing structs, so this means structs can't define virtual methods or abstract methods.

The next example defines a struct representing an IP address. Note the only difference from defining a class is that the keyword struct is used.

```
type IpAddress = struct
    val first : byte
    val second : byte
    val third : byte
    val fourth : byte
    new(first, second, third, fourth) =
        { first = first;
          second = second;
          third = third;
          fourth = fourth }
    override x.ToString() =
        Printf.sprintf "%0.%0.%0.%0" x.first x.second x.third x.fourth
    member x.GetBytes() = x.first, x.second, x.third, x.fourth
end
```

So, when should you use a classes, and when should you use a struct? A good rule of thumb is to avoid structs, using them only when really necessary, for example, when interoperating with unmanaged C/C++ code (for more details on this, see Chapter 13).

Enums

Enums allow you to define a type made up of a finite set of identifiers, with each identifier mapping to an integer. This defines a type that can then take the value associated with any one of the defined identifiers.

To define an enum, give the names of the identifiers followed by equals signs and then the values of the constants associated with the identifiers. The identifiers that are members of the enum are separated by vertical bars. To demonstrate this, an enum Scale is defined in the following example:

```
#light
type Scale =
  |   C = 1
  |   D = 2
  |   E = 3
  |   F = 4
  |   G = 5
  |   A = 6
  |   B = 7
```

It's quite common to define enums that are intended to be combined logically. To do this, choose constants so that each number is represented by a single bit, that is, the numbers 0, 1, 2, 4, 8, and so on. F#'s binary literals are a great help here, since you can easily see how the constants can combine.

```
#light
[<System.Flags>]
type ChordScale =
|    C = 0b0000000000000001
|    D = 0b0000000000000010
|    E = 0b0000000000000100
|    F = 0b0000000000001000
|    G = 0b0000000000010000
|    A = 0b0000000000100000
|    B = 0b0000000001000000
```

The module Enum provides functionality for dealing with enums in F#; I discuss it in Chapter 7.

Summary

You've now seen how to use the three major programming paradigms in F# and how flexible F# is for coding in any mix of styles. In the next chapter, you'll look at how code is organized in F# and how to annotate and "quote" it.

CHAPTER 6

■■■

Organizing, Annotating, and Quoting Code

An important part of any programming language is the ability to organize code into logical chunks. It's also important to be able to annotate code with notes about what it does, for future maintainers and even yourself.

It has also become common to use attributes and data structures to annotate assemblies and the types and values within them. Other libraries or the CLR can then interpret these attributes. I cover this technique of marking functions and values with attributes in the section "Attributes." The technique of compiling code into data structures is known as *quoting*, and I cover it in the section "Quoted Code" toward the end of the chapter.

Modules

F# code is organized into modules, which are basically a way of grouping values and types under a common name. This organization has an effect on the scope of identifiers. Inside a module, identifiers can reference each other freely. To reference identifiers outside a module, the identifier must be qualified with the module name, unless the module is explicitly opened with the open directive (see "Opening Namespaces and Modules" later in this chapter).

By default, each module is contained in a single source file. The entire contents of the source file make up the module, and if the module isn't explicitly named, it gets the name of its source file, with the first letter capitalized. (F# is case sensitive, so it's important to remember this.) It's recommended that such *anonymous* modules be used only for very simple programs.

To explicitly name a module, use the keyword module. The keyword has two modes of operation. One gives the same name to the whole of the source file. The other mode gives a name to a section of a source file; this way several modules can appear in a source file.

To include the entire contents of a source file in the same explicitly named module, you must place the module keyword at the top of the source file. A module name can contain dots, and these separate the name into parts. For example:

```
module Strangelights.Foundations.ModuleDemo
```

You can define nested modules within the same source file. Nested module names cannot contain dots. After the nested module's name comes an equals sign followed by the indented module definition. You can also use the keywords begin and end. To wrap the module definition, you can nest submodules. The following code defines three submodules, FirstModule, SecondModule, and ThirdModule. ThirdModule is nested within SecondModule.

```
#light
module FirstModule =
    let n = 1

module SecondModule =
    let n = 2
    module ThirdModule =
        let n = 3
```

Note that different submodules can contain the same identifiers without any problems. Modules affect the scope of an identifier. To access an identifier outside of its module, you need to qualify it with the module name so there is no ambiguity between identifiers in different modules. In the previous example, the identifier n is defined in all three modules. The following example shows how to access the identifier n specific to each of the modules:

```
let x = FirstModule.n
let y = SecondModule.n
let z = SecondModule.ThirdModule.n
```

A module will be compiled into a .NET class, with the values becoming methods and fields within that class. You can find more details about what an F# module looks like to other .NET programming languages in "Calling F# Libraries from C#" in Chapter 13.

Namespaces

Namespaces help organize your code hierarchically. To help keep module names unique across assemblies, the module name is qualified with a namespace name, which is just a character string with parts separated by dots. For example, F# provides a module named List, and the .NET BCL provides a class named List. There is no name conflict, because the F# module is in namespace Microsoft.FSharp, and the BCL class is in namespace System.Collections.Generic.

It's important that namespace names be unique. The most popular convention is to start namespace names with the name of a company or organization, followed by a specific name that indicates functionality. Although it's not obligatory to do this, the convention is so widely followed that if you intend to distribute your code, especially in the form of a class library, then you should adopt it too.

Note Interestingly, at the IL level, there is no real concept of namespaces. A name of a class or module is just a long identifier that might or might not contain dots. Namespaces are implemented at the compiler level. When you use an open directive, you tell the compiler to do some extra work; to qualify all your identifiers with the given name, if it needs to; and to see whether this results in a match with a value or type.

In the simplest case, you can place a module in a namespace simply by using a module name with dots in it. The module and namespace names will be the same. You can also explicitly define a namespace for a module with the namespace directive. For example, you could replace the following:

```
module Strangelights.Foundations.ModuleDemo
```

with this to get the same result:

```
namespace Strangelights.Foundations
module ModuleDemo
```

This might not be too useful for modules, but as noted in the previous section, submodules names cannot contain dots, so you use the namespace directive to place submodules within a namespace. For example:

```
#light
namespace Strangelights.Foundations
module FirstModule =
   let n = 1

module SecondModule =
   let n = 2
   module ThirdModule =
      let n = 3
```

This means that once compiled to the outside world, the first instance of n will be accessible using the identifier Strangelights.Foundation.FirstModule.n instead of just FirstModule.n.

It's possible to define a namespace without also using a module directive, but then the source file can contain only type definitions. For example:

```
#light
namespace Strangelights.Foundations

type MyRecord = { field : string }
```

The following example will not compile, because you can't place a value definition directly into a namespace without explicitly defining a module or submodule within the namespace.

```
#light
namespace Strangelights.Foundations

let value = "val"
```

In fact, the namespace directive has some interesting and subtle effects on what your code looks like to other languages; I cover this in "Calling F# Libraries from C#" in Chapter 13.

Opening Namespaces and Modules

As you have seen in the previous two sections, to specify a value or type that is not defined in the current module, you must use its qualified name. This can quickly become tedious because some qualified names can be quite long. Fortunately, F# provides the open directive so you can use simple names for types and values.

The open keyword is followed by the name of the namespace or module you want to open. For example, you could replace the following:

```
#light
System.Console.WriteLine("Hello world")
```

with this:

```
#light
open System

Console.WriteLine("Hello world")
```

Note that you don't need to specify the whole namespace name. You can specify the front part of it and use the remaining parts to qualify simple names. For example, you can specify System.Collections rather than the namespace, System.Collections.Generic, and then use Generic.List to create an instance of the generic List class, as follows:

```
#light
open System.Collections

let l = new Generic.Dictionary<string, int>()
```

Caution The technique of using partially qualified names, such as Generic.Dictionary, can make programs difficult to maintain. Either use the name and the full namespace or use just the name.

You can open F# modules, but you cannot open classes from non-F# libraries. If you open a module, it means you can reference values and types within it by just their simple names. For example, the following finds the length of an array and binds this to the identifier len:

```
#light
open Microsoft.FSharp.MLLib.Array

let len = length [| 1 |]
```

Some argue that this ability to open modules directly should be used sparingly because it can make it difficult to find where identifiers originated. In fact, modules can typically be divided into two categories: those that are designed to be accessed using qualified names and those that are designed to be opened directly. Most modules are designed to be accessed with qualified names; a few, such as Microsoft.FSharp.Core.Operators, are designed to be directly opened. The next example shows the using function from Operators being used directly:

```
#light
open System.IO
open Microsoft.FSharp.Core.Operators

using (File.AppendText("text.txt") ) (fun stream ->
    stream.WriteLine("Hello World"))
```

This example is slightly bogus because the `Microsoft.FSharp.Core.Operators` is opened by the compiler by default. I used this because modules designed to be opened directly are a rarity since it's almost always useful for anyone reading the code to know where the function originated.

If you open two namespaces that contain modules or classes of the same name, it won't cause a compile error. You can even use values from the modules or classes with the same name, as long as the names of the values are not the same. In Figure 6-1, the namespace `System` is opened. It contains the class `Array`, and a module, `Array`, is also available in F#'s libraries. In the figure you can see both static methods from BCL's `Array` class, all starting with a capital letter, and values from F#'s `Array` module, which start with a small letter.

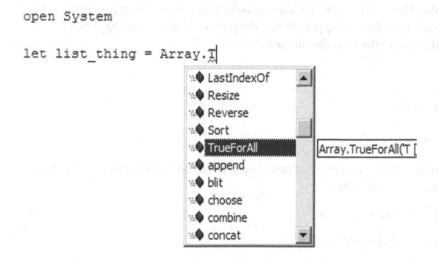

Figure 6-1. *Visual Studio's IntelliSense*

Giving Namespaces and Modules Aliases

It can sometimes be useful to give an alias to a namespace or module to avoid naming clashes. This is useful when two modules share the same name and value with a common name and can also be a convenient way of switching some of your code to use two different implementations of similar modules. It can be more common when using libraries not written in F#.

The syntax for this is the `module` keyword followed by an identifier, then an equals sign, and then the name of the namespace or module to be aliased. The following example defines `GColl` as the alias for the namespace `System.Collections.Generic`:

```
#light
module GColl = System.Collections.Generic

let l = new GColl.List<int>()
```

Signature Files

Signature files are a way of making function and value definitions private to a module. You've already seen the syntax for the definition of a signature file in Chapter 2. It is the source that the compiler generates when using the -i switch. Any definitions that appear in a signature file are public and can be accessed by anyone using the module. Any that are not in the signature file are private and can be used only inside the module itself. The typical way to create a signature file is to generate it from the module source and then go through and erase any values and functions that you want to be private.

The signature file name must be the same as the name of the module with which it is paired. It must have the extension .fsi or .mli. You must specify the signature file to the compiler. On the command line, you must give it directly before the source file for its module. In Visual Studio, the signature file must appear before the source file in Solution Explorer.

For example, if you have the following in the file Lib.fs:

```
#light
let funkyFunction x =
    x + ": keep it funky!"

let notSoFunkyFunction x = x + 1
```

and you want to create a library that exposes funkyFunction but not notSoFunkyFunction, you would use the signature code like this:

```
val funkyFunction : string -> string
```

and would use the command line like this:

```
fsc -a Lib.fsi Lib.fs
```

which results in an assembly named Lib.dll with one class named Lib, one public function named funkyFunction, and one private function named notSoFunkyFunction.

Module Scope

The order that modules are passed to the compiler is important, because it affects the scope of identifiers within the modules and the order in which the modules are executed. I cover scope in this section and execution order in the next.

Values and types within a module cannot be seen from another module unless the module they're in appears on the command line before the module that refers to them. This is probably easier to understand with an example. Suppose you have a source file, ModuleOne.fs, containing the following:

```
#light
module ModuleOne

let text = "some text"
```

and another module, ModuleTwo.fs, containing the following:

```
#light
module ModuleTwo

print_endline ModuleOne.text
```

These two modules can be compiled successfully with the following:

```
fsc ModuleOne.fs ModuleTwo.fs -o ModuleScope.exe
```

But the following command:

```
fsc ModuleTwo.fs ModuleOne.fs -o ModuleScope.exe
```

would result in this error message:

```
ModuleTwo.fs(3,17): error: FS0039: The namespace or module 'ModuleOne' is not
 defined.
```

This is because ModuleOne is used in the definition of ModuleTwo, so ModuleOne must appear before ModuleTwo in the command line, or else ModuleOne will not be in scope for ModuleTwo.

Visual Studio users should note that the order in which files appear in Solution Explorer is the order that they are passed to the compiler. This means it is sometimes necessary to spend a few moments rearranging the order of the files when adding a new file to a project.

Module Execution

Roughly speaking, execution in F# starts at the top of a module and works its way down to the bottom. Any values that are functions are calculated, and any top-level statements are executed. So, the following:

```
module ModuleOne

print_endline "This is the first line"

print_endline "This is the second"

let file =
    let temp = new System.IO.FileInfo("test.txt") in
    Printf.printf "File exists: %b\r\n" temp.Exists;
    temp
```

will give the following result:

```
This is the first line
This is the second
File exists: false
```

This is all pretty much as you might expect. When a source file is compiled into an assembly, none of the code in it will execute until a value from it is used by a currently executing function. Then, when the first value in the file is touched, all the let expressions and top-level statements in the module will execute in their lexical order. When a program is split over more than one module, the last module passed to the compiler is special. All the items in this module will execute, and the other items will behave as they were in an assembly. Items in other modules will execute only when a value from that module is used by the module currently executing. Suppose you create a program with two modules.

This is ModuleOne.fs:

```
#light
module ModuleOne

print_endline "This is the third and final"
```

This is ModuleTwo.fs:

```
#light
module ModuleTwo

print_endline "This is the first line"

print_endline "This is the second"
```

If this is compiled with the following:

```
fsc ModuleOne.fs ModuleTwo.fs -o ModuleExecution.exe
```

this will give the following result:

```
This is the first line
This is the second
```

This might not be what you expected, but it is important to remember that since ModuleOne was not the last module passed to the compiler, nothing in it will execute until a value from it is used by a function currently executing. In this case, no value from ModuleOne is ever used, so it never executes. Taking this into account, you can fix your program so it behaves more as you expect.

Here is ModuleOne.fs:

```
module ModuleOne

print_endline "This is the third and final"

let n = 1
```

Here is ModuleTwo.fs:

```
module ModuleTwo

print_endline "This is the first line"

print_endline "This is the second"

let funct() =
    Printf.printf "%i" ModuleOne.n

funct()
```

If this is compiled with the following:

```
fsc ModuleOne.fs ModuleTwo.fs -o ModuleExecution.exe
```

it will give the following result:

```
This is the first line
This is the second
This is the third and final
1
```

However, using this sort of trick to get the results you want is not recommended. It is generally best only to use statements at the top level in the last module passed to the compiler. In fact, the typical form of an F# program is to have one statement at the top level at the bottom of the last module that is passed to the compiler.

Optional Compilation

Optional compilation is a technique where the compiler can ignore various bits of text from a source file. Most programming languages support some kind of optional compilation. It can be handy, for example, if you want to build a library that supports both .NET 1.1 and 2.0 and want to include extra values and types that take advantage of the new features of version 2.0. However, you should use the technique sparingly and with great caution, because it can quickly make code difficult to understand and maintain.

In F# optional compilation is supported by the compiler switch --define FLAG and the command #if FLAG in a source file.

The following example shows how to define two different versions of a function, one for when the code is compiled for .NET 2.0 and the other for all other versions of .NET:

```
#light
open Microsoft.FSharp.Compatibility

#if FRAMEWORK_AT_LEAST_2_0
let getArray() = [|1, 2; 3|]
#else
```

```
let getArray() = CompatArray.of_array [|1; 2; 3|]
#endif
```

This example assumes that the compiler switch `--define FRAMEWORK_AT_LEAST_2_0` is defined when the code is being compiled for .NET 2.0. Chapter 13 gives more on the differences between .NET 1.0, 1.1, and 2.0 and covers compiler options.

Comments

F# provides two kinds of comments. *Multiline* comments start with a left parenthesis and an asterisk and end with an asterisk and a right parenthesis. For example:

```
(* this is a comment *)
```

or

```
(* this
   is a
   comment
*)
```

You cannot nest multiline comments, and you will get a compile error if a comment is left unclosed. *Single-line* comments start with two slashes and extend to the end of a line. For example:

```
// this is a single-line comment
```

Doc Comments

Doc comments allow comments to be extracted from the source file in the form of XML or HTML. This is useful because it allows programmers to browse code comments without having to browse the source. This is convenient for the vendors of APIs because it allows them to provide documentation about the code without having to provide the source itself, and it is just more convenient to be able to browse the docs without having to open the source. In addition, the documentation is stored alongside the source where it has more chance of being updated when code changes.

Doc comments start with three slashes instead of two. They can be associated only with top-level values or type definitions and are associated with the value or type they appear immediately before. The following code associates the comment `this is an explanation` with the value `myString`:

```
#light
/// this is an explanation
let myString = "this is a string"
```

To extract doc comments into an XML file, you use the `-doc` compiler switch. If this example were saved in a source file, `prog.fs`, the following command:

```
fsc -doc doc.xml Prog.fs
```

would produce the following XML:

```
<?xml version="1.0" encoding="utf-8"?>
<doc>
<assembly><name>Prog</name></assembly>
<members>
<member name="F:Prog.myString">
<summary>
 this is an explanation
</summary>

</member>
<member name="T:Prog">

</member>
</members>
</doc>
```

You can then process the XML using various tools, such as NDoc (ndoc.sourceforge.net), to transform it into a number of more readable formats. The compiler also supports the direct generation of HTML from doc comments. Although this is less flexible than XML, it can produce usable documentation with less effort. It can also produce better results, under some circumstances, because notations such as generics and union types are not always well supported by documentation generation tools. I cover the compiler switches that generate HTML in "Useful Command-Line Switches" in Chapter 12.

In F# there is no need to explicitly add any XML tags; for example, the <summary> and </summary> tags were added automatically. I find this useful because it saves a lot of typing and avoids wasted space in the source file; however, you can take control and write out the XML tags themselves if you want. The following is a doc comment where the tags have been explicitly written out:

```
#light
/// <summary>
/// divides the given parameter by 10
/// </summary>
/// <param name="x">the thing to be divided by 10</param>
let divTen x = x / 10
```

This will produce the following XML:

```
<?xml version="1.0" encoding="utf-8"?>
<doc>
<assembly><name>AnotherProg</name></assembly>
<members>
<member name="M:AnotherProg.divTen (System.Int32)">
<summary>
divides the given parameter by 10
</summary>
<param name="x">the thing to be divided by 10</param>
```

```
</member>
<member name="T:AnotherProg">

</member>
</members>
</doc>
```

If no signature file exists for the module file, then the doc comments are taken directly from the module file itself. However, if a signature file exists, then doc comments come from the signature file. This means that even if doc comments exist in the module file, they will not be included in the resulting XML or HTML if the compiler is given a signature file for it.

Custom Attributes

Custom attributes add information to your code that will be compiled into an assembly and stored alongside your values and types. This information can then be read programmatically via reflection or by the runtime itself.

Attributes can be associated with types, members of types, and top-level values. They can also be associated with do statements. An attribute is specified in brackets, with the attribute name in angle brackets. For example:

```
[<Obsolete>]
```

Attribute names, by convention, end with the string Attribute, so the actual name of the Obsolete attribute is ObsoleteAttribute.

An attribute must immediately precede what it modifies. The following code marks the function, functionOne, as obsolete:

```
#light
open System

[<Obsolete>]
let functionOne () = ()
```

An attribute is essentially just a class, and when you use an attribute, you are really just making a call to its constructor. In the previous example, Obsolete has a parameterless constructor, and it can be called with or without parentheses. In this case, we called it without parentheses. If you want to pass arguments to an attribute's constructor, then you must use parentheses and separate arguments with commas. For example:

```
#light
open System

 [<Obsolete("it is a pointless function anyway!")>]
let functionTwo () = ()
```

Sometimes an attribute's constructor does not expose all the properties of the attribute. If you want to set them, you need to specify the property and a value for it. You specify the property name, an equals sign, and the value after the other arguments to the constructor. The next example sets the Unrestricted property of the PrintingPermission attribute to true:

```
#light
open System.Drawing.Printing
open System.Security.Permissions

[<PrintingPermission(SecurityAction.Demand, Unrestricted = true)>]
let functionThree () = ()
```

You can use two or more attributes by separating the attributes with semicolons:

```
#light
open System
open System.Drawing.Printing
open System.Security.Permissions

[<Obsolete; PrintingPermission(SecurityAction.Demand)>]
let functionFive () = ()
```

So far, we've used attributes only with values, but using them with type or type members is just as straightforward. The following example marks a type and all its members as obsolete:

```
#light
open System

[<Obsolete>]
type OOThing = class
    [<Obsolete>]
    val stringThing : string
    [<Obsolete>]
    new() = {stringThing = ""}
    [<Obsolete>]
    member x.GetTheString () = x.string_thing
end
```

If you intend to use WinForms or Windows Presentation Foundation (WPF) graphics within your program, you must ensure that the program is a *single-thread apartment*. This is because the libraries that provide the graphical components use *unmanaged* (not compiled by the CLR) code under the covers. The easiest way to do this is by using the STAThread attribute. This must modify the first do statement in the last file passed to the compiler, that is, the first statement that will execute when the program runs. For example:

```
#light
open System
open System.Windows.Forms

let form = new Form()

[<STAThread>]
do Application.Run(form)
```

> **Note** The do keyword is usually required only when not using the #light mode; however, it is also required when applying an attribute to a group of statements.

Once attributes have been added to types and values, it's possible to use reflection to find which values and types are marked with which attributes. This is usually done with the IsDefined or GetCustomAttributes methods of the System.Reflection.MemberInfo class, meaning they are available on most objects used for reflection including System.Type. The next example shows how to look for all types that are marked with the Obsolete attribute:

```
#light
let obsolete = System.AppDomain.CurrentDomain.GetAssemblies()
            |> List.of_array
            |> List.map ( fun assm -> assm.GetTypes() )
            |> Array.concat
            |> List.of_array
            |> List.filter
                ( fun m ->
                    m.IsDefined((type System.ObsoleteAttribute), true))

print_any obsolete
```

The results are as follows:

```
[System.ContextMarshalException; System.Collections.IHashCodeProvider;
 System.Collections.CaseInsensitiveHashCodeProvider;
 System.Runtime.InteropServices.IDispatchImplType;
 System.Runtime.InteropServices.IDispatchImplAttribute;
 System.Runtime.InteropServices.SetWin32ContextInIDispatchAttribute;
 System.Runtime.InteropServices.BIND_OPTS;
 System.Runtime.InteropServices.UCOMIBindCtx;
 System.Runtime.InteropServices.UCOMIConnectionPointContainer;
...
```

Now that you've seen how you can use attributes and reflection to examine code, let's look at a similar but more powerful technique for analyzing compiled code, called *quotation*.

Quoted Code

Quotations are a way of telling the compiler, "Don't generate code for this section of the source file; turn it into a data structure, an *expression tree*, instead." This expression tree can then be interpreted in a number of ways, transformed or optimized, compiled into another language, or even just ignored.

Quotations come in two types, raw and typed, the difference being that typed quotations carry static type information whereas raw quotations do not. Both carry runtime type annotations. Typed quotations are designed for use in client programs, so usually you will want to use typed quotations. These are the only quotations covered in this section. Raw quotations are designed for implementing libraries based on quotations; these will generally be automatically typed quotations before they are consumed.

To quote an expression, place it between *guillemets* (also called *French quotes*), « ». To ensure the compiler recognizes these characters, you must save your file as UTF-8. Visual Studio users can do this with File ➤ Advanced Save. If you have some objection to using UTF-8, you can use an ASCII alternative: <@ @>. Both ways of quoting an expression are essentially just an operator defined in a module, so you need to open the module Microsoft. FSharp.Quotations.Typed to be able to use them. The next example uses a quotation and prints it:

```
#light
open Microsoft.FSharp.Quotations.Typed

let quotedInt = « 1 »

printf "%A\r\n" quotedInt
```

The result is as follows:

```
<@ Int32 1 @>
```

If you were to use the ASCII alternative, it would look like this:

```
#light
open Microsoft.FSharp.Quotations.Typed

let asciiQuotedInt = <@ 1 @>

printf "%A\r\n" asciiQuotedInt
```

The result is as follows:

```
<@ Int32 1 @>
```

As you can see, the code doesn't look very different and the results are the same, so from now I'll use guillemets. The following example defines an identifier and uses it in a quotation:

```
#light
open Microsoft.FSharp.Quotations.Typed

let n = 1
let quotedId = « n »

printf "%A\r\n" quotedId
```

The result is as follows:

```
<@ Prog.n @>
```

Next we'll quote a function applied to a value. Notice that since we are quoting two items, the result of this quotation is split into two parts. The first part represents the function, and the second represents the value to which it is applied.

```
#light
open Microsoft.FSharp.Quotations.Typed

let inc x = x + 1
let quotedFun = « inc 1 »

printf "%A\r\n" quotedFun
```

The result is as follows:

```
<@ Prog.inc (Int32 1) @>
```

The next example shows an operator applied to two values. Because the expression has three items, the result is split into three parts, one to represent each part of the expression.

```
#light
open Microsoft.FSharp.Quotations.Typed

let quotedOp = « 1 + 1 »

printf "%A\r\n" quotedOp
```

The result is as follows:

```
<@ Microsoft.FSharp.Operators.op_Addition (Int32 1) (Int32 1) @>
```

The next example quotes an anonymous function:

```
#light
open Microsoft.FSharp.Quotations.Typed

let quotedAnonFun = « fun x -> x + 1 »

printf "%A\r\n" quotedAnonFun
```

The result is as follows:

```
<@
fun  x#6142.1 ->
  Microsoft.FSharp.Operators.op_Addition x#6142.1 (Int32 1) @>
```

To interpret expressions, you must first convert them into raw expressions and then query the expression to see whether it is of a certain type. Querying the type returns an option type that will contain the value Some if it is of that type or None if it isn't. The next example defines a function, interpretInt, that queries the expression passed to it to see whether it is an integer. If it is, it prints the value of that integer; otherwise, it prints the string "not an int".

```
#light
open Microsoft.FSharp.Quotations
open Microsoft.FSharp.Quotations.Typed

let interpretInt exp =
    let uexp = to_raw exp in
    match uexp with
    | Raw.Int32 x -> printfn "%d" x
    | _ -> printfn "not an int"

interpretInt « 1 »
interpretInt « 1 + 1 »
```

The results are as follows:

```
1
not an int
```

We printed two expressions with interpretInt. The first was an integer value, so it printed out the value of that integer. The second was not an integer, although it contained integers.

Quotations are a very big topic, and we can't cover them completely in this section or even in this book. You will, however, return to them in "Meta-programming with Quotations" in Chapter 11.

Summary

In this chapter, you saw how to organize code in F#. You also saw how to comment, annotate, and quote code, but you just scratched the surface of both annotation and quoting.

This concludes the tour of the F# core language. The rest of the book will focus on how to use F#, from working with relational databases to creating user interfaces, after you look at the F# core libraries in the next chapter.

CHAPTER 7

■ ■ ■

The F# Libraries

Although F# can use all the classes available in the .NET BCL, it also ships with its own set of libraries.

The F# libraries are split into two, `FSLib.dll`, which is also referred to as the native F# library or just FSLib, and `MLLib.dll`, which is sometimes referred to as the ML compatibility library or MLLib. FSLib contains everything that the F# compiler really needs to work; for example, it contains the `Tuple` class that is used when you use a tuple. MLLib is a set of libraries for doing common programming tasks partially based on the libraries that ship with OCaml.

The objective of this chapter is not to completely document every nuance of every F# library type and function. It is to give you an overview of what the modules can do, with a particular focus on features that aren't readily available in the BCL. The F# online documentation (`http://research.microsoft.com/fsharp/manual/namespaces.html`) is the place to find detailed documentation about each function.

There is some crossover between the functionality provided by the F# libraries and the .NET BCL. Programmers often ask when should they use functions from the F# library and when should they use the classes and methods available in the .NET BCL. Both have their advantages and disadvantages, and a good rule of thumb is to prefer what is in FSLib over the classes available in the .NET Framework BCL and prefer what is available in the .NET Framework BCL over MLLib.

Libraries Overview

The following sections list all the modules that are contained in FSLib and MLLib; the modules covered in this chapter are highlighted in bold.

The Native F# Library FSLib.dll

These are the modules in FSLib:

- Microsoft.FSharp

    - Idioms

- **Reflection**

- Microsoft.FSharp.Collections

    - Array
    - ComparisonIdentity
    - LazyList
    - ReadonlyArray
    - Set

    - Array2
    - HashIdentity
    - List
    - ResizeArray

    - Array3
    - IEnumerable
    - Map
    - **Seq**

- Microsoft.FSharp.Collections.Tags

    - Optimizations

- Microsoft.FSharp.Compatibility

    - CompatArray
    - CompatMatrix
    - MATLAB

- Microsoft.FSharp.Control

    - IEvent
    - Lazy
    - LazyStatus

- Microsoft.FSharp.Core

    - Byte
    - Float
    - Int32
    - LanguagePrimitives
    - Option
    - UInt16
    - UInt8

    - Char
    - Float32
    - Int64
    - Operators
    - SByte
    - UInt32

    - **Enum**
    - Int16
    - Int8
    - OptimizedClosures
    - String
    - UInt64

- Microsoft.FSharp.Math

    - BigInt
    - **Complex**
    - LinearAlgebra
    - RawMatrixOps

    - BigNum
    - GlobalAssociations
    - Matrix
    - RowVector

    - BigRational
    - Instances
    - Notation
    - Vector

- Microsoft.FSharp.Math.Primitive

  - BigNat   • FFT

- Microsoft.FSharp.NativeInterop

  - NativePtr   • Ref

- Microsoft.FSharp.Primitives

  - Basics

- Microsoft.FSharp.Quotations

  - Raw   • RawTypes   • Typed   • Utilities

- Microsoft.FSharp.Text

  - **Printf**   • PrintfImpl

- Microsoft.FSharp.Text.StructuredFormat

  - Display   • LayoutOps

- Microsoft.FSharp.Tools.FsYacc

  - ParseHelpers

The ML Compatibility Library MLLib.dll

These are the modules in MLLib:

- Microsoft.FSharp.Compatibility.OCaml

  - **Arg**

  - Big_int

  - Buffer

  - Bytearray

  - Filename

  - Hashtbl

  - Lexing

  - Num

  - Obj

  - Parsing

  - **Pervasives**

  - Printexc

  - Sys

The Native F# Library FSLib.dll

FSLib contains all the classes that you need to make the compiler work, such as the definition of the type into which F#'s list literal compiles. I'll cover the following modules:

Microsoft.FSharp.Core.Operators: A module containing functions similar to useful C# constructs such as using and lock.

Microsoft.FSharp.Reflection: A module containing functions that supplement the .NET Framework's reflection classes to give a more accurate view of F# types and values.

Microsoft.FSharp.Collections.Seq: A module containing functions for any type that supports the IEnumerable interface.

Microsoft.FSharp.Core.Enum: A module containing functions for .NET enumeration types.

Microsoft.FSharp.Text.Printf: A module for formatting strings.

Microsoft.FSharp.Control.IEvent: A module for working with events in F#.

Microsoft.FSharp.Math: A namespace that contains several modules related to mathematics. These include arbitrary precision integers and rationales, vectors, matrices, and complex numbers.

The Microsoft.FSharp.Core.Operators Module

In F#, operators are defined by libraries rather than built into the language; this module contains some of the language's operators. It also contains some useful operators such as functions, and it is these that I'll be covering here. The module is open by default, which means the user can use these functions with no prefix. Specifically, I will cover the following functions:

The using *function*: A function that helps you ensure that unmanaged or limited resources are disposed of in a timely manner

The lock *function*: A function that helps you ensure that any resources that need to be shared between threads are dealt with correctly

Tuple functions: Functions on tuples

The using Function

The IDisposable interface has one member, Dispose; typically this interface is used when a class that wraps some unmanaged or limited resource, such as a database connection, calling Dispose ensures that the resource can always be reclaimed in a timely manner and you do not have to wait for garbage collection. The using function is a great way to ensure that the Dispose method of the IDisposable interface is always called when you are finished with the class, even if an exception is thrown.

The using function has the type 'a -> ('a -> 'b) -> 'b when 'a :> IDisposable. It therefore has two parameters: the first must implement the IDisposable interface, and the second is a function that must take a parameter of type IDisposable interface and that can return a parameter of any type. The parameter returned from this function is the return type of the using function. The following example illustrates this by opening a file to append to it:

```
#light
open System.IO

using (File.AppendText("test.txt"))
    (fun streamWriter ->
        streamWriter.WriteLine("A safe way to write to a file"))
```

The call to the BCL's method File.AppendText will return a System.IO.StreamWriter, which is a way of writing to a file. A file is managed by the operating system, so it has an "unmanaged" aspect. This is why System.IO.StreamWriter implements IDisposable. A System.IO.StreamWriter is passed to the function, which itself makes up the second parameter passed to the using function. This is a neat way of ensuring that the streamWriter is available only inside a limited scope of the function and that it is disposed of straightaway when the function ends. If you did not write your file access using the using function, you would have to explicitly call the Dispose method, or your text would not be flushed from memory into the file. Similarly, there would be a risk that an exception could occur. Although the risk is limited, there is a real risk that a file would not be closed properly and the text not written to it.

It's worth noting that using returns unit because the call to StreamWriter.WriteLine returns unit. If you were performing an operation that didn't return unit, say reading from a file or database, you could return a value from the using function. The following example illustrates this by reading from a file and then binding the contents of the first line of that file to the identifier text:

```
#light
open System.IO
let text =
    using (File.OpenText("test.txt")) (fun streamReader ->
        streamReader.ReadLine()
    )
```

The lock Function

The lock function operates in a fashion similar to using. The purpose of the function is to lock a section of code so that only one thread can pass through it at a time. This issue arises in multi-threaded programming because a thread can context switch at any time, leaving operations that should have been atomic half done. This is controlled by locking on an object; the idea is that as soon as the lock is taken, any thread attempting to enter the section of code will be blocked until the lock is released by the thread that holds it. Code protected in this way is sometimes called a *critical section*. This is achieved by calling System.Threading.Monitor.Enter at the start of the code that is to be protected and System.Threading.Monitor.Exit at the end; it is important to guarantee that Monitor.Exit is called, or this could lead to threads being locked forever. The lock function is a nice way to ensure that Monitor.Exit is always called if Monitor.Enter has been called. It takes two parameters; the first is the object to be locked on, and the second is a function that contains the code to be protected. This function should take unit as its parameter, and it can return any value.

The following example demonstrates the subtle issues involved in locking. It needs to be quite long and has been deliberately written to exaggerate the problem of context switching. The idea is that two threads will run at the same time, both trying to write the console. The aim of the sample is to write the string "One ... Two ... Three ... " to the console atomically; that is, one thread should be able to finish writing its message before the next one starts. The example has a function, called makeUnsafeThread, that creates a thread that will not be able to write to the console atomically and a second one, makeSafeThread, that writes to the console atomically by using a lock.

```
#light
open System
open System.Threading

// function to print to the console character by character
// this increases the chance of there being a context switch
// between threads.
let printSlowly (s : string) =
    s.ToCharArray()
    |> Array.iter print_char


// create a thread that prints to the console in an unsafe way
let makeUnsafeThread() =
    new Thread(fun () ->
        for x = 1 to 100 do
            printSlowly "One ... Two ... Three ... "
            print_newline()
        done)

// the object that will be used as a lock
let lockObj = new Object()

// create a thread that prints to the console in a safe way
let makeSafeThread() =
    new Thread(fun () ->
        for x = 1 to 100 do
            // use lock to ensure operation is atomic
            lock lockObj (fun () ->
                printSlowly "One ... Two ... Three ... "
                print_newline()
            )
        done)
```

```
// helper function to run the test to
let runTest (f : unit -> Thread) message =
    print_endline message;
    let t1 = f() in
    let t2 = f() in
    t1.Start()
    t2.Start()
    t1.Join()
    t2.Join()

// runs the demonstrations
let main() =
    runTest
        makeUnsafeThread
        "Running test without locking ..."
    runTest
        makeSafeThread
        "Running test with locking ..."

main ()
```

The part of the example that actually uses the lock is repeated next to highlight the important points. You should note a couple of important factors. First, the declaration of the lockObj will be used to create the critical section. Second, the use of the lock function is embedded in the makeSafeThread function. The most important thing to notice is how the printing functions you want to be atomic are placed inside the function that is passed to lock.

```
// the object that will be used as a lock
let lockObj = new Object()

// create a thread that prints to the console in a safe way
let makeSafeThread() =
    new Thread(fun () ->
        for x = 1 to 100 do
            // use lock to ensure operation is atomic
            lock lockObj (fun () ->
                printSlowly "One ... Two ... Three ... "
                print_newline()
            )
        done)
```

The results of the first part of the test will vary each time it is run, since it depends on when a thread context switches. It might also vary based on the number of processors, because if a machine has two or more processors, then threads can run at the same time, and therefore the messages will be more tightly interspersed. On a single-processor machine, things will look less messy, because the messages will go wrong only when a content switch takes place. The results of the first part of the sample, run on a single-processor machine, are as follows:

```
Running test without locking ...
...
One ... Two ... Three ...
One One ... Two ... Three ...
One ... Two ... Three ...
...
```

The results of the second half of the example will not vary at all, because of the lock, so it will always look like this:

```
Running test with locking ...
One ... Two ... Three ...
One ... Two ... Three ...
One ... Two ... Three ...
...
```

Locking is an important aspect of concurrency. Any resource that will be written to and shared between threads should be locked. A resource is often a variable, but it could also be a file or even the console, as shown in this example. You should not think of locks as a magical solution to concurrency. Although they work, they also can also create problems of their own since they can create a deadlock, where different threads lock resources that each other needs and neither can advance. The simplest solution to concurrency is often to simply avoid sharing a resource that can be written to between threads.

■**Note** You can find more information about concurrency at http://www.strangelights.com/fsharp/foundations/default.aspx/FSharpFoundations.Concurrency.

Tuple Functions

The Operators module also offers two useful functions that operate on tuples. You can use the functions fst and snd to break up a tuple with two items in it. The following example demonstrates their use:

```
printf "(fst (1, 2)): %i\r\n" (fst (1, 2))
printf "(snd (1, 2)): %i\r\n" (snd (1, 2))
```

The results of this code are as follows:

```
(fst (1, 2)): 1
(snd (1, 2)): 2
```

The Microsoft.FSharp.Reflection Module

This module contains F#'s own version of reflection. F# contains some types that are 100 percent compatible with the CLR type system but aren't precisely understood with .NET reflection. For example, F# uses some sleight of hand to implement its union type, and this is transparent in 100 percent F# code but can look a little strange when you use the BCL to reflect over it. The F# reflection system addresses this kind of problem. But, it blends with the BCL's System.Reflection namespace, so if you are reflecting over an F# type that uses BCL types, you will get the appropriate object from the System.Reflection namespace.

In F#, you can reflect over types or over values. The difference is a bit subtle and is best explained with an example. Those of you familiar with .NET reflection might like to think of reflection over types as using the Type, EventInfo, FieldInfo, MethodInfo, and PropertyInfo types and reflections over values as calling their members such as GetProperty or InvokeMember to get values dynamically, but reflection over values offers a high-level, easy-to-use system.

- *Reflection over types* lets you examine the types that make up a particular value or type.

- *Reflection over values* lets you examine the values that make up a particular composite value.

Reflection Over Types

The following example shows a function that will print the type of any tuple:

```
#light
open Microsoft.FSharp.Reflection

let printTupleTypes x =
    match  Value.GetTypeInfo(x) with
    | TupleType types ->
        print_string "("
        types
        |> List.iteri
            (fun i t ->
                if i <> List.length types - 1 then
                    Printf.printf " %s * " t.Name
                else
                    print_string t.Name)
        print_string " )"
    | _ -> print_string "not a tuple"

printTupleTypes ("hello world", 1)
```

First you use the function Value.GetTypeInfo() to get a TypeInfo value that represents the object passed to the function. This is similar to calling GetType() on a BCL object. If you had a System.Type object instead of a value, you could have used Type.GetTypeInfo to retrieve the same TypeInfo value. TypeInfo is a union type, so you pattern-match over it. In this case, you are interested only in tuples, so you print "not a tuple" if you receive anything else. The TupleType constructor contains a list of System.Type values that represent the members of a tuple, so by printing the Name property of System.Type, you can print the names of the types that make up the tuple. This means when compiled and run, the sample outputs the following:

```
( String * Int32 )
```

Reflection Over Values

Imagine instead of displaying the types of a tuple that you wanted to display the values that make up the tuple. To do this, you would use reflection over values, and you would need to use the function GetValueInfo to retrieve a value of type ValueInfo that is similar to TupleType, except that instead of containing information about types, it contains information about values. To print out the values within a tuple, you use the TupleValue constructor, which contains a list of values that make up the tuple. The following example implements such a function:

```
#light
open Microsoft.FSharp.Reflection

let printTupleValues x =
    match Value.GetInfo(x) with
    | TupleValue vals ->
        print_string "("
        vals
        |> List.iteri
            (fun i v ->
                if i <> List.length vals - 1 then
                    Printf.printf " %s, " (any_to_string v)
                else
                    print_any v)
        print_string " )"
    | _ -> print_string "not a tuple"

printTupleValues ("hello world", 1)
```

The result of this code, when compiled and executed, is as follows:

```
( "hello world", 1 )
```

Reflection is used both within the implementation of fsi, the interactive command-line tool that is part of the F# tool suite (see Chapter 11), and within the F# library functions any_to_string and print_any. If you want to learn more about the way you can use reflection, take a look at the source for any_to_string and print_any, available in the distribution in the file \lib\mllib\layout.fs.

The Microsoft.FSharp.Collections.Seq Module

The Microsoft.FSharp.Collections.Seq module contains functions that work with any collection that supports the IEnumerable interface, which is most of the collections in the .NET Framework's BCL. The module is called Seq because F# gives the alias seq to the IEnumerable interface to shorten it and make it easier to type and read; this alias is used when type definitions are given.

■ **Note** FSLib contains several modules designed to work with various types of collections. These include Array, Array2 (two-dimensional arrays), Array3 (three-dimensional arrays), Hashtbl (a hash table implementation), IEnumerable, LazyList, List, Map, and Set. I'll cover only Seq because it should generally be favored over these collections because of its ability to work with lots of different types of collections. Also, although each module has functions that are specific to it, many functions are common to them all.

Some of these functions can be replaced by the list comprehension syntax covered in Chapters 3 and 4. For simple tasks and working with untyped collections, it's generally easier to use list comprehension, but for more complicated tasks you will want to stick to these functions. You will take a look at the following functions:

map and iter: These two functions let you apply a given function to every item in the collection.

concat: This function lets you concatenate a collection of collections into one collection.

fold: This function lets you create a summary of a list by folding the items in the collection together.

exists and for_all: These function let you make assertions about the contents of a collection.

filter, find and tryfind: These functions let you pick elements in the list that meet certain conditions.

choose: This function lets you perform a filter and map at the same time.

init_finite and init_infinite: These functions let you initialize collections.

unfold: This provides a more flexible way to initialize lists.

untyped: This gives you a look at the functions that are designed to work with the non-generic version of IEnumerable, rather than IEnumerable<T>.

The map and iter Functions

You'll look at map and iter first. These apply a function to each element in a collection. The difference between them is that map is designed to create a new collection by transforming each element in the collection, while iter is designed to apply an operation that has a side effect to each item in the collection. A typical example of a side effect would be writing the element to the console. The following example shows both map and iter in action:

```
#light

let myArray = [|1; 2; 3|]

let myNewCollection =
    myArray |>
    Seq.map (fun x -> x * 2)

print_any myArray
print_newline()

myNewCollection |> Seq.iter (fun x -> printf "%i ... " x)
```

The results of this code, when compiled and executed, are as follows:

```
[|1; 2; 3|]
2 ... 4 ... 6 ...
```

The concat Function

The previous example used an array, because it was convenient to initialize this type of collection, but you could use any of the collection types available in the BCL. The next example uses the List type provided in the System.Collections.Generic namespace and demonstrates how to use the concat function, which has type #seq< #seq<'a> > -> seq<'a> and which collects IEnumerable values into one IEnumerable value:

```
#light
open System.Collections.Generic

let myList =
    let temp = new List<int[]>()
    temp.Add([|1; 2; 3|])
    temp.Add([|4; 5; 6|])
    temp.Add([|7; 8; 9|])
    temp

let myCompleteList = Seq.concat myList

myCompleteList |> Seq.iter (fun x -> printf "%i ... " x)
```

The results of this code, when compiled and executed, are as follows:

```
1 ... 2 ... 3 ... 4 ... 5 ... 6 ... 7 ... 8 ... 9 ...
```

The fold Function

The next example demonstrates the fold function, which has type (`'b -> 'a -> 'b) -> 'b -> #seq<'a> -> 'b`. This is a function for creating a summary of a collection by threading an accumulator value through each function call. The function takes two parameters. The first of these is an accumulator, which is the result of the previous function, and the second is an element from the collection. The function body should combine these two values to form a new value of the same type as the accumulator. In the next example, the elements of myPhrase are concatenated to the accumulator so that all the strings end up combined into one string.

```
#light
let myPhrase = [|"How"; "do"; "you"; "do?"|]

let myCompletePhrase =
    myPhrase |>
    Seq.fold (fun acc x -> acc + " " + x) ""

print_endline myCompletePhrase
```

The result of this code, when compiled and executed, is as follows:

```
How do you do?
```

The exists and for_all Functions

The next example demonstrates two functions that you can use to determine facts about the contents of collections. These functions are exists and for_all, which both have the type (`'a -> bool) -> #seq<'a> -> bool`. You can use the exists function to determine whether any element in the collection exists that meets certain conditions. The conditions that must be met are determined by the function passed to exists, and if any of the elements meet this condition, then exists will return true. The function for_all is similar except that all the elements in the collection must meet the condition before it will return true. The following example first uses exists to determine whether there are any elements in the collections that are multiples of 2 and then uses for_all to determine whether all items in the collection are multiples of 2:

```
#light
let intArray = [|0; 1; 2; 3; 4; 5; 6; 7; 8; 9|]

let existsMultipleOfTwo =
    intArray |>
    Seq.exists (fun x -> x % 2 = 0)

let allMultipleOfTwo =
    intArray |>
    Seq.exists (fun x -> x % 2 = 0)

printfn "existsMultipleOfTwo: %b" existsMultipleOfTwo
printfn "allMultipleOfTwo: %b" allMultipleOfTwo
```

The results of this code, when compiled and executed, are as follows:

```
existsMultipleOfTwo: true
allMultipleOfTwo: false
```

The filter, find, and tryfind Functions

The next example looks at three functions that are similar to exists and for_all; these functions are filter of type ('a -> bool) -> #seq<'a> -> seq<'a>, find of type ('a -> bool) -> #seq<'a> -> 'a and tryfind of type ('a -> bool) -> #seq<'a> -> 'a option. They are similar to exists and for_all because they use functions to examine the contents of a collection, but instead of returning a Boolean, these functions actually return the item or items found. The function filter uses the function passed to it to check every element in the collection. The filter function then returns a list that contains all the elements that have met the condition of the function. If no elements meet the condition, then an empty list is returned. The functions find and tryfind both return the first element in the collection to meet the condition specified by the function passed to them. Their behavior is altered when no element in the collection meets the condition; find throws an exception, whereas tryfind returns an option type that will be None if no element is found. Since exceptions are relatively expensive in .NET, you should prefer tryfind over find.

In the following example, you'll look through a list of words; first you use filter to create a list containing only the words that end in *at*. Then you'll use find to find the first word that ends in *ot*. Finally, you'll use tryfind to check whether any of the words end in *tt*.

```
#light
let shortWordList = [|"hat"; "hot"; "bat"; "lot"; "mat"; "dot"; "rat";|]

let atWords =
    shortWordList
    |> Seq.filter (fun x -> x.EndsWith("at"))

let otWord =
    shortWordList
    |> Seq.find (fun x -> x.EndsWith("ot"))

let ttWord =
    shortWordList
    |> Seq.tryfind (fun x -> x.EndsWith("tt"))

atWords |> Seq.iter (fun x -> printf "%s ... " x)
print_newline()
print_endline otWord
print_endline (match ttWord with | Some x -> x | None -> "Not found")
```

The results of this code, when compiled and executed, are as follows:

```
hat ... bat ... mat ... rat ...
hot
Not found
```

The choose Function

The next Seq function you'll look at is a clever function that allows you to do a filter and a map at the same time. This function is called choose and has the type ('a -> 'b option) -> #seq<'a> -> seq<'b>. To do this, the function that is passed to choose must return an option type. If the element in the list can be transformed into something useful, the function should return Some containing the new value, and when the element is not wanted, the function returns None.

In the following example, you'll take a list of floating-point numbers and multiply them by 2. If the value is an integer, it is returned; otherwise, it is filtered out. This leaves you with just a list of integers.

```
#light
let floatArray = [|0.5; 0.75; 1.0; 1.25; 1.5; 1.75; 2.0 |]

let integers =
    floatArray |>
    Seq.choose
        (fun x ->
            let y = x * 2.0
            let z = floor y
            if y - z = 0.0 then
                Some (int_of_float z)
            else
                None)

integers |> Seq.iter (fun x -> printf "%i ... " x)
```

The results of this code, when compiled and executed, are as follows:

```
1 ... 2 ... 3 ... 4 ...
```

The init_finite and init_infinite Functions

Next you'll look at two functions for initializing collections, init_finite of type int -> (int -> 'a) -> seq<'a> and init_infinite of type (int -> 'a) -> seq<'a>. You can use the function init_finite to make a collection of a finite size; it does this by calling the function passed to it the number of times specified by the number passed to it. You can use the function init_infinite to create a collection of an infinite size. It does this by calling the function passed to it each time it is asked for a new element this way; in theory, a list of unlimited size can be created, but in reality you are constrained by the limits of the machine performing the computation.

The following example shows `init_finite` being used to create a list of ten integers, each with the value 1. It also shows a list being created that should contain all the possible 32-bit integers and demonstrates using the function `take` to create a list of the first ten.

```
#light
let tenOnes = Seq.init_finite 10 (fun _ -> 1)
let allIntegers = Seq.init_infinite (fun x -> System.Int32.MinValue + x)
let firstTenInts = Seq.take 10 allIntegers

tenOnes |> Seq.iter (fun x -> printf "%i ... " x)
print_newline()
print_any firstTenInts
```

The results of this code, when compiled and executed, are as follows:

```
1 ... 1 ... 1 ... 1 ... 1 ... 1 ... 1 ... 1 ... 1 ... 1 ...
[-2147483648; -2147483647; -2147483646; -2147483645; -2147483644; -2147483643;
 -2147483642; -2147483641; -2147483640; -2147483639]
```

The unfold Function

You already met `unfold` in Chapter 3; it is a more flexible version of the functions `init_finite` and `init_infinite`. The first advantage of `unfold` is that it can be used to pass an accumulator through the computation, which means you can store some state between computations and do not simply have to rely on the current position in the list to calculate the value, like you do with `init_finite` and `init_infinite`. The second advantage is that it can be used to produce a list that is either finite or infinite. Both of these advantages are achieved by using the return type of the function passed to `unfold`; the return type of the function is `'a * 'b option`, meaning an option type that contains a tuple of values. The first value in the option type is the value that will be placed in the list, and the second is the accumulator. If you want to continue the list, you return Some with this tuple contained within it. If want to stop it, you return None.

The following example, repeated from Chapter 2, shows `unfold` being used to compute the Fibonacci numbers. You can see the accumulator being used to store a tuple of values representing the next two numbers in the Fibonacci sequence. Because the list of Fibonacci numbers is infinite, you never return None.

```
#light
let fibs =
    (1,1) |> Seq.unfold
        (fun (n0, n1)  ->
            Some(n0, (n1, n0 + n1)))

let first20 = Seq.take 20 fibs

print_any first20
```

The results of this code, when compiled and executed, are as follows:

```
[1; 1; 2; 3; 5; 8; 13; 21; 34; 55; 89; 144; 233; 377; 610; 987;
 1597; 2584; 4181; 6765]
```

The example demonstrates using unfold to produce a list that terminates. Imagine you want to calculate a sequence of numbers where the value decreases by half its current value, such as a nuclear source decaying. Imagine beyond a certain limit the number becomes so small that you are no longer interested in it. You can model such a sequence in the following example by returning None when the value has reached its limit:

```
#light
let decayPattern =
    Seq.unfold
        (fun x ->
            let limit = 0.01
            let n = x - (x / 2.0)
            if n > limit then
                Some(x, n)
            else
                None)
        (10.0)

decayPattern |> Seq.iter (fun x -> printf "%f ... " x)
```

The results of this code, when compiled and executed, are as follows:

```
10.000000 ... 5.000000 ... 2.500000 ... 1.250000 ...
0.625000 ... 0.312500 ... 0.156250 ... 0.078125 ... 0.039063 ...
```

The generate and generate_using Functions

The generate function of type (unit -> 'b) -> ('b -> 'a option) -> ('b -> unit) -> seq<'a> and the generate_using function of type (unit -> 'a) -> ('a -> 'b option) -> seq<'b> when 'a :> IDisposable are two useful functions of creating IEnumerable collections. They allow you to generate collections from some kind of cursor. The cursor can be a file stream, as shown in these examples, or perhaps more commonly a database cursor; or it can be any type that will generate a sequence of elements. The generate function takes three functions: one to open the cursor (the opener function in the following example), one to do the work of actually generating the collection (the generator function), and one to close the cursor (the closer function). The collection can then be treated as any other IEnumerable collection, but behind the scenes, the functions you have defined will be called to go to the data source and read the elements from it. The following example shows the function being used to read a comma-separated list of words from a file:

```
#light
open System
open System.Text
open System.IO

// test.txt: the,cat,sat,on,the,mat
let opener() = File.OpenText("test.txt")

let generator (stream : StreamReader) =
    let endStream = ref false
    let rec generatorInner chars =
        match stream.Read() with
        | -1 ->
            endStream := true
            chars
        | x ->
            match Convert.ToChar(x) with
            | ',' -> chars
            | c -> generatorInner (c :: chars)
    let chars = generatorInner []
    if List.length chars = 0 && !endStream then
        None
    else
        Some(new string(List.to_array (List.rev chars)))

let closer (stream : StreamReader) =
    stream.Dispose()

let wordList =
    Seq.generate
        opener
        generator
        closer

wordList |> Seq.iter (fun s -> print_endline s)
```

The results of this code, when compiled and executed, are as follows:

```
the
cat
sat
on
the
mat
```

The generate_using function is the same as the generate function, except that the type used to create the collection must support the IDisposable interface, and this will be called when the last item has been read from the collection instead of the closer function. This saves you the trouble of explicitly defining a closer function, leading to short programs. I consider the generate_using function very useful because most types you want to generate collections from will support the IDisposable interface; its usage is demonstrated here:

```
#light
open System
open System.Text
open System.IO

// test.txt: the,cat,sat,on,the,mat
let opener() = File.OpenText("test.txt")

let generator (stream : StreamReader) =
    let endStream = ref false
    let rec generatorInner chars =
        match stream.Read() with
        | -1 ->
            endStream := true
            chars
        | x ->
            match Convert.ToChar(x) with
            | ',' -> chars
            | c -> generatorInner (c :: chars)
    let chars = generatorInner []
    if List.length chars = 0 && !endStream then
        None
    else
        Some(new string(List.to_array (List.rev chars)))

let closer (stream : StreamReader) =
    stream.Dispose()

let wordList =
    Seq.generate_using
        opener
        generator

wordList |> Seq.iter (fun s -> print_endline s)
read_line()
```

The results of this code, when compiled and executed, are as follows:

```
the
cat
sat
on
the
mat
```

The untyped_ Functions

The .NET Framework's BCL contains two versions of the IEnumerable interface, one defined in System.Collections.Generic and an older one defined in System.Collections. All the samples shown so far have been designed to work with the new generic version from System.Collections.Generic. However, sometimes it might be necessary to work with collections that are not generic, so the F# IEnumerable module also provides a number of functions to work with nongeneric collections. These functions all start with the prefix untyped and then have the same name as their generic counterpart. The big disadvantage of using these functions is that they do not contain any type information; therefore, the compiler cannot type check them properly, which can mean some code might throw an invalid cast exception at runtime.

Before using these functions, I strongly recommend that you see whether you can use the list comprehension syntax covered in Chapters 3 and 4 instead. This is because the list comprehension syntax can infer the types of many untyped collections, usually by looking at the type of the Item indexer property, so there is less need for type annotations, which generally makes programming easier.

The following example looks at an array list that stores a sequence of integers and then uses untyped_map to double each of the integers in the list:

```
#light
open System.Collections

let arrayList =
    let temp = new ArrayList()
    temp.AddRange([| 1; 2; 3 |])
    temp

let doubledArrayList =
    arrayList |>
    Seq.untyped_map (fun x -> x * 2)

doubledArrayList |> Seq.untyped_iter (fun x -> printf "%i ... " x)
```

The results of this code, when compiled and executed, are as follows:

```
2 ... 4 ... 6 ...
```

As you can see from the previous example, when the programmer gets the types right, using the untyped functions is pretty straightforward. However, consider the following example that tries to perform the same operation on the list, except this time it contains strings:

```
#light
open System.Collections

let stringArrayList =
    let temp = new ArrayList()
    temp.AddRange([| "one"; "two"; "three" |])
    temp
```

```
let invalidCollection =
    stringArrayList |>
    Seq.untyped_map (fun x -> x * 2)

invalidCollection |> Seq.untyped_iter (fun x -> printf "%O ... " x)
```

The results of this code, when compiled and executed, are as follows:

```
System.InvalidCastException: Specified cast is not valid.
 at Microsoft.FSharp.Collections.IEnumerator.untyped_map@25.get_Current()
 at Microsoft.FSharp.Collections.IEnumerator.untyped_iter@12[A,U](FastFunc`2 f, U e)
 at <StartupCode>.FSI_0011._main()
stopped due to error
```

It's easy to see that using untyped collections places an extra burden on the programmer to ensure the types in the collection are correct. So, I highly recommend that if for some reason you must use an untyped collection, then it is best to convert it to a typed collection. This is done using the function untyped_to_typed, which is demonstrated in the following example:

```
#light
open System.Collections
open System.Collections.Generic

let floatArrayList =
    let temp = new ArrayList()
    temp.AddRange([| 1.0; 2.0; 3.0 |])
    temp

let (typedIntList : seq<float>) =
    Seq.untyped_to_typed floatArrayList
```

Using untyped_to_typed always required using type annotations to tell the compiler what type of list you are producing. Here you have a list of floats, so you use the type annotation IEnumerable<float> to tell the compiler it will be an IEnumerable collection containing floating-point numbers.

The Microsoft.FSharp.Core.Enum Module

The Enum module is a simple module to help deal with enumerations in F#. I will cover the following functions:

to_int and of_int: Functions for converting to and from integers

combine and test: Functions for combining enums with a bitwise "and" and testing whether a bit is set

The to_int and of_int Functions

The following example shows how to convert from an enumeration to an integer and then convert it back to an enumeration. Converting from an enumeration to an integer is straight-forward; you just use the `to_int` function. Converting back is slightly more complicated; you use the `of_int` function, but you must provide a type annotation so that the compile knows which type of enumeration to convert it to. You can see this in the following sample where you add the annotation DayOfWeek to the identifier dayEnum:

```
#light
open System
let dayInt = Enum.to_int DateTime.Now.DayOfWeek
let (dayEnum : DayOfWeek) = Enum.of_int dayInt

print_int dayInt
print_newline ()
print_any dayEnum
```

The results of this code, when compiled and executed, are as follows:

```
0
Sunday
```

The combine and test Functions

The other common tasks that you need to perform with enumerations is to combine them using a logical "or" and then test them using a logical "and." The functions `combine` and `test` are provided to fulfill these roles. The function `combine` takes a list of enumerations and combines them into one enumeration. The function test tests whether a particular enumeration is part of a combined enumeration.

The following example combines two enumeration values, AnchorStyles.Left and AnchorStyles.Left, and then uses test to test the resulting enumeration:

```
#light
open System.Windows.Forms
let anchor = Enum.combine [AnchorStyles.Left ; AnchorStyles.Left]

printfn "(Enum.test anchor AnchorStyles.Left): %b"
    (Enum.test anchor AnchorStyles.Left)
printfn "(Enum.test anchor AnchorStyles.Right): %b"
    (Enum.test anchor AnchorStyles.Right)
```

The results of this code, when compiled and executed, are as follows:

```
(Enum.test anchor AnchorStyles.Left): true
(Enum.test anchor AnchorStyles.Right): false
```

Enum types marked with the System.Flags attribute also support the use of the &&& and ||| operators to perform these operations directly. For example, you could write the previous code as follows:

```
#light
open System.Windows.Forms
let anchor = AnchorStyles.Left ||| AnchorStyles.Left

printfn "test AnchorStyles.Left: %b"
    (anchor &&& AnchorStyles.Left <> Enum.of_int 0)
printfn "test AnchorStyles.Right: %b"
    (anchor &&& AnchorStyles.Right <> Enum.of_int 0)
```

The Microsoft.FSharp.Text.Printf Module

The Printf module provides functions for formatting strings in a type-safe way. The functions in the Printf module take a string with placeholders for values as their first argument. This returns another function that expects values for the placeholders. You form placeholders by using a percentage sign and a letter representing the type that they expect. Table 7-1 shows the full list.

Table 7-1. Printf *Placeholders and Flags*

Flag	Description
%b	bool, formatted as "true" or "false."
%s	string, formatted as its unescaped contents.
%d, %i	Any basic integer type (that is, sbyte, byte, int16, uint16, int32, uint32, int64, uint64, nativeint, or unativeint) formatted as a decimal integer, signed if the basic integer type is signed.
%u	Any basic integer type formatted as an unsigned decimal integer.
%x, %X, %o	Any basic integer type formatted as an unsigned hexadecimal, (a-f)/Hexadecimal (A-F)/Octal integer.
%e, %E	Any basic floating-point type (that is, float or float32), formatted using a C-style floating-point format specification, signed value having the form [-]d.dddde[sign]ddd where *d* is a single decimal digit, *dddd* is one or more decimal digits, *ddd* is exactly three decimal digits, and *sign* is + or –.
%f	Any basic floating-point type, formatted using a C-style floating-point format specification, signed value having the form [-]dddd.dddd, where *dddd* is one or more decimal digits. The number of digits before the decimal point depends on the magnitude of the number, and the number of digits after the decimal point depends on the requested precision.
%g, %G	Any basic floating-point type, formatted using a C-style floating-point format specification, signed value printed in f or e format, whichever is more compact for the given value and precision.
%M	System.Decimal value.
%O	Any value, printed by boxing the object and using its ToString method(s).
%A	Any value, printed using the any_to_string method that pretty prints F# types.

continued

Table 7-1. *Continued*

Flag	Description
%a	A general format specifier; requires two arguments: A function that accepts two arguments: a context parameter of the appropriate type for the given formatting function (such as a System.IO.TextWriter) and a value to print and that either outputs or returns appropriate text. The particular value to print.
%t	A general format specifier; requires one argument: a function that accepts a context parameter of the appropriate type for the given formatting function (such as a System.IO.TextWriter) and that either outputs or returns appropriate text.
0	A flag that adds zeros instead of spaces to make up the required width.
-	A flag that left justifies the result within the width specified.
+	A flag that adds a + character if the number is positive (to match the – sign for negatives).
' '	Adds an extra space if the number is positive (to match the – sign for negatives).

The following example shows how to use the printf function. It creates a function that expects a string and then passes a string to this function.

```
#light
Printf.printf "Hello %s" "Robert"
```

The results of this code are as follows:

```
Hello Robert
```

The significance of this might not be entirely obvious, but the following example will probably help explain it; if a parameter of the wrong type is passed to the printf function, then it will not compile:

```
#light
Printf.printf "Hello %s" 1
```

The previous code will not compile, giving the following error:

```
Prog.fs(4,25): error: FS0001: This expression has type
    int
but is here used with type
    string
```

This also has an effect on type inference. If you create a function that uses printf, then any arguments that are passed to printf will have their types inferred from this. For example, the function myPrintInt, shown here, has the type int -> unit because of the printf function contained within it:

```
#light
let myPrintInt x =
    Printf.printf "An integer: %i" x
```

The basic placeholders in a Printf module function are %b for a Boolean; %s for a string; %d or %i for an integer; %u for an unsigned integer; and %x, %X, or %o for an integer formatted as a hexadecimal. It is also possible to specify the number of decimal places that are displayed in numeric types. The following example demonstrates this:

```
#light
let pi = System.Math.PI

Printf.printf "%f\r\n" pi
Printf.printf "%1.1f\r\n" pi
Printf.printf "%2.2f\r\n" pi
Printf.printf "%2.8f\r\n" pi
```

The results of this code are as follows:

```
3.141593
3.1
3.14
3.14159265
```

The Printf module also contains a number of other functions that allow a string to be formatted in the same ways as printf itself but allow the result to be written to a different destination. The following example shows some of the different versions available:

```
#light
// write to a string
let s = Printf.sprintf "Hello %s\r\n" "string"
print_string s

// prints the string to the given channel
Printf.fprintf stdout "Hello %s\r\n" "channel"

// prints the string to a .NET TextWriter
Printf.twprintf System.Console.Out "Hello %s\r\n" "TextWriter"

// create a string that will be placed
// in an exception message
Printf.failwithf "Hello %s" "exception"
```

The results of this code are as follows:

```
Hello string
Hello channel
Hello TextWriter
Microsoft.FSharp.FailureException: Hello exception
   at Microsoft.FSharp.Text.Printf.failwithf@60.Invoke(String s)
   at Microsoft.FSharp.Text.PrintfImpl.Make@188.Invoke(A inp))
   at <StartupCode>.FSI_0003._main()
stopped due to error
```

The Microsoft.FSharp.Control.IEvent Module

You can think of an event in F# as a collection of functions that can be triggered by a call to a function. The idea is that functions will register themselves with the event, the collection of functions, to await notification that the event has happened. The trigger function is then used to give notice that the event has happened, causing all the functions that have added themselves to the event to be executed.

I will cover the following features of the IEvent module:

Creating and handling events: The basics of creating and handling events using the create and add functions

The filter *function*: A function to filter the data coming into events

The partition *function*: A function that splits the data coming into events into two

The map *function*: A function that maps the data before it reaches the event handler

Creating and Handling Events

The first example looks at a simple event being created using the IEvent module's create function. This function returns a tuple containing the trigger function as its first item and the event itself as its second item. Often you need to add type annotations to say what type of event you want, that is, what type of parameter your event's handler functions should take. After this, you use the event's Add function to add a handler method, and finally you trigger the event using the trigger function:

```
#light

let trigger, event = IEvent.create<string>()
event.Add(fun x -> printfn "%s" x)
trigger "hello"
```

The result of this code is as follows:

```
hello
```

In addition to this basic event functionality, the F# IEvent module provides a number of functions that allow you to filter and partition events to give fine-grained control over which data is passed to which event handler.

The filter Function

The following example demonstrates how you can use the IEvent module's filter function so that data being passed to the event is filtered before it reaches the event handlers. In this example, you filter the data so that only strings beginning with *H* are sent to the event handler:

```
#light

let trigger, event = IEvent.create<string>()
let newEvent = event |> IEvent.filter (fun x -> x.StartsWith("H"))
newEvent.Add(fun x -> printfn "new event: %s" x)

trigger "Harry"
trigger "Jane"
trigger "Hillary"
trigger "John"
trigger "Henry"
```

The results of this code, when compiled and executed, are as follows:

```
new event: Harry
new event: Hillary
new event: Henry
```

The partition Function

The IEvent module's partition function is similar to the filter function except two events are
returned, one where data caused the partition function to return false and one where data
caused the partition function to return true. The following example demonstrates this:

```
#light

let trigger, event = IEvent.create<string>()
let hData, nonHData = event |> IEvent.partition (fun x -> x.StartsWith("H"))
hData.Add(fun x -> printfn "H data: %s" x)
nonHData.Add(fun x -> printfn "None H data: %s" x)

trigger "Harry"
trigger "Jane"
trigger "Hillary"
trigger "John"
trigger "Henry"
```

The results of this code are as follows:

```
H data: Harry
None H data: Jane
H data: Hillary
None H data: John
H data: Henry
```

The map Function

It is also possible to transform the data before it reaches the event handlers. You do this using the map function provided in the IEvent module. The following example demonstrates how to use it:

```
#light

let trigger, event = IEvent.create<string>()
let newEvent = event |> IEvent.map (fun x -> "Mapped data: " + x)
newEvent.Add(fun x -> print_endline x)

trigger "Harry"
trigger "Sally"
```

The results of this code are as follows:

```
Mapped data: Harry
Mapped data: Sally
```

This section has just provided a brief overview of events in F#. You will return to them in more detail in Chapter 8 when I discuss user interface programming, because that is where they are most useful.

The Microsoft.FSharp.Math Namespace

The Microsoft.FSharp.Math namespace is designed to enable F# to ensure that the F# libraries include definitions of some of the foundational constructs used across a wide range of graphics, mathematical, scientific, and engineering applications. First you will look briefly at the modules that make it up, and then you'll dive into a more detailed example.

It contains arbitrary precision numbers; these are numbers whose values have no upper limit and include the modules BigInt and BigNum. A typical use of these would be in a program that searches for large prime numbers, perhaps for use in cryptography.

The modules Matrix, Vector, RowVector, and Notations all contain operations related to matrices and vectors. *Matrices* are sets of numbers arranged in rows and columns to form a rectangular array. Vectors are a column of numbers and are like a matrix with one column but are a separate type. A *vector* is a quantity characterized by magnitude and direction, so a two-dimensional vector is specified by two coordinates, a three-dimensional vector by three coordinates, and so on; therefore, vectors are represented as a matrix made up of one column with the number of rows depending on the dimension of the vector.

There is a module, Complex, for working with complex numbers. The complex numbers are the base for many types of fractal images, so I will demonstrate how you can use the F# complex number library to draw the most famous fractal of all, the Mandelbrot set. The Mandelbrot set is generated by repeated iteration of the following equation:

$$C_{n+1} = C_n^2 + c$$

The next number in the series is formed from the current number squared plus the original number. If repeated iteration of this equation stays between the complex number C(1, 1i) and C(–1, –1i), then the original complex number is a member of the Mandelbrot set. This can be implemented in F# with the following:

```
#light
open Microsoft.FSharp.Math
open Microsoft.FSharp.Math.Notation

let cMax = complex 1.0 1.0
let cMin = complex -1.0 -1.0
let iterations = 18
let isInMandelbrotSet c0 =
    let rec check n c =
        (n = iterations)
        or (cMin < c) && (c < cMax) && check (n + 1) ((c * c) + c0)
    check 0 c0
```

The function isInMandelbrotSet tests whether a complex number is in the Mandelbrot set by recursively calling the check function with the new c value of ((c * c) + c0) until either the complex number passes one of the constants cMax or cMin or the number of iterations exceeds the constant iterations. If the number of iterations specified by iterations is reached, then number is a member of the set; otherwise, it is not.

Because the complex numbers consist of two numbers, they can be represented in a two-dimensional plane. The Mandelbrot complex numbers exist between C(1, 1i) and C(–1, –1i) so the plane that you need to draw has the origin, which is the point 0, 0, in the center, and its axis extends out in either direction until reaching a maximum of 1.0 and a minimum of –1.0, such as the plane on the right of Figure 7-1. However, when it comes to pixels on a computer screen, you must deal with a plane where the origin is in the top-right corner and it extends rightward and downward. Because this type plane is made up of pixels, which are discrete values, it is represented by integers typically somewhere in the range 0 to 1600. Such a plane appears on the left of Figure 7-1.

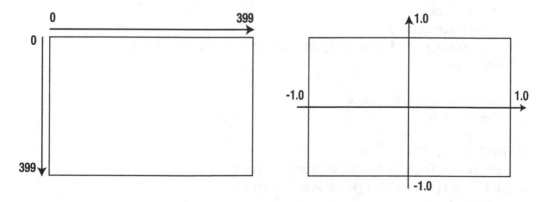

Figure 7-1. *A bitmap plane vs. a complex plane*

So, the application must map the points in the bitmap plane to points in the complex plane so that you can tell whether a pixel is part of the complex plane.

It is easy to perform this mapping in just a few lines of F# code:

```
#light
open Microsoft.FSharp.Math
open Microsoft.FSharp.Math.Notation

let scalingFactor = 1.0 / 200.0
let offset = -1.0

let mapPlane (x, y) =
    let fx = ((float x) * scalingFactor) + offset
    let fy = ((float y) * scalingFactor) + offset
    complex fx fy
```

Once this is complete, you just need to cycle through all the points in your bitmap plane, mapping them to the complex plane using the mapPlane function. Then you need to test whether the complex number is in the Mandelbrot set using the function isInMandelbrotSet. Then you set the color of the pixel. The full program is as follows:

```
#light
open System
open System.Drawing
open System.Windows.Forms
open Microsoft.FSharp.Math
open Microsoft.FSharp.Math.Notation

let cMax = complex 1.0 1.0
let cMin = complex -1.0 -1.0
let iterations = 18

let isInMandelbrotSet c0 =
    let rec check n c =
        (n = iterations)
        or (cMin < c) && (c < cMax) && check (n + 1) ((c * c) + c0)
    check 0 c0

let scalingFactor = 1.0 / 200.0
let offset = -1.0

let mapPlane (x, y) =
    let fx = ((float x) * scalingFactor) + offset
    let fy = ((float y) * scalingFactor) + offset
    complex fx fy
```

```
let form =
    let image = new Bitmap(400, 400)
    for x = 0 to image.Width - 1 do
        for y = 0 to image.Height - 1 do
            let isMember = isInMandelbrotSet ( mapPlane (x, y) )
            if isMember then
                image.SetPixel(x,y, Color.Black)
    let temp = new Form() in
    temp.Paint.Add(fun e -> e.Graphics.DrawImage(image, 0, 0))
    temp

[<STAThread>]
do Application.Run(form)
```

This program produces the image of the Mandelbrot set in Figure 7-2.

Figure 7-2. *The Mandelbrot set*

The ML Compatibility Library MLLib.dll

The MLLib library was designed to allow cross-compilation with code written in OCaml. It contains implementations of a subset of the modules that are distributed with OCaml. This played an important role in the development of F# because the compiler was originally written in OCaml and then cross-compiled into F# to produce a .NET assembly.

It contains many functions that are really useful, even to programmers who have no intention of cross-compiling their code; the most useful of these is the Arg module. Here, I will cover the following modules:

Microsoft.FSharp.MLLib.Pervasives: A module containing some floating-point functions and some simple functions to help the programmer manage I/O

Microsoft.FSharp.MLLib.Arg: A module for processing command-line arguments

The Microsoft.FSharp.Compatibility.OCaml.Pervasives Module

The word *pervasive* means thoroughly penetrating or permeating, which is a good description for the Pervasives module. It is automatically opened by the compiler, and its functions permeate through most F# code, since functions that it contains can be used automatically without a qualifier. You have already met some of the functions in many examples in this book, especially the print_string, print_endline, and print_int functions that were often used to write to the console.

It's hard to categorize the type of functions found in the Pervasives module; because they are generally the sort of thing a programmer will find useful, I will cover the following topics:

Arithmetic operators: Operators for basic arithmetic operations such as addition and subtraction

Floating-point arithmetic functions: More advanced arithmetic functions including logarithms and trigonometry

Mutable integer functions: Functions on mutable integers

Streams: Functions to help the programmer mange I/O

Arithmetic Operators

As already covered in Chapter 2, in F# operators can be defined by the programmer, so all the arithmetic operators are defined in the Pervasives module rather than built into the language. Therefore, the majority of operators that you will use in your day-to-day programming in F# are defined in the Pervasives module. I imagine that operators such as + and - need little explanation, since their usage is straightforward:

```
let x1 = 1 + 1
let x2 = 1 - 1
```

However, the F# equality operator is a bit more subtle. This is because in F# equality is *structural* equality, meaning that the contents of the objects are compared to check whether the items that make up the object are the same. This is opposed to *referential* equality, which determines whether two identifiers are bound to the same object or the same physical area of memory; a referential equality check can be performed using the method obj.ReferenceEquals. The structural equality operator is =, and the structural inequality operator is <>. The next example demonstrates this. The records robert1 and robert2 are equal, because even though they are separate objects, their contents are the same. On the other hand, robert1 and robert3 are not equal because their contents are different.

```
#light
type person = { name : string ; favoriteColor : string }

let robert1 = { name = "Robert" ; favoriteColor = "Red" }
let robert2 = { name = "Robert" ; favoriteColor = "Red" }
let robert3 = { name = "Robert" ; favoriteColor = "Green" }

printf "(robert1 = robert2): %b\r\n" (robert1 = robert2)
printf "(robert1 <> robert3): %b\r\n" (robert1 <> robert3)
```

The results of this code, when compiled and executed, are as follows:

```
(robert1 = robert2): true
(robert1 <> robert3): true
```

Structural comparison is also used to implement the > and < operators, which means they too can be used to compare F#'s record types. This is demonstrated here:

```
#light
let robert2 = { name = "Robert" ; favoriteColor = "Red" }
let robert3 = { name = "Robert" ; favoriteColor = "Green" }

printf "(robert2 > robert3): %b\r\n" (robert2 > robert3)
```

The results of this code, when compiled and executed, are as follows:

```
(robert2 > robert3): true
```

If you need to determine whether two objects are physically equal, then you can use the eq function available in the Obj module, as in the following example:

```
#light
let robert1 = { name = "Robert" ; favoriteColor = "Red" }
let robert2 = { name = "Robert" ; favoriteColor = "Red" }

printfn "(Obj.eq robert1 robert2): %b" (Obj.eq robert1 robert2)
```

Floating-Point Arithmetic Functions

The Pervasives module also offers a number of functions (see Table 7-2) specifically for floating-point numbers, some of which are used in the following sample:

```
#light
printfn "(sqrt 16.0): %f" (sqrt 16.0)
printfn "(log 160.0): %f" (log 160.0)
printfn "(cos 1.6): %f" (cos 1.6)
```

The results of this code, when compiled and executed, are as follows:

```
(sqrt 16.0): 4.000000
(log 160.0): 5.075174
(cos 1.6): -0.029200
```

Table 7-2. *Arithmetic Functions for Floating-Point Numbers*

Function	Description
abs_float	Returns the absolute value of the argument
acos	Returns the inverse cosine (arccosine) of the argument, which should be specified in radians
asin	Returns the inverse sine (arcsine) of the argument, which should be specified in radians
atan	Returns the inverse tangent (arctangent) of the argument, which should be specified in radians
atan2	Returns the inverse tangent (arctangent) of the two arguments, which should both be specified in radians
ceil	Returns the next highest integer value by rounding up the value if necessary; the value returned is still of type float
floor	Returns the next lowest integer value by rounding up the value if necessary; the value returned is still of type float
exp	Returns the exponential
infinity	Returns the floating-point number that represents infinity
ldexp	Returns the floating-point number from the mantissa and exponent
log	Returns the natural log of the floating-point number
log10	Returns the base 10 log of the floating-point number
max_float	Returns the maximum floating-point number
min_float	Returns the minimum floating-point number
mod_float	Returns the remainder of the first parameter with respect to the second parameter
modf	Returns the floating-point number split into the integer and fractional part
nan	Returns the floating-point number that represents "not a number"
neg_infinity	Returns the floating-point number that represents negative infinity
sqrt	Returns the square root of the number
cos	Returns the cosine of the parameter, which should be specified in radians
cosh	Returns the hyperbolic cosine of the parameter, which should be specified in radians
sin	Returns the sine of the parameter, which should be specified in radians

Function	Description
sinh	Returns the hyperbolic sine of the parameter, which should be specified in radians
tan	Returns the tangent of the parameter, which should be specified in radians
tanh	Returns the hyperbolic tangent of the parameter, which should be specified in radians
truncate	Returns the parameter converted to an integer
float	Takes an integer and returns it as a float
float32	Takes an integer and returns it as a float32

Mutable Integer Functions

The Pervasives module also offers two useful functions that operate on mutable integers. The incr and decr functions increment and decrement a mutable integer, respectively. The use of these functions is demonstrated here:

```
#light
let i = ref 0
(incr i)
print_int !i
print_newline ()
(decr i)
print_int !i
```

The results of this code are as follows:

```
1
0
```

Streams

Finally, you've come to the last major set of functions within the Pervasives module—functions that read from and write to streams. *Streams* are a way of managing I/O that allows a file, a network connection, or an area of memory to be written to in a homogeneous fashion. A stream is a value that provides functions to either read from it or write to it. A stream is an abstract concept, because no matter whether it represents a file, a connection, or memory, you can use the same methods to write to it. You have already seen the functions print_endline, print_newline, print_string, print_int, and printf used throughout the examples in this book. These are all examples of functions that write to the *standard output* stream, typically the console. The Pervasives module also provides several functions for reading from the *standard input* stream, typically the keyboard:

```
#light
let myString = read_line ()
let myInt = read_int ()
let myFloat = read_float ()
```

When executed, this sample will bind the identifier myString to a string input by the user. It will also bind myInt and myFloat to the integer and float values input by the user, provided the user types a correctly formed integer and float.

The fact that these functions read from and write to streams is not entirely obvious because they don't take stream parameters. This is because they are wrapper methods that hide that they are reading from or writing to a stream. They are built on top of some more general functions for reading from and writing to a stream. The next example demonstrates how to use the stream stdout, which defaults to the console, and shows how this can be written to in the same manner as writing to a file, using the output_string function:

```
#light
let getStream() =
    print_string "Write to a console (y/n): "
    let input = read_line ()
    match input with
    | "y" | "Y" -> stdout
    | "n" | "N" ->
        print_string "Enter file name: "
        let filename = read_line ()
        open_out filename
    | _ -> failwith "Not an option"

let main() =
    let stream = getStream()
    output_string stream "Hello"
    close_out stream
    read_line() |> ignore

main()
```

The function getStream allows the user to switch between writing to the console and writing to a file. If the user chooses to write to the console, the stream stdout is returned; otherwise, it asks the user to provide a filename so open_out can be used to open a file stream.

The implementation of streams is based on the classes available in System.IO namespace; the out_channel is an alias for TextWriter, and in_channel is an alias for TextReader. These aliases were included for compatibility purposes; you probably want to consider the classes available in the BCL's System.IO namespace directly, because this often gives you more flexibility.

The Microsoft.FSharp.Compatibility.OCaml.Arg Module

The Arg module allows users to quickly build a command-line argument parser. It does this by using F#'s union and list types to create a little language that is then interpreted by a number of functions provided in the Arg module.

The Arg module exposes a tuple type called argspec, which consists of two strings and a union type called spec. The first string in the tuple specifies the name of the command-line argument. The second item in the tuple is the union type spec, which specifies what the command-line argument is; for example, is it followed by a string value, or is it just a flag? It also specifies what should be done if and when the command-line token is found. The final string in the tuple is a text description of what the flag does. This will be printed to the console in the case of a mistake in the command-line arguments. It also serves as a useful note to the programmer.

The Arg module exposes two functions for parsing arguments: parse, which parses the command passed in on the command line, and parse_argv, which requires the arguments to be passed directly to it. Both should be passed a list of type argspec describing the command-line arguments expected, a function that will be passed all the command-line arguments not prefixed with -, and finally a string to describe the usage.

The module also exposes a third function usage, which can be passed a list of type argspec and will just directly write out the usage.

The following example demonstrates an argument parser built in this manner. The parameters collected from the command line are stored in identifiers for later use, in this case being written to the console.

```
#light

let myFlag = ref true
let myString = ref ""
let myInt = ref 0
let myFloat = ref 0.0
let (myStringList : string list ref) = ref []

let argList =
    [
      ("-set", Arg.Set myFlag, "Sets the value myFlag");
      ("-clear", Arg.Clear myFlag, "Clears the value myFlag");
      ("-str_val", Arg.String(fun x -> myString := x), "Sets the value myString");
      ("-int_val", Arg.Int(fun x -> myInt := x), "Sets the value myInt");
      ("-float_val", Arg.Float(fun x -> myFloat := x), "Sets the value myFloat");
    ]

if Sys.argv.Length <> 1 then
    Arg.parse
        argList
        (fun x -> myStringList := x :: !myStringList)
        "Arg module demo"
else
    Arg.usage
        argList
        "Arg module demo"
    exit 1

printfn "myFlag: %b" !myFlag
printfn "myString: %s" !myString
printfn "myInt: %i" !myInt
printfn "myFloat: %f" !myFloat
printfn "myStringList: "
print_any !myStringList
```

When run with no command-line arguments or faulty command-line arguments, the program will output this:

```
Arg module demo
        -set: Sets the value my_flag
        -clear: Clears the value my_flag
        -str_val <string>: Sets the value my_string
        -int_val <int>: Sets the value my_int
        -float_val <float>: Sets the value my_float
        --help: display this list of options
        -help: display this list of options
```

When run with the command line args.exe -clear -str_val "hello world" -int_val 10 -float_val 3.14 "file1" "file2" "file3", the program will output the following:

```
myFlag: false
myString: hello world
myInt: 10
myFloat: 3.140000
myStringList: ["file3"; "file2"; "file1"]
```

The Arg module is an excellent example of how creating a little language can make programming tasks easier and quicker and the resulting code easier to understand and more maintainable. You'll find more details on this style of programming in Chapter 11.

Summary

I covered a lot ground in this chapter, since the F# libraries have a diverse range of functionalities. First you looked through the FSLib.dll library with its useful Collections, Reflection, and Math modules. Then you looked at MLLib.dll, which provides functions that are excellent building blocks for all applications. Its Seq module is something that any nontrivial F# program will not be able to do without.

The next three chapters will look at how you can use F# with various .NET APIs for common programming tasks. You'll start with a look at implementing user interfaces in Chapter 8, and then you'll move to data access in Chapter 9 and distributed applications in Chapter 10.

User Interfaces

In this chapter, you will look at one of the most common tasks a programmer needs to perform—the art of putting pixels on the screen. In F# this is all about the libraries and API that you call, and you have a lot of choices in this area. You can create WinForms, a set of classes found in `System.Windows.Form.dll`. These classes allow you to create desktop applications based on forms and controls. You can create ASP.NET applications. This library is contained in `System.Web.dll`, which is a simple way to create server-based dynamic HTML applications. You also have the option to use Windows Presentation Foundation (WPF), which is a new library distributed with .NET 3.0 that allows you to design interfaces in an XML-based language called XAML. These three technologies (WinForms, ASP.NET, and WPF) will be the focus of this chapter. Since whole books have been written on each topic, I won't be able to cover them all in detail. Instead, you'll look at techniques for working with these technologies in F#.

F# can also use a lot of other graphics libraries—some designed to work with the technologies already mentioned and others, such as the DirectX or GTK# libraries, designed to replace them.

Introducing WinForms

WinForms are based on the `System.Windows.Forms.Form` class. By creating an instance of this class, you essentially create a new window. You must then create an *event loop*, a way of ensuring user interactions with the window are responded to. You do this by calling the `System.Windows.Application.Run` method and passing it the form object you have created. You can control the look of the form by setting its properties and calling its methods. The following example demonstrates this:

```
#light
open System.Drawing
open System.Windows.Forms

let form = new Form(BackColor = Color.Purple, Text = "Introducing WinForms")

Application.Run(form)
```

This example will not work with F# interactive, fsi, because you cannot start an event loop from within fsi. So to work with forms in fsi, you simply call the form's Show method or set the form's Visible property to true. This example shows the second technique:

```
> #light
open System.Drawing
open System.Windows.Forms

let form = new Form(BackColor=Color.Purple,
                    Text="Introducing WinForms",
                    Visible=true);;
```

Either way, you have the advantage that you can dynamically interact with your form object. For example:

```
> form.Text <- "Dynamic !!!";;
```

When working with WinForms, you can take one of two approaches: drawing forms yourself or using controls to build them. First you'll look at drawing your own forms, and then you'll move on to using controls.

Drawing WinForms

Drawing your own forms means you take responsibility for the pixels that actually appear on the screen. This low-level approach might appeal to many F# users, because they might find that many controls that come with the WinForms library are not perfectly suited to displaying their data structures and the results of functions and algorithms. However, be warned that this approach can be time-consuming, and your time is usually better spent looking for a graphics library that abstracts some of the presentation logic.

To draw a WinForm, you attach an event handler to the form's or the control's Paint event. This means every time Windows requests the form to be drawn, your function will be called. The event argument that is passed into this function has a property called Graphics, which contains an instance of a class also called Graphics. This class has methods (such as DrawLine) that allow you to draw pixels on the form. The following example shows a simple form where you draw a pie on it:

```
#light
open System.Drawing
open System.Windows.Forms

let brush = new SolidBrush(Color.Red)

let form =
    let temp = new Form()
    temp.Resize.Add(fun _ -> temp.Invalidate())
    temp.Paint.Add
        (fun e ->
            if temp.Width - 64 > 0 && temp.Height - 96 > 0 then
                e.Graphics.FillPie
                    (brush,
                        32,
                        32,
```

```
                    temp.Width - 64,
                    temp.Height - 64,
                    0,
                    290))
    temp

Application.Run(form)
```

Figure 8-1 shows the resulting form.

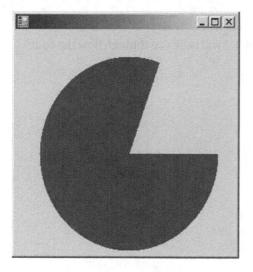

Figure 8-1. *A WinForm containing a pie shape*

Because this image is linked to the size of the form, you must tell the form to redraw itself whenever the form is resized. You do this by attaching an event handling function to the Resize event. In this function, you call the form's Invalidate method, which tells the form that it needs to redraw itself.

You'll now look at a more complete WinForms example. Imagine you want to create a form to display the Tree type defined in the next code example and displayed in Figure 8-2.

```
// The tree type
type 'a Tree =
| Node of 'a Tree * 'a Tree
| Leaf of 'a

// The definition of the tree
let tree =
    Node(
        Node(
            Leaf "one",
            Node(Leaf "two", Leaf "three")),
        Node(
            Node(Leaf "four", Leaf "five"),
            Leaf "six"))
```

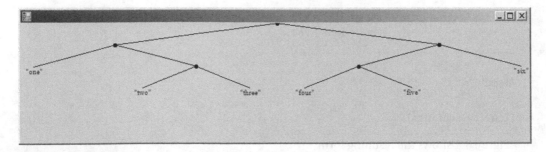

Figure 8-2. *A WinForm showing a tree structure*

You can draw this tree with the code in Listing 8-1. I will walk you through how the code works directly after the listing.

Listing 8-1. *Drawing a Tree*

```
#light
open System
open System.Drawing
open System.Windows.Forms

// The tree type
type 'a Tree =
| Node of 'a Tree * 'a Tree
| Leaf of 'a

// The definition of the tee
let tree =
    Node(
        Node(
            Leaf "one",
            Node(Leaf "two", Leaf "three")),
        Node(
            Node(Leaf "four", Leaf "five"),
            Leaf "six"))

// A function for finding the maximum depth of a tree
let getDepth t =
    let rec getDepthInner t d =
        match t with
        | Node (l, r) ->
            max
                (getDepthInner l d + 1.0F)
                (getDepthInner r d + 1.0F)
        | Leaf x -> d
    getDepthInner t 0.0F
```

```
// Constants required for drawing the form
let brush = new SolidBrush(Color.Black)
let pen = new Pen(Color.Black)
let font = new Font(FontFamily.GenericSerif, 8.0F)

// a useful function for calculating the maximum number
// of nodes at any given depth
let raise2ToPower (x : float32) =
    Convert.ToSingle(Math.Pow(2.0, Convert.ToDouble(x)))

let drawTree (g : Graphics) t =
    // constants that relate to the size and position
    // of the tree
    let center = g.ClipBounds.Width / 2.0F
    let maxWidth = 32.0F * raise2ToPower (getDepth t)

    // function for drawing a leaf node
    let drawLeaf (x : float32) (y : float32) v =
        let value = any_to_string v
        let l = g.MeasureString(value, font)
        g.DrawString(value, font, brush, x - (l.Width / 2.0F), y)

    // draw a connector between the nodes when necessary
    let connectNodes (x : float32) y p =
        match p with
        | Some(px, py) -> g.DrawLine(pen, px, py, x, y)
        | None -> ()

    // the main function to walk the tree structure drawing the
    // nodes as we go
    let rec drawTreeInner t d w p =
        let x = center - (maxWidth * w)
        let y = d * 32.0F
        connectNodes x y p
        match t with
        | Node (l, r) ->
            g.FillPie(brush, x - 3.0F, y - 3.0F, 7.0F, 7.0F, 0.0F, 360.0F)
            let d = (d + 1.0F)
            drawTreeInner l d (w + (1.0F / d)) (Some(x, y))
            drawTreeInner r d (w - (1.0F / d)) (Some(x, y))
        | Leaf v -> drawLeaf x y v

    drawTreeInner t 0.0F 0.0F None
```

```
// create the form object
let form =
    let temp = new Form(WindowState = FormWindowState.Maximized)
    temp.Resize.Add(fun _ -> temp.Invalidate())
    temp.Paint.Add
        (fun e ->
            e.Graphics.Clip <-
                new Region(new Rectangle(0, 0, temp.Width, temp.Height))
            drawTree e.Graphics tree)
    temp

Application.Run(form)
```

You define a function, drawTree, that has two parameters: the Graphics object and the tree to be drawn:

```
let drawTree (g : Graphics) t =
```

This is a common pattern when drawing WinForms. Creating a function that takes the Graphics object and a data type to be drawn allows the function to be easily reused by different forms and controls.

To implement drawTree, you first calculate a couple of constants to be used by the function, center and maxWidth. These are nice—since they can't be seen by functions outside drawTree yet, they can be used within all its inner functions without having to be passed around as parameters.

```
// constants that relate to the size and position
// of the tree
let center = g.ClipBounds.Width / 2.0F
let maxWidth = 32.0F * raise2ToPower (getDepth t)
```

The rest of the function is implemented by breaking it down into inner functions. You define drawLeaf to take care of drawing leaf nodes:

```
// function for drawing a leaf node
let drawLeaf (x : float32) (y : float32) v =
    let value = any_to_string v
    let l = g.MeasureString(value, font)
    g.DrawString(value, font, brush, x - (l.Width / 2.0F), y)
```

You use connectNodes to take care of drawing the connections between nodes, where appropriate:

```
// draw a connector between the nodes when necessary
let connectNodes (x : float32) y p =
    match p with
    | Some(px, py) -> g.DrawLine(pen, px, py, x, y)
    | None -> ()
```

Finally, you define drawTreeInner as a recursive function that does the real work of walking the Tree type and drawing it:

```
// the main function to walk the tree structure drawing the
// nodes as we go
let rec drawTreeInner t d w p =
    let x = center - (maxWidth * w)
    let y = d * 32.0F
    connectNodes x y p
    match t with
    | Node (l, r) ->
        g.FillPie(brush, x - 3.0F, y - 3.0F, 7.0F, 7.0F, 0.0F, 360.0F)
        let d = (d + 1.0F)
        drawTreeInner l d (w + (1.0F / d)) (Some(x, y))
        drawTreeInner r d (w - (1.0F / d)) (Some(x, y))
    | Leaf v -> drawLeaf x y v
```

This function uses parameters to store values between recursive calls. Because it is an inner function, you know that the outside world cannot misuse it by initializing its initial values incorrectly; this is because the outside world cannot see it. Hiding parameters to store working values between recursive function calls is another common pattern in functional programming.

In some ways this tree-drawing function is satisfactory; it gives a nice hierarchical overview of the tree in a fairly concise 86 lines of F# code. However, there is a limit to how well this approach scales. As you draw more complicated images, the number of lines of code can grow rapidly, and working out all the geometry can become time-consuming. To help manage this complexity, F# can use controls, as discussed in the next section.

Caution Although you can use these techniques to produce animation, such animations will flicker. To avoid this flicker, you must use a technique called *double buffering*, which requires you to understand a lot about how Windows draws forms. For more information about double buffering, please see http:// strangelights.com/FSharp/Foundations/default.aspx/FSharpFoundations.DoubleBuffering.

To make the most of drawing on WinForms, you should get to know the System.Drawing namespace contained in System.Drawing.dll. You should concentrate on two areas, first learning how to use the Graphics object, particularly the overloads of methods prefixed with either Draw or Fill. To help you get started, Table 8-1 summaries them.

Table 8-1. *Important Methods on the* System.Drawing.Graphics *Object*

Method Name	Description
DrawArc	Draws a portion of an ellipse.
DrawBezier	Draws a Bézier spline, which is a curve represented by two endpoints and two free-floating points controlling the angle of the curve.
DrawCurve	Draws a curved line defined by an array of points.
DrawClosedCurve	Draws a closed curved line defined by an array of points.

continued

Table 8-1. *Continued*

Method Name	Description
DrawEllipse	Draws the outline of an ellipse represented by a rectangle or rectangular set of points.
DrawPie	Draws a portion of the outline of an ellipse, represented by a rectangle and two radial lines representing the start and finish angles.
DrawLine	Draws a single line from two points.
DrawLines	Draws a set of lines from an array of points.
DrawPolygon	Draws the outline of a polygon, which is a closed set of lines from an array of points.
DrawRectangle	Draws the outline of a rectangle represented by a coordinate and its width and height.
DrawRectangles	Draws the outline of a set of rectangles from an array of rectangles.
FillClosedCurve	Draws a solid closed curve defined by an array of points.
FillEllipse	Draws a solid ellipse represented by a rectangle or rectangular set of points.
FillPie	Draws a portion of a solid ellipse, represented by a rectangle and two radial lines representing the start and finish angles.
FillPolygon	Draws a solid polygon, which is a closed set of lines from an array of points.
FillRectangle	Draws a solid rectangle represented by a coordinate and its width and height.
FillRectangles	Draws a solid set of rectangles from an array of rectangles.
DrawIcon	Draws an image specified by the System.Drawing.Icon type.
DrawImage	Draws an image specified by the System.Drawing.Image type.
DrawImageUnscaled	Draws an image specified by the System.Drawing.Image type with no scaling.
DrawString	Draws a string of characters.
MeasureString	Gives the dimensions of the string of characters so the programmer can calculate where it should be placed on the image.
DrawPath	Draws an outline represented by the System.Drawing.Drawing2D.GraphicsPath. This is a class that allows you to add geometric constructs such as the curves, rectangle, ellipses, and polygons described earlier to save you from recalculating them each time. This is useful if you want to draw something that is complicated but fairly static.
FillPath	Provides the same functionality as DrawPath, except draws an image that is solid rather than an outline.

The second area is closely related to the System.Drawing.Graphics object; it is the creation of the Icon, Image, Pen, and Brush objects that are used by its methods. Table 8-2 shows examples of how to create these objects via their constructors.

Table 8-2. *Important Methods on the* System.Drawing.Graphics *Object*

Snippet	Description
Color.FromArgb(33, 44, 55)	Creates a color from its red, green, and blue components
Color.FromKnownColor(KnownColor.Crimson)	Creates a color from a member of the KnownColor enumeration
Color.FromName("HotPink")	Creates a color from its name in string form
new Font(FontFamily.GenericSerif, 8.0f)	Creates a new font that is a generic serif font and 8 points tall
Image.FromFile("myimage.jpg")	Creates a new image from a file
Image.FromStream(File.OpenRead ("myimage.gif"))	Creates a new image from a stream
new Icon("myicon.ico")	Creates a new icon from a file
new Icon(File.OpenRead("myicon.ico"))	Creates a new icon from a stream
new Pen(Color.FromArgb(33, 44, 55))	Creates a pen, used to draw lines, from a color
new Pen(SystemColors.Control, 2.0f)	Creates a pen, used to draw lines, from a color and with a width of 2 pixels
new SolidBrush(Color.FromName("Black"))	Creates a solid brush that can be used to draw filled shapes
new TexturedBrush(Image.FromFile ("myimage.jpg"))	Creates a new textured brush from an image and draws a filled shape with an image mapped across it

If you prefer to use standard objects, you can use several classes in the System.Drawing namespace that contain predefined objects. These are Brushes, Pens, SystemBrushes, SystemColors, SystemFonts, SystemIcons, and SystemPens; the following is a quick example of using these:

```
#light
open System.Drawing

let myPen = Pens.Aquamarine
let myFont = SystemFonts.DefaultFont
```

Working with Controls in WinForms

A *control* is simply a class that derives from System.Windows.Forms.Control. Any class that derives from this can be displayed in a form by adding it to the Controls collection on the form object.

You'll now look at a way to draw the tree using controls. The WinForms library defines a TreeView class, which is specifically for displaying tree-like structures, so you'll use this control to display the tree. To use TreeView, you create an instance of it and configure it by setting its properties and calling its methods. Most important, you add to its Nodes collection the nodes you want to display. Once the control is ready to be displayed, you add it to the form's Controls collection.

The TreeView class uses TreeNode objects to represent nodes, so you'll define the function mapTreeToTreeNode to recursively walk the tree structure and create a TreeNode graph. The program in Listing 8-2 produces the tree in Figure 8-3.

Listing 8-2. *Drawing a Tree via a* TreeView *Control*

```
#light
open System.Windows.Forms

// The tree type
type 'a Tree =
| Node of 'a Tree * 'a Tree
| Leaf of 'a

// The definition of the tee
let tree =
    Node(
        Node(
            Leaf "one",
            Node(Leaf "two", Leaf "three")),
        Node(
            Node(Leaf "four", Leaf "five"),
            Leaf "six"))

// A function to transform our tree into a tree of controls
let mapTreeToTreeNode t =
    let rec mapTreeToTreeNodeInner t (node : TreeNode) =
        match t with
        | Node (l, r) ->
            let newNode = new TreeNode("Node")
            node.Nodes.Add(newNode) |> ignore
            mapTreeToTreeNodeInner l newNode
            mapTreeToTreeNodeInner r newNode
        | Leaf x ->
            node.Nodes.Add(new TreeNode(any_to_string x)) |> ignore
    let root = new TreeNode("Root")
    mapTreeToTreeNodeInner t root
    root
```

```
// create the form object
let form =
    let temp = new Form()
    let treeView = new TreeView(Dock = DockStyle.Fill)
    treeView.Nodes.Add(mapTreeToTreeNode tree) |> ignore
    treeView.ExpandAll()
    temp.Controls.Add(treeView)
    temp

Application.Run(form)
```

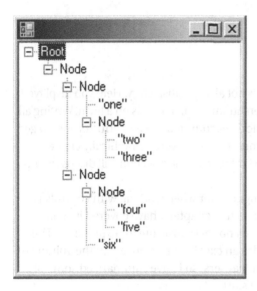

Figure 8-3. *A* TreeView *control used to view a tree*

This code is about half the length of Listing 8-1, when you drew the tree yourself. It is also more functional, because it allows you to fold away parts of the tree in which you're not interested. This greatly improves the size of tree that can be manageably displayed.

In this example, you use the "dock style" to control how the control looks. You do this by setting the control's Dock property with a member of the DockStyle enumeration. Docking means that the control will take up as much space as available in the form that contains it on the left side if you use DockStyle.Left, on the right side if you use DockStyle.Right, at the top if you use DockStyle.Top, on the bottom if you use DockStyle.Bottom, and on the whole form if you use DockStyle.Fill. This is great when you have just a few controls, because it creates a nice dynamic effect because the controls are resized when the user resizes the form; however, it does not work well with a lot of controls because it is difficult to get lots of controls to fit together nicely using this technique. For example, if you have two controls that are docked to the left, it's confusing which one is supposed to be the leftmost one and how much of the left side they both take up. A better solution with a lot of controls is to explicitly control their layout using the Top and Left properties. You can create a dynamic effect by using the Anchor property to anchor the control to the edge of the containing form. The following example creates a form with a single textbox on it that will grow and shrink as the user resizes the form.

```
#light
open System
open System.Windows.Forms

let form =
    let temp = new Form()
    let textBox = new TextBox(Top=8,Left=8, Width=temp.Width - 24.
                               Anchor = (AnchorStyles.Left |||
                                         AnchorStyles.Right |||
                                         AnchorStyles.Top))
    temp.Controls.Add(textBox)
    temp

[<STAThread>]
do Application.Run(form)
```

However, this method of working with controls is not always satisfactory. Here you displayed only one control. Often you want to display tens, even hundreds, of controls on a form. Writing all the code to create and configure the controls can quickly become tedious and error-prone. To get around this, Visual Studio provides some form designers that allow you to graphically create forms. However, a designer is not currently available for F#, so the next section will discuss working in F# with forms created with the C# designer.

One of the difficulties facing the WinForms programmer when working with controls is that there are many controls from which to choose. In this chapter, I have covered just one control. Unfortunately, in learning what works, there's no real substitute for experience. The MSDN library (http://msdn.microsoft.com) provides an excellent reference, but the volume of information there can also be a little off-putting for learners, so I have summarized some of the most useful ones in Table 8-3 to give you a head start.

Table 8-3. *Common WinForm Controls and Their Usages*

Control	Description
Label	A control for displaying text information to the user; generally most other controls should be accompanied by a Label to explain their usage. Placing an & in the text of the Text property of the Label will underline the letter directly after it and allow the keyboard user to hop to the control associated with the Label (the control next in the tab order) by pressing Alt+<letter>; this is good for improving application usability.
TextBox	A box for entering text. The default is a single line of text but can be changed to support multiline entry if you set the Multiline property to true; in this case, also check that the WordWrap and ScrollBar properties are to your liking. This is also useful for displaying text to the user that you want them to be able to copy and paste; in this case, set the ReadOnly property to true.
MaskedTextBox	A textbox similar in a lot of respects to the previous control; it allows you limit the data a user can enter via setting the Mask property.
Button	A button for the user to click; as with the Label control, placing an & in the text of the Text property of the Button control will allow underline the letter directly after it and allow the keyboard user to hop to the Button by pressing Alt+<letter>. Again, this is great for usability.

Control	Description
LinkLabel	Not really to be used as a label as the name might suggest but as a type of button that looks like an HTML link. This is great for users who are used to a web environment or to indicate that clicking the button leads to opening a web page.
CheckBox	A box for the users to check if you have a set of options that are not mutually exclusive.
RadioButton	Similar to a CheckBox but for options that are mutually exclusive. Several of these placed in the same container are automatically mutually exclusive. The container is usually a Form.
DateTimePicker	A control to allow the user to pick a date via a drop-down calendar.
MonthCalander	A control to allow a user to pick a date from a calendar that is permanently on display.
ComboBox	A control to allow a user to make a selection from a drop-down list; this is great for showing a dynamic set of data via data binding. For more details on this, see Chapter 9.
ListBox	Similar to a ComboBox but the list of items is displayed within the form rather than as a drop-down list. Favor this one if your form has lots of free space.
DataGridView	A control to provide an excellent way to display information from a database table, though this can be used to display any kind of tabular data. This should always be used in preference to the older DataGrid. I'll discuss this further in Chapter 9.
TreeView	Another control great for showing dynamic data, but this time it is most useful for data in a tree-like form.
ProgressBar	Giving your users feedback about any long-running activity is vital for a usable application, and this control provides a good way to do this.
RichTextBox	A control for providing a way to display and edit rich text documents, which is useful if your users want a little more formatting than offered by the standard textbox.
WebBrowser	A control for displaying HTML documents; this is useful since a lot of information is available in HTML format.
Panel	A control for breaking your form into different sections; this is highly effective when used with HScrollBar and VScrollBar.
HScrollBar	A horizontal scroll bar, used to fit more information on a Form or Panel.
VScrollBar	A vertical scroll bar, used to fit more information on a Form or Panel.
TabControl	A form that uses a series of tabs to display user controls.

Using the Visual Studio Form Designer's Forms in F#

F# does not yet have a form designer of its own; however, thanks to the great interoperability of .NET, it is easy to use forms created with the designer in F#. You have two approaches. You can create an F# library and call functions from this library in your Windows form, or you can create a library of forms and use them from your F# application. You'll look first at creating an

F# library, and then you will look at creating a forms library. Then I'll compare the two techniques. Both examples will be based on the same Fibonacci calculator shown in Figure 8-4.

Caution This book is about F#, and for the majority of the material, knowledge of no other programming language is necessary. However, for this topic, it will be necessary to understand a little of another .NET programming language, in this case C#. Specifically, you'll see two short listings in C# in this section. You can easily replace the C# code with Visual Basic .NET code if you feel more comfortable with that language.

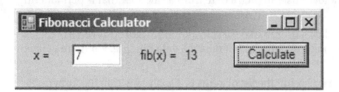

Figure 8-4. *A Fibonacci calculator form created with the Visual Studio designer*

The main consideration in creating an F# library to be used from a form is making it easy to use from the form. In this case, you'll create a function to calculate the Fibonacci number, so this will take an integer and return an integer. This makes things simple since a form has no problem using the .NET integer type. You want the library to be reasonably efficient, so create a lazy list of Fibonacci numbers and define a function that can get the *n*th number:

```
#light
module Strangelights.Fibonacci
let fibs =
    (1,1) |> Seq.unfold
        (fun (n0, n1) ->
            Some(n0, (n1, n0 + n1)))

let getFib n =
    Seq.nth n fibs
```

Using this function from a form is pretty straightforward; you just need to reference your F# .dll from the Visual Studio form project. You can use the module Strangelights.Fibonacci by opening the Strangelights namespace and treating Fibonacci as if it were a class in C#. The following example shows how to call the function in C# and place the result in a control. Note that because this form was created with Visual Studio 2005, the control definitions are in a separate source file.

```
using System;
using System.Windows.Forms;
using Strangelights;
```

```
namespace CSApp
{
    public partial class FibForm : Form
    {
        public FibForm()
        {
            InitializeComponent();
        }

        private void calculate_Click(object sender, EventArgs e)
        {
            int n = Convert.ToInt32(input.Text);
            n = Fibonacci.get(n);
            result.Text = n.ToString();
        }
    }
}
```

If you want to be able to use the form created in C# from F#, you need to expose certain controls as properties. Not all controls need to be exposed—just the ones that you want to interact with from F#. The following example shows how to do this in C#; again, any designer-generated code is hidden in a separate file:

```
using System;
using System.Windows.Forms;

namespace Strangelights.Forms
{
    public partial class FibForm : Form
    {
        public FibForm()
        {
            InitializeComponent();
        }

        public Button Calculate
        {
            get { return calculate; }
        }

        public Label Result
        {
            get { return result; }
        }
    }
}
```

```
        public TextBox Input
        {
            get { return input; }
        }
    }
}
```

It is then very straightforward to reference the C# .dll from F# and create an instance of the form and use it. The following example demonstrates the code you use to do this:

```
#light
open System.Windows.Forms
open Strangelights.Forms

let fibs =
    (1,1) |> Seq.unfold
        (fun (n0, n1) ->
            Some(n0, (n1, n0 + n1)))

let getFib n =
    Seq.nth n fibs

let form =
    let temp = new FibForm()
    temp.Calculate.Click.Add
        (fun _ ->
            let n = int_of_string temp.Input.Text
            let n = getFib n
            temp.Result.Text <- string_of_int n)
    temp
```

```
Application.Run(form)
```

As you have seen, you can use both techniques to produce similar results, so which is best to use when? The problem with a C# form calling F# is that you will inevitably end up writing quite a bit of C# to glue everything together. It can also be difficult to use some F# types, such as union types, from C#. Considering these two facts, I generally create a C# forms library and use this from F#. I discuss the problem of making F# libraries ready for use with other .NET languages in Chapter 13.

Working with WinForms Events and the IEvent Module

The IEvent module, first discussed in Chapter 7, can be useful when working with events in WinForms. When working with events in a WinForm, there is often not an event that exactly fits what you want. For example, the MouseButton event is raised when either the left or right mouse button is clicked, but you might want to respond only to the click of the left mouse button. In this case, it can be useful to use the IEvent.filter function to create a new event that responds only to the left mouse button click. The next example demonstrates how to do this:

```
light
open System.Windows.Forms

let form =
    let temp = new Form()
    temp.MouseClick
    |> IEvent.filter (fun e -> e.Button = MouseButtons.Left)
    |> IEvent.listen
        (fun _ ->
            MessageBox.Show("Left button") |> ignore)
    temp

Application.Run(form)
```

Here the filter function is used with a function that checks whether the left mouse button is pressed; the resulting event is then piped forward to the listen function that adds an event handler to the event, exactly as if you had called the event's .Add method. You could have implemented this using an if expression within the event handler, but this technique has the advantage of separating the logic that controls the event firing and what happens during the event itself. If you want, several event handlers can reuse the new event.

Listing 8-3 demonstrates using more of IEvent's functions to create a simple drawing application (shown in Figure 8-5). Here you want to use the MouseDown event in different ways, first to monitor whether the mouse is pressed at all and then to split the event into left or right button presses using the IEvent.partition function. This is used to control the drawing color, either red or black.

Listing 8-3. *Using Events to Implement a Simple Drawing Application*

```
#light
open System
open System.Drawing
open System.Windows.Forms

let form =
    let temp = new Form(Text = "Scribble !!")

    let pointsMasterList = ref []
    let pointsTempList = ref []
    let mouseDown = ref false
    let pen = ref (new Pen(Color.Black))

    temp.MouseDown.Add(fun _ -> mouseDown := true)
```

```
    let leftMouse, rightMouse =
        temp.MouseDown
        |> IEvent.partition (fun e -> e.Button = MouseButtons.Left)

    leftMouse.Add(fun _ -> pen := new Pen(Color.Black))
    rightMouse.Add(fun _ -> pen := new Pen(Color.Red))

    temp.MouseUp
    |> IEvent.listen
        (fun _ ->
            mouseDown := false
            if List.length !pointsTempList > 1 then
                let points = List.to_array !pointsTempList
                pointsMasterList :=
                    (!pen, points) :: !pointsMasterList
            pointsTempList := []
            temp.Invalidate())

    temp.MouseMove
    |> IEvent.filter(fun _ -> !mouseDown)
    |> IEvent.listen
        (fun e ->
            pointsTempList := e.Location :: !pointsTempList
            temp.Invalidate())

    temp.Paint
    |> IEvent.listen
        (fun e ->
            if List.length !pointsTempList > 1 then
                e.Graphics.DrawLines
                    (!pen, List.to_array !pointsTempList)
            !pointsMasterList
            |> List.iter
                (fun (pen, points) ->
                    e.Graphics.DrawLines(pen, points)))
    temp

[<STAThread>]
do Application.Run(form)
```

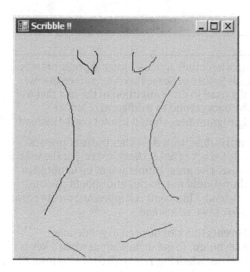

Figure 8-5. *Scribble: a simple drawing application implemented using events*

Events created this way can also be published on the form's interface so that code consuming the form can also take advantage of these events.

Again, a big problem facing a programmer working with events in WinForms is the volume of events available, which can make choosing the right one difficult. Perhaps surprisingly, most events are defined on the class Control, with each specialization providing only a handful of extra events. This generally makes life a bit easier, because if you have used an event with a control, odds are it will also be available on another. To help beginners with the most common events on the Control class, I have provided a summary in Table 8-4.

Table 8-4. *A Summary of Events on the Control Class*

Event	Description
Click	This event is caused by the user clicking the control. It is a high-level event, and although it is ordinarily caused by the user clicking with the mouse, it might also be caused by the user pressing Enter or the spacebar when on a control. There are a series of events called MouseDown, MouseClick, and MouseUp that provide more detailed information about the actions of the mouse, but because these events just provide information about the mouse actions, generally the Click should be handled instead of these events. Otherwise, this will lead to the control responding in ways users expect, because it will respond to keystrokes and mouse clicks.
DoubleClick	This is raised when the mouse is clicked twice in quick succession; the amount of time is determined by the user's operating system settings. Programmers should be careful when handling this event because every time this event is raised, a Click event will have been raised before it, so in general programmers should handle either this event or the Click event.

continued

Table 8-4. *Continued*

Event	Description
Enter	This event is raised when the control becomes active—either the user presses Tab to enter it, the programmer calls Select or SelectNextControl, or the user clicks it with the mouse. It is usually used to draw attention to the fact that the control is active, such as setting the background to a different color. It is suppressed on the Form class, and programmers should use Activated instead.
Leave	This event is raised when the control is deactivated—either the user presses Tab to leave it, the programmer calls Select or SelectNextControl, or the user clicks another control with the mouse. The programmer might be tempted to use this event for validation, but they should not do this and should use the Validating and Validated events instead. This event is suppressed on the Form class, and programmers should use Activated instead.
KeyPress	This event is part of a sequence of events that can be used to get detailed information about the state of the keyboard. To get details about when a key is first pressed, use KeyDown, and to find out when it is released, use KeyUp instead.
Move	This event is raised whenever the control is moved by the user.
MouseHover	This event is useful to find out whether the mouse is hovering over a control so can be used to give users more information about the control. The events MouseEnter and MouseLeave are also useful for this.
Paint	This event occurs when the form will be repainted by Windows; handle this event if you want to take care of drawing the control yourself. For more information about this, see the section "Drawing WinForms" earlier in this chapter.
Resize	This event occurs when the user resizes the form; it can be useful to handle this event to adjust the layout of the form to the new size.

Creating New Forms Classes

So far you've looked only at a script style of programming, using an existing form and controls to quickly put forms together. This style of programming is great for the rapid development of single-form applications but has some limitations when creating applications composed of multiple forms or creating libraries of forms for use with other .NET languages. In these cases, you must take a more component-oriented approach.

Typically, when creating a large WinForms application, you'll want to use some forms repeatedly; furthermore, these forms typically communicate with each other by adjusting their properties and calling their methods. You usually do this by defining a new form class that derives from System.Windows.Forms. Listing 8-4 shows a simple example of this, using the class syntax introduced in Chapter 5.

Listing 8-4. *A Demonstration of Creating a New Type of Form*

```
#light
open System
open System.Windows.Forms
```

```
type MyForm() as x = class
    inherit Form(Width=174, Height=64)
    let label = new Label(Top=8, Left=8, Width=40, Text="Input:")
    let textbox = new TextBox(Top=8, Left=48, Width=40)
    let button = new Button(Top=8, Left=96, Width=60, Text="Push Me!")
    do button.Click.Add
            (fun _ ->
                let form = new MyForm(Text=textbox.Text)
                form.Show())
    do x.Controls.Add(label)
    do x.Controls.Add(textbox)
    do x.Controls.Add(button)
    member x.Textbox = textbox
end

let form =
    let temp = new MyForm(Text="My Form")
    temp.Textbox.Text <- "Next!"
    temp

[<STAThread>]
do Application.Run(form)
```

Figure 8-6 shows the resulting forms.

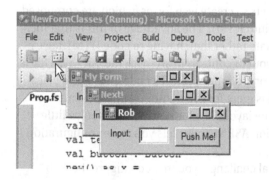

Figure 8-6. *A demonstration of creating a new type of form for easy reuse*

In this example, you created a form that has three fields: label, textbox, and button. These fields can then be manipulated by external code. At the end of the example, you created a new instance of this form and then set the Text property of the textbox field.

Events can be exposed on the interface of a form much the same way that fields can. This takes a little more work because of some restrictions. The idea is to create a new event, then store this event in a field in the class, and finally make this event a subscriber to the filtered event. This is demonstrated in the next example, where you filter the MouseClick event to create a LeftMouseClick:

```
#light
open System.Windows.Forms

type LeftClickForm() as x = class
    inherit Form()
    let trigger, event = IEvent.create()
    do x.MouseClick
        |> IEvent.filter (fun e -> e.Button = MouseButtons.Left)
        |> IEvent.listen (fun e -> trigger e)
    member x.LeftMouseClick = event
end
```

Forms created in this component-based manner will undoubtedly be easier to use than forms created with a more scripted approach, but there are still pitfalls when creating libraries for other .NET languages. Please refer to Chapter 13 for more information about making F# libraries usable by other .NET languages.

Introducing ASP.NET 2.0

ASP.NET 2.0 is a technology designed to simplify creating dynamic web pages. The simplest way to do this is to implement an interface called IHttpHandler. This interface allows the implementer to describe how an HTTP request should be responded to; the next section of the chapter will concentrate on how this works.

Merely implementing the IHttpHandler interface will not allow you to take full advantage of the ASP.NET 2.0 feature set. ASP.NET allows users to create web forms, which are composed of controls that know how to render themselves into HTML. The advantage of this is that the programmer has a nice object model to manipulate rather than having to code HTML tags. It also allows a programmer to separate out the layout of controls in an .aspx file. An .aspx file is basically all the static HTML you don't want to worry about in your F# code, plus a few place-holders for the dynamic controls. This approach is great for programming in F#, because it allows you to separate the code that represents the layout of a form, which can look a little long in F#, from the code that controls its behavior. ASP.NET also lets you store configuration values in an XML-based web.config file.

Working with ASP.NET presents an additional challenge; you must configure the web server that will host the ASP.NET application. Your configuration will vary depending on your development environment.

Visual Studio 2005 comes with a built-in web server, so to create a new web site, it is just a matter of selecting File ➤ New ➤ Web Site and then choosing the location for the web site. This site will run only those pages written in C# or Visual Basic .NET, so you need to add an F# proj-ect to the solution and then manually alter the solution file so that it lives inside the web site directory. This is easier than it sounds. You just need to copy the .fsharpp file to the web site directory, open the .sln file in Notepad, and alter the path to the .fsharpp file. After this you merely need to configure the project file to output a library and write this to a bin subdirectory. This might seem like a lot of effort, but after this you will just be able to press F5, and your proj-ect will compile and run.

If you do not have Visual Studio 2005, then the next best thing to do is host the site in IIS. In some ways, this is easier than hosting in Visual Studio but doesn't have the convenience of just being able to execute your code once coding is completed. To host your code in IIS, you need to create an IIS virtual directory with a subdirectory called bin. You then need to copy your .aspx pages and your web.config file to the virtual directory.

■**Note** Getting ASP.NET to work with F# and Apache is possible but is more difficult than the situation either with or without Visual Studio 2005. Please see the following site for more details of how to do this: http://strangelights.com/FSharp/Foundations/default.aspx/FSharpFoundations.Apache.

Creating an IHttpHandler

Creating an IHttpHandler is the simplest way to take advantage of ASP.NET 2.0. It is a simple interface with just two members. The first of these members is a read-only Boolean property called IsReusable that the programmer should use to indicate whether the runtime can reuse the instance of the object. It is generally best to set this to false.

The other member of the interface is the ProcessRequest method, and this is called when a web request is received. It takes one parameter of HttpContent type; you can use this type to retrieve information about the request being made through its Request property and also to respond to the request via its Response property. The following code is a simple example of an IHttpHandler that just responds to a request with the string "<h1>Hello World</h1>":

```
#light
namespace Strangelights.HttpHandlers
open System.Web

type SimpleHandler() = class
    interface IHttpHandler with
        member x.IsReusable = false
        member x.ProcessRequest(c : HttpContext) =
            c.Response.Write("<h1>Hello World</h1>")
    end
end
```

After this, you must configure the URL where the IHttpHandler is available. You do this by adding an entry to the web.config file. If a web.config file is not already in the project, you can add one by right-clicking the web project and choosing Add New Item. The handlers are added to the httpHandlers section, and you need to configure four properties for each handler: path, which is the URL of the page; verb, which configures which HTTP verbs the handler will respond to; type, which is the name of the type that will be used to handle the request; and finally validate, which tells the runtime whether it should check the availability of the type when the application is first loaded.

```
<configuration>
  <system.web>
    <httpHandlers>
      <add
        path="hello.aspx"
        verb="*"
        type="Strangelights.HttpHandlers.SimpleHandler"
        validate="True" />
    </httpHandlers>
</configuration>
```

Figure 8-7 shows the resulting web page.

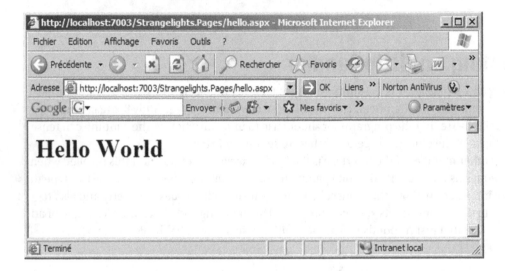

Figure 8-7. *The resulting web page when the* SimpleHandler *is executed*

This technique is unsatisfactory for creating web pages, because it requires the HTML tags to be mixed into the F# code. It does have some advantages, though. You can use this technique to put together documents other than HTML documents; for example, you can use it to dynamically create images on the server. The following example shows an IHttpHandler that generates a JPEG image of a pie shape. The amount of pie shown is determined by the angle value that that is passed in on the query string.

```
#light
namespace Strangelights.HttpHandlers
open System.Drawing
open System.Drawing.Imaging
open System.Web
```

```
type PictureHandler() = class
    interface IHttpHandler with
        member x.IsReusable = false
        member x.ProcessRequest(c : HttpContext) =
            let bitmap = new Bitmap(200, 200)
            let graphics = Graphics.FromImage(bitmap)
            let brush = new SolidBrush(Color.Red)
            let x = int_of_string(c.Request.QueryString.Get("angle"))
            graphics.FillPie(brush, 10, 10, 180, 180, 0, x)
            bitmap.Save(c.Response.OutputStream, ImageFormat.Gif)
    end
end
```

Again, you still need to register this type in the web.config file; the required configuration is as follows:

```
<configuration>
  <system.web>
    <httpHandlers>
      <add
        path="pic.aspx"
        verb="*"
        type="Strangelights.HttpHandlers.PictureHandler"
        validate="True" />
    </httpHandlers>
  </system.web>
</configuration>
```

Figure 8-8 shows the resulting image. In this case, I passed in an angle of 200.

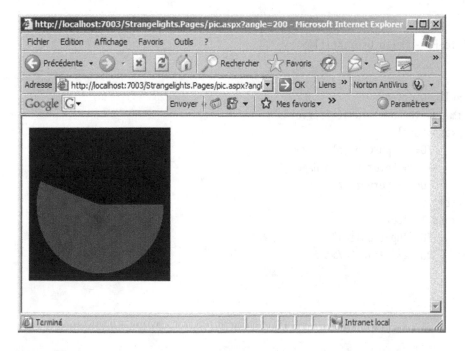

Figure 8-8. *Using an* IHttpHandler *to dynamically generate a picture*

Although this is a great technique for spicing up web sites, you should be careful when using it. Generating images can be very processor intensive, especially if the images are large or complicated. This can lead to web sites that do not scale up to the required number of concurrent users; therefore, if you do use this technique, ensure you profile your code correctly. For more information about profiling your applications and for some general performance enhancements, please see Chapter 13.

Working with ASP.NET Web Forms

If you want to create dynamic web pages, then you will probably have an easier time using ASP.NET forms than implementing your own IHttpHandler. The main advantage of web forms is that you do not need to deal with HTML tags in F# code; most of this is abstracted away for you. There are other, smaller advantages too, such as that you do not have to register the page in web.config.

To create an ASP.NET web form, you generally start by creating the user interface, defined in an .aspx file. The .aspx file is all the static HTML, plus some placeholders for the dynamic controls. An .aspx file always starts with a Page directive; you can see this at the top of the next example. The Page directive allows you to specify a class that the page will inherit from; you do this by using the Inherits attribute and giving the full name of the class. This will be a class in F# that provides the dynamic functionality.

If you look at the following example, in among the regular HTML tags you'll find some tags that are prefixed with asp:. These are ASP.NET web controls, and these provide the dynamic functionality. A web control is a class in the .NET Framework that knows how to render itself into HTML, so for example, the <asp:TextBox /> tag will become an HTML <input /> tag. You will be able to take control of these controls in your F# class and use them to respond to user input.

```
<%@ Page Inherits="Strangelights.HttpHandlers.HelloUser" %>
<html>
    <head>
        <title>F# - Hello User</title>
    </head>
    <body>
        <p>Hello User</p>
        <form id="theForm" runat="server">
            <asp:Label
                ID="OutputControl"
                Text="Enter you're name ..."
                runat="server" />
            <br />
            <asp:TextBox
                ID="InputControl"
                runat="server" />
```

```
            <br />
            <asp:LinkButton
                ID="SayHelloButton"
                Text="Say Hello ..."
                runat="server"
                OnClick="SayHelloButton_Click" />
        </form>
    </body>
</html>
```

When designing your class, you need to provide mutable fields with the same name as the controls you want to manipulate. Although the HTML page you created had three controls in it, you provide only two mutable fields, because you don't want to manipulate the third control, a link button. You just want it to call the SayHelloButton_Click function when you click it. You do this by adding the function name to the OnClick attribute of the asp:LinkButton control.

When the other two controls are created, a label and a textbox, they will be stored in the mutable fields OutputControl and InputControl, respectively. It is the code contained in the .aspx page, not your class, that is responsible for creating these controls. This is why you explicitly initialize these controls to null in the constructor. Finally, all that remains in SayHelloButton_Click is to take the input from InputControl and place it into OutputControl.

```
#light
namespace Strangelights.HttpHandlers

open System
open System.Web.UI
open System.Web.UI.WebControls

type HelloUser = class
    inherit Page
    val mutable OutputControl : Label
    val mutable InputControl : TextBox
    new() =
        { OutputControl = null
          InputControl = null }

    member x.SayHelloButton_Click((sender : obj), (e : EventArgs)) =
        x.OutputControl.Text <- ("Hello ... " + x.InputControl.Text)
end
```

Figure 8-9 shows the resulting web page.

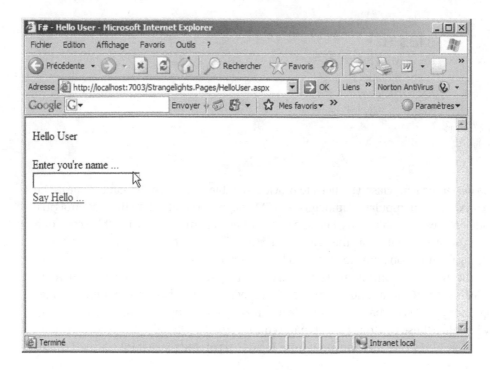

Figure 8-9. *A page created using an ASP.NET form*

This form doesn't look great, but the nice thing about your application being defined in HTML is that you can quickly use images and Cascading Style Sheets (CSS) to spice up the application. Figure 8-10 shows the results of a little CSS magic.

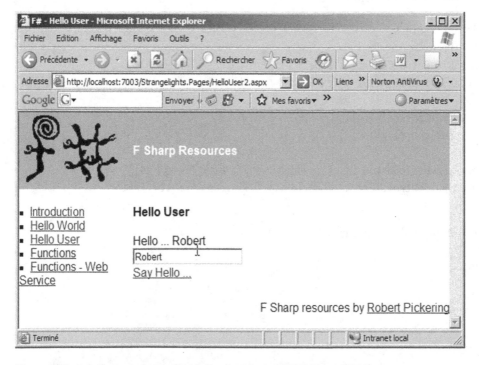

Figure 8-10. *A web page that takes full advantage of HTML and CSS*

You have taken only a brief look at all the functionality offered by ASP.NET. To give beginners a starting point for investigating this further, Table 8-5 summarizes all the namespaces available in `System.Web.dll` that contains the ASP.NET functionality.

Table 8-5. *A Summary of the Namespaces Available in* `System.Web.dll`

Namespace	Description
`System.Web`	This namespace provides types that are the basis to the HTML rendering process that is ASP.NET; this is where the `IHttpHander` interface, which I have already discussed in this chapter, lives.
`System.Web.Mail`	This namespace provides types that can be used to send emails from ASP.NET applications.
`System.Web.HtmlControls`	This namespace provides controls that are exact copies of HTML tags.
`System.Web.WebControls`	This namespace provides controls that are like HTML tags but are more abstract. For example, the `TextBox` control is rendered as an `input` tag if its `TextMode` property is set to `TextBoxMode.SingleLine` and as a `textarea` if it is set to `TextBoxMode.MultiLine`.
`System.Web.WebControls.Adapters`	This namespace provides adapters that can be used to affect the rendering of other controls to alter their behavior or render different HTML tags for different types of browsers.
`System.Web.WebControls.WebParts`	This namespace provides *web parts*, controls that support a system where users can add, remove, and dynamically configure them within a page to give a personalized experience.

Introducing Windows Presentation Foundation

WPF is a library that offers a completely new programming model for user interfaces. It is aimed at creating desktop applications that have more pizzazz than the ones that are created with WinForms. WPF also comes with a new XML-based language called XAML, which can be used to code the bulk of the layout of the form, leaving F# code free to describe the interesting parts of the application.

■**Note** Several XAML designers are now available; these allow F# users to design their interface using a graphical WYSWIG tool and then add the interactivity to it using F#. Mobiform offers a designer called Aurora (`http://www.mobiform.com/eng/aurora.html`), and Microsoft offers a designer called Expression Blend (`http://www.microsoft.com/products/expression/en/expression-blend/default.mspx`).

The first example you'll look at is how to create a simple form in XAML and then display it to the user using F#. Listing 8-5 shows the XAML definition of a form with four controls: two labels, a textbox, and a button.

Listing 8-5. *A Simple Form Created in XAML*

```
<Window
  xmlns="http://schemas.microsoft.com/winfx/2006/xaml/presentation"
  xmlns:sys="clr-namespace:System;assembly=mscorlib"
  xmlns:x="http://schemas.microsoft.com/winfx/2006/xaml" >
  <Grid>
  <Grid.ColumnDefinitions>
    <ColumnDefinition Width="64" />
    <ColumnDefinition Width="128" />
    <ColumnDefinition Width="128" />
    <ColumnDefinition Width="128" />
  </Grid.ColumnDefinitions>
  <Grid.RowDefinitions>
    <RowDefinition Height="24"/>
  </Grid.RowDefinitions>

    <Label Grid.Row="0" Grid.Column="0" >Input: </Label>
    <TextBox Name="input" Grid.Column="1" Text="hello" />
    <Label Name="output" Grid.Row="0" Grid.Column="2" ></Label>
    <Button Name="press" Grid.Column="3" >Press Me</Button>
  </Grid>
</Window>
```

To make this XAML definition of a form useful, you need to do two things. You must load the form's definition and show it to the user, but just doing this will offer no interaction with the user, so the other thing you need to do is make the form interactive. To do this, you use F# to add event handlers to the controls, in this case to add an event handler to the button to place the contents of the textbox into the second label. The function createWindow is a general-purpose function for loading an XAML form. You then use this function to create the value window, and you pass this value to the form's FindName method to find the controls within the form so you can interact with them. Finally, in the main function you create an instance of the Application class and use this to show the form (see Listing 8-6).

Listing 8-6. *Displaying the XAML Form and Adding Event Handlers to It*

```
#light
open System
open System.Collections.Generic
open System.Windows
open System.Windows.Controls
open System.Windows.Markup
open System.Xml

// creates the window and loads the given XAML file into it
let createWindow (file : string) =
    using (XmlReader.Create(file)) (fun stream ->
            (XamlReader.Load(stream) :?> Window))
```

```
// create the window object and add event handler
// to the button control
let window =
    let temp = createWindow "Window1.xaml"
    let press = temp.FindName("press") :?> Button
    let textbox = temp.FindName("input") :?> TextBox
    let label = temp.FindName("output") :?> Label
    press.Click.Add (fun _ -> label.Content <- textbox.Text )
    temp

// run the application
let main() =
    let app = new Application()
    app.Run(window) |> ignore

[<STAThread>]
do main()
```

To get this program to compile, you must add references to PresentationCore.dll, PresentationFramework.dll, and WindowsBase.dll, which are usually found in the directory C:\Program Files\Reference Assemblies\Microsoft\Framework\v3.0. In the other examples in this chapter, you didn't need to add references, since the libraries were automatically referenced by the compiler. The form appears as in Figure 8-11.

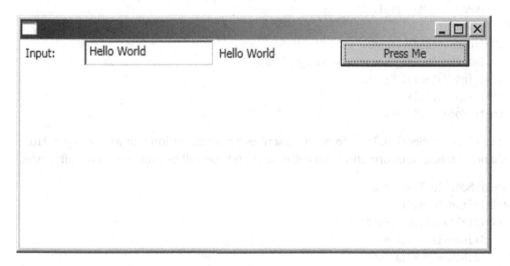

Figure 8-11. *A form created using XAML and F#*

Introducing Windows Presentation Foundation 3D

Another great advantage of WPF is the huge number of controls it offers. One control that you'll dig a little deeper into is Viewport3D, which offers the ability to create impressive 3D graphics, something not readily available with the WinForms library. You'll learn how you can display a 3D plane and then map an equation over it.

The example (shown later in Listing 8-7) starts with the XAML script. Both XAML and 3D graphics are huge topics; my aim is not to cover them in detail but to give you enough of an idea of what they involve and to give you the basis for your own experiments. The following XAML script describes a window with one control, a Viewport3D, on it. The script is fairly lengthy because there are quite a few elements required to make a 3D scene. First you must define a camera so you know which direction you are looking at the scene from. You do this using the <Viewport3D.Camera> element:

```
<Viewport3D.Camera>
  <PerspectiveCamera Position="0,0,2" LookDirection="0,0,-1" FieldOfView="60" />
</Viewport3D.Camera>
```

The tags inside <Model3DGroup> describe what the scene will look like. The <AmbientLight Color="White" /> tag describes how the scene will be lit, and the <GeometryModel3D.Geometry> tag describes the 3D shape in the scene:

```
<GeometryModel3D.Geometry>
  <MeshGeometry3D />
</GeometryModel3D.Geometry>
```

Here you could describe all the objects that make up the scene by giving the points that make them up using the <MeshGeometry3D /> tag; however, you don't describe the points that make up the shape since it is a lot easier to do this in F# than in XAML. The <GeometryModel3D.Material> tag describes what the surface of the shape will look like:

```
<GeometryModel3D.Material>
  <DiffuseMaterial>
    <DiffuseMaterial.Brush>
      <ImageBrush ImageSource="venus.jpg" />
    </DiffuseMaterial.Brush>
  </DiffuseMaterial>
</GeometryModel3D.Material>
```

The <GeometryModel3D.Transform> tag describes a transformation that will be applied to the shape, that is, a transformation that will mean the shape will be rotated by a certain angle:

```
<GeometryModel3D.Transform>
  <RotateTransform3D>
    <RotateTransform3D.Rotation>
      <AxisAngleRotation3D
        x:Name="MyRotation3D"
        Angle="45"
        Axis="0,1,0"/>
    </RotateTransform3D.Rotation>
  </RotateTransform3D>
</GeometryModel3D.Transform>
```

You do this mainly so you can use the <Viewport3D.Triggers> tag to define an animation that will alter the angle it is shown at over time:

```
<Viewport3D.Triggers>
  <EventTrigger RoutedEvent="Viewport3D.Loaded">
    <EventTrigger.Actions>
      <BeginStoryboard>
        <Storyboard>
          <DoubleAnimation
            From="-80"
            To="80"
            Duration="0:0:12"
            Storyboard.TargetName="MyRotation3D"
            Storyboard.TargetProperty="Angle"
            RepeatBehavior="Forever"
            AutoReverse="True" />
        </Storyboard>
      </BeginStoryboard>
    </EventTrigger.Actions>
  </EventTrigger>
</Viewport3D.Triggers>
```

To demonstrate how these various sections hang together, Listing 8-7 shows the complete example.

Listing 8-7. *An XAML Definition of a 3D Scene*

```
<Window
  xmlns="http://schemas.microsoft.com/winfx/2006/xaml/presentation"
  xmlns:x="http://schemas.microsoft.com/winfx/2006/xaml">

<Viewport3D Name="ViewPort">
  <Viewport3D.Camera>
    <PerspectiveCamera Position="0,0,2" LookDirection="0,0,-1" FieldOfView="60" />
  </Viewport3D.Camera>

  <Viewport3D.Children>
    <ModelVisual3D>
      <ModelVisual3D.Content>
        <Model3DGroup >
          <Model3DGroup.Children>
            <AmbientLight Color="White" />
            <GeometryModel3D>
              <GeometryModel3D.Geometry>
                <MeshGeometry3D />
              </GeometryModel3D.Geometry>
```

```xml
                        <GeometryModel3D.Transform>
                          <RotateTransform3D>
                            <RotateTransform3D.Rotation>
                              <AxisAngleRotation3D
                                x:Name="MyRotation3D"
                                Angle="45"
                                Axis="0,1,0"/>
                            </RotateTransform3D.Rotation>
                          </RotateTransform3D>
                        </GeometryModel3D.Transform>

                        <GeometryModel3D.Material>
                          <DiffuseMaterial>
                            <DiffuseMaterial.Brush>
                              <ImageBrush ImageSource="venus.jpg" />
                            </DiffuseMaterial.Brush>
                          </DiffuseMaterial>
                        </GeometryModel3D.Material>

                      </GeometryModel3D>
                    </Model3DGroup.Children>
                  </Model3DGroup>
                </ModelVisual3D.Content>
              </ModelVisual3D>
            </Viewport3D.Children>

            <Viewport3D.Triggers>
              <EventTrigger RoutedEvent="Viewport3D.Loaded">
                <EventTrigger.Actions>
                  <BeginStoryboard>
                    <Storyboard>
                      <DoubleAnimation
                        From="-80"
                        To="80"
                        Duration="0:0:12"
                        Storyboard.TargetName="MyRotation3D"
                        Storyboard.TargetProperty="Angle"
                        RepeatBehavior="Forever"
                        AutoReverse="True" />
                    </Storyboard>
                  </BeginStoryboard>
                </EventTrigger.Actions>
              </EventTrigger>
            </Viewport3D.Triggers>
          </Viewport3D>
        </Window>
```

The example continues later in Listing 8-8, with the F# script, which borrows a couple of functions from Listing 8-6; it also assumes that Listing 8-7 is saved in a file called Window2.xaml. You use the createWindow function to load the window and use a similar main function to display the window. You then use the findMeshes function to find any meshes in the picture (a *mesh* is a set of points used to describe the 3D plane). You find the meshes by walking the various objects in the Viewport3D and building up a list:

```
// finds all the MeshGeometry3D in a given 3D view port
let findMeshes ( viewport : Viewport3D ) =
    viewport.Children
    |> Seq.choose
        (function :? ModelVisual3D as c -> Some(c.Content) | _ -> None)
    |> Seq.choose
        (function :? Model3DGroup as mg -> Some(mg.Children) | _ -> None)
    |> Seq.concat
    |> Seq.choose
        (function :? GeometryModel3D as mg -> Some(mg.Geometry) | _ -> None)
    |> Seq.choose
        (function :? MeshGeometry3D as mv -> Some(mv) | _ -> None)
```

I kept this function generic so it could work with any Viewport3D. It is highly likely that you will want to grab a list of all the meshes in your 3D scene in any 3D work you do in XAML and F# because it is likely that you will want to manipulate your meshes in some way in F#. Then you use createPlaneItemList, createSquare, createPlanePoints, createIndicesPlane, and addPlaneToMesh to add a flat plane to the mesh object in the scene. The function mapPositionsCenter centers the plane so it is in the middle of the scene. Finally, a clever little function called changePositions maps the function movingWaves repeatedly across the plane ten times a second. The core of this function creates a new Point3DCollection from the Point3D objects contained within the old one using the function movingWaves to decide what the new Z position should be.

```
let changePositions () =
    let dispatcherTimer = new DispatcherTimer()
    dispatcherTimer.Tick.Add
        (fun e ->
            let t = (float_of_int DateTime.Now.Millisecond) / 2000.0
            let newPositions =
                mesh.Positions
                |> Seq.map
                    (fun position ->
                        let z = movingWaves t position.X position.Y
                        new Point3D(position.X, position.Y, z))
            mesh.Positions <- new Point3DCollection(newPositions))
    dispatcherTimer.Interval <- new TimeSpan(0,0,0,0,100)
    dispatcherTimer.Start()
```

Using the DispatcherTimer class means that the code is executed on the thread that created the form, meaning there is no need to call back to this thread to update the form. It needs to be

called at least ten times a second to create a smooth animation effect. Listing 8-8 shows the
complete example.

Listing 8-8. *Displaying and Interacting with a 3D XAML Scene*

```
#light
open System
open System.Collections.Generic
open System.IO
open System.Windows
open System.Windows.Controls
open System.Windows.Markup
open System.Windows.Media
open System.Windows.Media.Media3D
open System.Windows.Threading
open System.Xml

// creates the window and loads the given XAML file into it
let createWindow (file : string) =
    using  (XmlReader.Create(file))
        (fun stream ->
            let temp = XamlReader.Load(stream) :?> Window
            temp.Height <- 400.0
            temp.Width <- 400.0
            temp.Title <- "F# meets Xaml"
            temp)

// finds all the MeshGeometry3D in a given 3D view port
let findMeshes ( viewport : Viewport3D ) =
    viewport.Children
    |> Seq.choose
        (function :? ModelVisual3D as c -> Some(c.Content) | _ -> None)
    |> Seq.choose
        (function :? Model3DGroup as mg -> Some(mg.Children) | _ -> None)
    |> Seq.concat
    |> Seq.choose
        (function :? GeometryModel3D as mg -> Some(mg.Geometry) | _ -> None)
    |> Seq.choose
        (function :? MeshGeometry3D as mv -> Some(mv) | _ -> None)

// loop function to create all items necessary for a plane
let createPlaneItemList f (xRes : int) (yRes : int) =
    let list = new List<_>()
    for x = 0 to xRes - 1 do
        for y = 0 to yRes - 1 do
            f list x y
    list
```

```
// function to initialize a point
let point x y = new Point(x, y)
// function to initialize a "d point
let point3D x y = new Point3D(x, y, 0.0)

// create all the points necessary for a square in the plane
let createSquare
    f (xStep : float) (yStep : float) (list : List<_>) (x : int) (y : int) =
    let x' = Float.of_int x * xStep
    let y' = Float.of_int y * yStep
    list.Add(f x' y')
    list.Add(f (x' + xStep) y')
    list.Add(f (x' + xStep) (y' + yStep))
    list.Add(f (x' + xStep) (y' + yStep))
    list.Add(f x' (y' + yStep))
    list.Add(f x' y')

// create all items in a plane
let createPlanePoints f xRes yRes =
    let xStep = 1.0 / Float.of_int xRes
    let yStep = 1.0 / Float.of_int yRes
    createPlaneItemList (createSquare f xStep yStep) xRes yRes

// create the 3D positions for a plane, i.e., the thing that says where
// the plane will be in 3D space
let createPlanePositions xRes yRes =
    let list = createPlanePoints point3D xRes yRes
    new Point3DCollection(list)

// create the texture mappings for a plane, i.e., the thing that
// maps the 2D image to the 3D plane
let createPlaneTextures xRes yRes =
    let list = createPlanePoints point xRes yRes
    new PointCollection(list)

// create indices list for all our triangles
let createIndicesPlane width height =
    let list = new System.Collections.Generic.List<int>()
    for index = 0 to width * height * 6 do
        list.Add(index)
    new Int32Collection(list)

// center the plane in the field of view
let mapPositionsCenter (positions : Point3DCollection) =
    let newPositions =
        positions
        |> Seq.map
```

```fsharp
                    (fun position ->
                        new Point3D(
                                    (position.X - 0.5 ) * -1.0 ,
                                    (position.Y - 0.5 ) * -1.0,
                                     position.Z))
        new Point3DCollection(newPositions)

// create a plane and add it to the given mesh
let addPlaneToMesh (mesh : MeshGeometry3D) xRes yRes =
    mesh.Positions <- mapPositionsCenter
                        (createPlanePositions xRes yRes)
    mesh.TextureCoordinates <- createPlaneTextures xRes yRes
    mesh.TriangleIndices <- createIndicesPlane xRes yRes

let movingWaves (t : float) x y =
    (Math.Cos((x + t) * Math.PI * 4.0) / 3.0) *
        (Math.Cos(y * Math.PI * 2.0) / 3.0)

// create our window
let window = createWindow "Window2.xaml"

let mesh =
    // grab the 3D view port
    let viewport = window.FindName("ViewPort") :?> Viewport3D
    // find all the meshes and get the first one
    let meshes = findMeshes viewport
    let mesh = Seq.hd meshes
    // add plane to the mesh
    addPlaneToMesh mesh 20 20
    mesh

let changePositions () =
    let dispatcherTimer = new DispatcherTimer()
    dispatcherTimer.Tick.Add
        (fun e ->
            let t = (float_of_int DateTime.Now.Millisecond) / 2000.0
            let newPositions =
                mesh.Positions
                |> Seq.map
                    (fun position ->
                        let z = movingWaves t position.X position.Y
                        new Point3D(position.X, position.Y, z))
            mesh.Positions <- new Point3DCollection(newPositions))
    dispatcherTimer.Interval <- new TimeSpan(0,0,0,0,100)
    dispatcherTimer.Start()
```

```
let main() =
    let app = new Application()
    changePositions()
    // show the window
    app.Run(window) |> ignore


[<STAThread>]
do main()
```

Figure 8-12 shows the resulting window. It doesn't show off the animated results, so I encourage you to try the application yourself.

Figure 8-12. *A 3D scene created using XAML and F#*

One other thing I encourage you to do is play with this sample in fsi. You can subtly alter the sample to run inside fsi, and then the function applied to the plane can be altered dynamically. The original script must be altered in several small ways.

First, you must set the reference to the .dll files in an fsi style:

```
#I @"C:\Program Files\Reference Assemblies\Microsoft\Framework\v3.0" ;;
#r @"PresentationCore.dll" ;;
#r @"PresentationFramework.dll" ;;
#r @"WindowsBase.dll" ;;
```

Then, you must alter the changePositions function to use a mutable function:

```
// mutable function that is used within changePositions function
let mutable f  = (fun (t : float) (x : float) (y : float) -> 0.0)
```

```
// function for changing the plane over time
let changePositions () =
    let dispatcherTimer = new DispatcherTimer()
    dispatcherTimer.Tick.Add
        (fun e ->
            let t = (float_of_int DateTime.Now.Millisecond) / 2000.0
            let newPositions =
                mesh.Positions
                |> Seq.map
                    (fun position ->
                        let z = f t position.X position.Y
                        new Point3D(position.X, position.Y, z))
            mesh.Positions <- new Point3DCollection(newPositions))
    dispatcherTimer.Interval <- new TimeSpan(0,0,0,0,100)
    dispatcherTimer.Start()
```

Then, finally, you show the window using its .Show() method rather than the Application class's Run method, not forgetting to set its Topmost property to true so that it is easy to interact with the window and see the results:

```
// show the window, set it the top, and activate the function that will
// set it moving
window.Show()
window.Topmost <- true
changePositions ()
```

Finally, you need to define some other functions to map across the plane. This can be any function that takes three floating-point numbers (the first representing the time and the next two representing the X and Y coordinates, respectively) and returns a third floating-point representing the Z coordinate. I'm practically fond of using sine and cosine functions because these generate interesting wave patterns. Here are some examples of what you could use, but please feel free to invent your own:

```
let cosXY _ x y =
    Math.Cos(x * Math.PI) * Math.Cos(y * Math.PI)
```

```
let movingCosXY (t : float) x y =
    Math.Cos((x + t) * Math.PI) * Math.Cos((y - t) * Math.PI)
```

You can then easily apply these functions to the plane by updating the mutable function:

```
f <- movingCosXY
```

Using this technique produces the image in Figure 8-13.

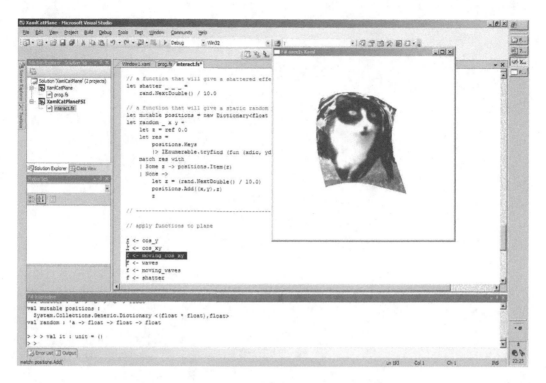

Figure 8-13. *Controlling a 3D XAML scene interactively using F# interactive*

The WPF framework contains lots of types and controls that will take any programmer some time to learn. Fortunately, many resources are available on the Internet to help you do this. A good resource is the NetFx3 WPF site (http://wpf.netfx3.com) and of course the WPF section of MSDN (http://msdn2.microsoft.com/en-us/netframework/aa663326.aspx).

Summary

This chapter provided an overview of various options for creating user interfaces with F#. Because of the scope of this topic, I didn't cover all the options for user interface programming in F#. For example, there are hundreds of third-party components, built on ASP.NET, WinForms, or WPF. These help raise the level of abstraction when creating user interfaces. There are also libraries that offer complete alternative programming models, such as DirectX, which is designed for high-performance 3D graphics, and the GTK# library, which is designed to give better cross-platform support.

The next chapter will take a look at another important programming task—how to access data.

CHAPTER 9

■ ■ ■

Data Access

Since computers are designed to process data, it's a rare program that doesn't require some form of data access, whether it's reading a small configuration file or accessing a full-scale relational database management system. In this chapter, you will investigate the wide range of options that are available for data access in F#.

The System.Configuration Namespace

Whenever you execute any program written in any .NET language, the .NET runtime will automatically check whether a configuration file is available. This is a file with the same name as the executable plus the extension .config that must be placed in the same directory as the executable, meaning the configuration file for MyApp.exe would be MyApp.exe.config. In ASP.NET applications, these files are called web.config files because there is no executable, and they live in the web root. These files are useful for storing settings that you want to be able to change without recompiling the application—a classic example of this is a connection string to a database. You should be careful not to store values that are specific to a user in the configuration file, because any changes to the file will affect all users of the application. The best place to store user-specific settings is in a relational database. I'll cover relational database access in the "ADO.NET" section.

■**Note** You can use configuration files to do much more than store data for your program to access. You can also use them to control various settings with the .NET Framework, such as controlling which version of the .NET runtime should be used or directing a program to automatically look for a new version of a .dll. I don't cover this functionality in this chapter, but you can find more information online at http://strangelights.com/FSharp/Foundations/default.aspx/FSharpFoundations.Config.

The System.Configuration namespace provides an easy way to access configuration values, and the simplest way of accessing configuration data is with ConfigurationManager. The next example shows how to load a simple key-value pair from a configuration file. Imagine you have the following configuration file and want to read "MySetting" from the file:

```
<configuration>
  <appSettings>
    <add key="MySetting" value="An important string" />
  </appSettings>
</configuration>
```

The following code loads the setting by using ConfigurationManager's static AppSettings property:

```
#light
#r "System.Configuration.dll";;
open System.Configuration

let setting = ConfigurationManager.AppSettings.Item("MySetting")

print_string setting
```

The result is as follows:

```
An important string
```

Note The way to access these values in .NET version 1.1 was through the ConfigurationSettings type in System.dll. This type is still available in .NET 2.0 but has been depreciated, so it is best to avoid using it.

Since the most common use for these name-value pairs is to store connection strings, it is customary to use a separate section specifically for this purpose to help separate them from other configuration settings. The providerName property allows you to store information about which database provider the connection string should be used with. The next example shows how to load the connection string "MyConnectionString" from the following configuration file:

```
<configuration>
  <connectionStrings>
    <add
      name="MyConnectionString"
      connectionString=" Data Source=server;
          Initial Catalog=pubs;
          Integrated Security=SSPI;"
      providerName="System.Data.SqlClient" />
  </connectionStrings>
</configuration>
```

The following example loads the connection string via another static property on the ConfigurationManager class, the ConnectionString property. This is a collection that gives access to a type called ConnectionStringSettings, which has a ConnectionString property giving access to the connection string and a `ProviderName` property giving access to the provider name string.

```
#light
#r "System.Configuration.dll";;

let connectionStringDetails =
    ConfigurationManager.ConnectionStrings.Item("MyConnectionString")
let connectionString = connectionStringDetails.ConnectionString
let providerName = connectionStringDetails.ProviderName

printfn "%s\r\n%s"
    connectionString
    providerName
```

The results are as follows:

```
Data Source=server;
        Initial Catalog=pubs;
        Integrated Security=SSPI;
System.Data.SqlClient
```

■ **Caution** Notice that because I added spaces and newline characters to the configuration file to improve the formatting, these were also added to the connection string, which can be seen when output to the console. Most libraries consuming the connection string will correct for this, but some may not, so be careful when formatting your configuration file.

You'll explore the possibility of choosing between different relational databases at runtime in "The EntLib Data Access Block" section later in this chapter.

It's also possible to load configuration files associated with other programs or web applications and even `machine.config`, which contains the default settings for .NET on a particular machine. These files can be queried, updated, and then saved. The following sample shows how to open `machine.config` and enumerate the various sections within it:

```
#light
#r "System.Configuration.dll";;

let config =
    ConfigurationManager.OpenMachineConfiguration()

for x in config.Sections do
  print_endline x.SectionInformation.Name
```

The results, when executed on my machine, are as follows:

```
system.data
windows
system.webServer
mscorlib
system.data.oledb
system.data.oracleclient
system.data.sqlclient
configProtectedData
satelliteassemblies
system.data.dataset
startup
system.data.odbc
system.diagnostics
runtime
system.codedom
system.runtime.remoting
connectionStrings
assemblyBinding
appSettings
system.windows.forms
```

This section has shown how to work with configuration files, a particular kind of XML file. The next section will show how to use the System.Xml namespace to work with any kind of XML file.

The System.IO Namespace

The main purpose of the System.IO namespace is to provide types that give easy access to the files and directories of the operating system's file store, although it also provides ways of writing to memory and network streams too.

The namespace offers two main ways to deal with files and directories. FileInfo and DirectoryInfo objects are used to get or alter information about a file or directory. There are also File and Directory classes that offer the same functionality but that are exposed as static members that require the filename to be passed to each method. Generally, you will use the File and Directory classes if you want a single piece of information about a file system object and use the FileInfo and DirectoryInfo classes if you need lots of information about a single file system object. The two techniques are complementary; for example, you might use the Directory type to get information about all the files in a directory and then use the FileInfo object to find out the name and other information about the file. Here's an example of doing this:

```
#light
open System.IO

let files = Directory.GetFiles(@"c:\")
```

```
for filepath in files do
    let file = new FileInfo(filepath)
    printfn "%s\t%d\t%O"
        file.Name
        file.Length
        file.CreationTime
```

The results, when executed on my machine, are as follows:

addadmin.bat	95	01/10/2003	02:08:10
ATTDialer.doc	297472	03/11/2003	20:12:54
AUTOEXEC.BAT	0	12/05/2003	20:21:21
avapower.gif	1056	07/07/2004	01:27:05
boot.ini	211	12/05/2003	12:58:01
CONFIG.SYS	0	12/05/2003	20:21:21
dpst.bat	17	01/10/2003	02:08:10
imagefaq.bat	21	01/10/2003	02:08:10
IO.SYS	0	12/05/2003	20:21:22
MSDOS.SYS	0	12/05/2003	20:21:22
NTDETECT.COM	47564	23/08/2001	14:00:00
Ntldr	250032	23/08/2001	14:00:00
NavCClt.Log	35152	13/05/2003	00:44:02

The namespace also provides an extremely convenient way to work with the contents of files. Files are open and are represented as streams, which provide a way to read or write bytes, characters, or strings from a file. Opening a file and reading text from it could not be simpler—just call the File.OpenText method, and you get access to a StreamReader object that allows you to read the file line by line. The following example demonstrates reading a comma-separated file, containing three columns of data:

```
#light
open System.IO
//test.csv:
//Apples,12,25
//Oranges,12,25
//Bananas,12,25
using (File.OpenText("test.csv"))
    (fun f ->
        while not f.EndOfStream do
            let line = f.ReadLine()
            let items = line.Split([|',','|])
            printfn "%O     %O     %O"
                items.[0]
                items.[1]
                items.[2])
```

The results, when executed with the text file in the comments, are as follows:

Apples	12	25
Oranges	12	25
Bananas	12	25

> **Note** The `File.OpenText` method assumes your file has a UTF-8 encoding. If your file does not use this text encoding, you should call the `OpenRead` method and then wrap the resulting `FileStream` object in a `StreamReader`, passing in the appropriated encoding object. For example, if your file used the encoding Windows-1252 for Western languages, you should open it via `new StreamReader(File.OpenRead ("accents.txt"), Encoding.GetEncoding(1252))`.

The System.Xml Namespace

XML has become a popular data format for a number of reasons, probably because for most people it is a convenient format to represent their data and because the resulting files tend to be reasonably human readable. Programmers tend to like that you can have both files be unstructured (that is, don't follow a set pattern) or have the files be structured and have the data conform to a contract defined by an *XSD schema*. Programmers also like the convenience of being able to query the data using *XPath*, which means that writing custom parsers for new data formats is rarely necessary, and files can quickly be converted between different XML formats using the powerful *XSLT language* to transform data.

The `System.Xml` namespace contains classes for working with XML files using all the different technologies I have described and more besides this. You'll look at the most common way to work with XML files—the .NET implementation of the W3C recommendation for the XML Document Object Model (DOM), which is generally represented by the class `XmlDocument`. The first example in this section will read information from the following short XML file, `fruits.xml`:

```
<fruits>
  <apples>2</apples>
  < oranges >3</oranges>
  <bananas>1</bananas>
</fruits>
```

The following code loads `fruits.xml`, binds it to the identifier `fruitsDoc`, and then uses a loop to display the data:

```
#light
open System.Xml

let fruitsDoc =
    let temp = new XmlDocument()
    temp.Load("fruits.xml")
    temp
```

```
let fruits = fruitsDoc.SelectNodes("/fruits/*")

for x in fruits do
    printfn "%s = %s " x.Name x.InnerText
```

The results are as follows:

```
apples = 2
oranges = 3
bananas = 1
```

The next example looks at how to build up an XML document and then write it to disk. Say you have a set of data, bound to the identifier animals, and you'd like to write it as XML to the file animals.xml. You start by creating a new XmlDocument object, and then you build the document by creating the root node via a call to the XmlDocument instance member CreateElement method and then append to the document object using its AppendChild method. The rest of the document is built up by enumerating over the animals list and creating and appending nodes.

```
#light
open System.Xml

let animals = [ "ants", "6"; "spiders", "8"; "cats", "4" ]

let animalsDoc =
    let temp = new XmlDocument()
    let root = temp.CreateElement("animals")
    temp.AppendChild(root) |> ignore
    animals
    |> List.iter (fun x ->
        let element = temp.CreateElement(fst x)
        element.InnerText <- (snd x)
        root.AppendChild(element) |> ignore )
    temp

animalsDoc.Save("animals.xml")
```

The result of this code is a file, animals.xml, containing the following XML document:

```
<animals>
  <ants>6</ants>
  <spiders>8</spiders>
  <cats>4</cats>
</animals>
```

The System.Xml namespace is large, with many interesting classes to help you work with XML data. Table 9-1 describes some of the most useful ones.

Table 9-1. *Summary of Useful Classes from the* System.XML *Namespace*

Class	Description
System.Xml.XmlDocument	The Microsoft .NET implementation of the W3C's XML DOM.
System.Xml.XmlNode	This class can't be created directly but is often used; it is the result of the XmlDocument's SelectSingle node method.
System.Xml.XmlNodeList	This class is a collection of nodes and is the result of the XmlDocument's SelectNode method.
System.Xml.XmlTextReader	This provides forward-only, read-only access to an XML document. Although not as easy to use as the XmlDocument class, it does not require the whole document to be loaded into memory. When working with big documents, it can often provide better performance than the XmlDocument.
System.Xml.XmlTextWriter	This class provides a forward-only way to write to an XML document. If you must start your XML document from scratch, this is often the easiest way to create it.
System.Xml.Schema.XmlSchema	This provides a way of loading an XML schema into memory and then allows the user to validate XML documents with it.
System.Xml.Serialization.XmlSerializer	This allows a user to serialize .NET objects directly to and from XML. However, unlike the BinarySerializer available elsewhere in the framework, this class serializes only public fields.
System.Xml.XPath.XPathDocument	This class is designed to be the most efficient way to work with XPath expressions. This class is just the wrapper for the XML document; the programmer must use the XPathExpression and XPathNavigator to actually do the work.
System.Xml.XPath.XPathExpression	This class represents an XPath expression to be used with an XPathDocument; it can be compiled to make it more efficient when used repeatedly.
System.Xml.XPath.XPathNavigator	Once an XPathExpression has been executed against the XPathDocument, this class can be used to navigate the results; the advantage of this class is that it pulls only one node at a time into memory, making it efficient in terms of memory.
System.Xml.Xsl.XslTransform	This class can be used to transform XML using XSLT style sheets.

ADO.NET

Relational database management systems are the most pervasive form of data storage. ADO.NET, in System.Data and associated namespaces, makes it easy to access relational data. In this section, you'll look at various ways you can use F# with ADO.NET.

Note All database providers use a connection string to specify the database to which to connect. You can find a nice summary of the connection strings you need to know at http://www.connectionstrings.com.

All examples in this section use the AdventureWorks sample database and SQL Server 2005 Express Edition, both freely available for download from http://www.microsoft.com. It should be easy to port these samples to other relational databases. To use this database with SQL Server 2005 Express Edition, you can use the following connection settings or an adaptation of them appropriate to your system:

```
<connectionStrings>
  <add
    name="MyConnection"
    connectionString="
        Database=AdventureWorks;
        Server=.\SQLExpress;
        Integrated Security=SSPI;
        AttachDbFilename=
C:\Program Files\Microsoft SQL Server\MSSQL.1\MSSQL\Data\AdventureWorks_Data.mdf"
    providerName="System.Data.SqlClient" />
</connectionStrings>
```

I'll discuss options for accessing other relational databases in the section "ADO.NET Extensions." The following example shows a simple way of accessing a database:

```
#light
#r "System.Configuration.dll";;
open System.Configuration
open System.Data
open System.Data.SqlClient

let connectionSetting =
    ConfigurationManager.ConnectionStrings.Item("MyConnection")
let connectionString =
    connectionSetting.ConnectionString

using (new SqlConnection(connectionString))
    (fun connection ->
        let command =
            let temp = connection.CreateCommand()
            temp.CommandText <- "select * from Person.Contact"
            temp.CommandType <- CommandType.Text
            temp

        connection.Open()
```

```
            using (command.ExecuteReader())
                (fun reader ->
                    let title = reader.GetOrdinal("Title")
                    let firstName = reader.GetOrdinal("FirstName")
                    let lastName = reader.GetOrdinal("LastName")
                    let getString (r : #IDataReader) x =
                        if r.IsDBNull(x) then
                            ""
                        else
                            r.GetString(x)
                    while reader.Read() do
                        printfn "%s %s %s"
                            (getString reader title )
                            (getString reader firstName)
                            (getString reader lastName)))
```

The results are as follows:

```
Mr. Gustavo Achong
Ms. Catherine Abel
Ms. Kim Abercrombie
Sr. Humberto Acevedo
Sra. Pilar Ackerman
Ms. Frances Adams
Ms. Margaret Smith
Ms. Carla Adams
Mr. Jay Adams
Mr. Ronald Adina
Mr. Samuel Agcaoili
Mr. James Aguilar
Mr. Robert Ahlering
Mr. François Ferrier
Ms. Kim Akers
...
```

In the previous example, first you find the connection string you are going to use; after this, you create the connection:

```
using (new SqlConnection(connectionString))
```

You wrap it in the using function to ensure it is closed after you have finished what you're doing. The connection is used to create a SqlCommand class and use its CommandText property to specify which command you want to execute:

```
temp.CommandText <- "select * from Person.Contact"
```

Then you execute the command to create a SqlDataReader class that is used to do the work of actually reading from the database:

```
using (command.ExecuteReader())
```

This tool is called through the using function to ensure it is closed correctly.

You probably wouldn't write data access code in F# if you had to write this amount of code for every query. One way to simplify things is to create a library function to execute commands for you, allowing you to parameterize which command to run and which connection to use.

The following example shows how to write such a function. You implement the execCommand function via Seq.generate_using, which is a way of generating an IEnumerable sequence collection. The generate_using function takes two arguments. The first is a function to open a connection to the database and is called each time you enumerate the resulting collection. This function is called the *opener* and could just as well open a connection to a file. The second is a function to generate the items in the collection, called the *generator*. In this case, this creates a Dictionary object for a row of data.

```
#light
#r "System.Configuration.dll";;

open System.Configuration
open System.Collections.Generic
open System.Data
open System.Data.SqlClient
open System.Data.Common
open System

/// Create and open an SqlConnection object using the connection string found
/// in the configuration file for the given connection name
let openSQLConnection(connName:string) =
    let connSetting = ConfigurationManager.ConnectionStrings.Item(connName)
    let connString = connSetting.ConnectionString
    let conn = new SqlConnection(connString)
    conn.Open();
    conn

/// Create and execute a read command for a connection using
/// the connection string found in the configuration file
/// for the given connection name
let openConnectionReader connName cmdString =
    let conn = openSQLConnection(connName)
    let cmd = conn.CreateCommand(CommandText=cmdString,
                                 CommandType = CommandType.Text)
    let reader = cmd.ExecuteReader(CommandBehavior.CloseConnection)
    reader
```

```
let readOneRow (reader: #DbDataReader) =
    if reader.Read() then
        let dict = new Dictionary<string, obj>()
        for x = 0 to (reader.FieldCount - 1) do
            dict.Add(reader.GetName(x), reader.Item(x))
        Some(dict)
    else
        None

let execCommand  (connName : string) (cmdString : string) =
    Seq.generate_using
        // This function gets called to open a connection and create a reader
        (fun () -> openConnectionReader connName cmdString)
        // This function gets called to read a single item in
        // the enumerable for a reader/connection pair
        (fun reader -> readOneRow(reader))
```

After defining a function such as execCommand, accessing a database becomes pretty easy.
You call execCommand, passing the chosen connection and command, and then enumerate the
results. This is as follows:

```
let contactsTable =
    execCommand
        "MyConnection"
        "select * from Person.Contact"

for row in contactsTable do
    for col in row.Keys do
        printfn "%s = %O" col (row.Item(col))
```

The results are as follows:

```
...
ContactID = 18
NameStyle = False
Title = Ms.
FirstName = Anna
MiddleName = A.
LastName = Albright
Suffix =
EmailAddress = anna0@adventure-works.com
EmailPromotion = 1
Phone = 197-555-0143
PasswordHash = 6Hwr3vf9bo8CYMDbLuUt78TXCr182Vf8Zf0+uil0ANw=
PasswordSalt = SPfSr+w=
AdditionalContactInfo =
rowguid = b6e43a72-8f5f-4525-b4c0-ee84d764e86f
ModifiedDate = 01/07/2002 00:00:00
...
```

One thing you should be careful about when dealing with relational databases is ensuring that the connection is closed in a timely manner. Closing the connection quickly makes the connection available to other database users, improving concurrent access. Let's look at how the previous sample creates connections and how they are "cleaned up" automatically. In the previous example, the opener function openConnectionReader is called every time the collection is enumerated using Seq.iter. This uses an IEnumerator object to iterate the data, which in turn uses the generator function to generate individual results. Each call to Seq.iter creates one SqlDataReader and one SqlDataReader object. These must be closed at the end of the iteration or if the iteration terminates abruptly for some reason. Fortunately, the F# library implementation of Seq.iter and Seq.generate_using are careful to invoke the right functions to clean up resources on both complete and partial iterations. They do this by calling IDisposable.Dispose methods on the intermediate IEnumerator objects, which in turn cause the SqlDataReader to be closed. You must also close the corresponding SqlConnection object, which is done by linking the closing of the database connection to the closing of the SqlDataReader:

```
command.ExecuteReader(CommandBehavior.CloseConnection)
```

To avoid keeping the connection open for too long, you should avoid complicated or time-consuming operations while iterating the resulting IEnumerable collection, and you should especially avoid any user interaction with the collection. For example, rewriting the previous example so the user can move on to the next record by pressing Enter would be bad for database performance, as shown here:

```
for row in contactsTable do
    for col in row.Keys do
        printfn "%s = %O" col (row.Item(col))
    printfn "Press <enter> to see next record"
    read_line() |> ignore
```

If you want to use the collection more than once or let the user interact with it, you should generally convert it to a list or an array; an example of this is as follows:

```
let contactsTable =
  execCommand
        "select * from Person.Contact"
        "MyConnection"

let contactsList = Seq.to_list contactsTable
```

Although connections will be closed when the cursors are garbage collected, this generally takes too long, especially if a system is under stress. For example, if the code you are writing will run in a server application that will handle lots of concurrent users, then not closing connections will cause errors because the server will run out of database connections.

The EntLib Data Access Block

The Enterprise Library (EntLib) is a library produced by the Microsoft Patterns and Practices department and is available for download at http://www.microsoft.com. This section uses EntLib 2.0. It includes a *data access block*, which is designed to help programmers conform to best practices when writing data access code.

EntLib includes a configuration console, which allows you to configure connection strings without having to deal directly with the XML .config file. Figure 9-1 shows the configuration console.

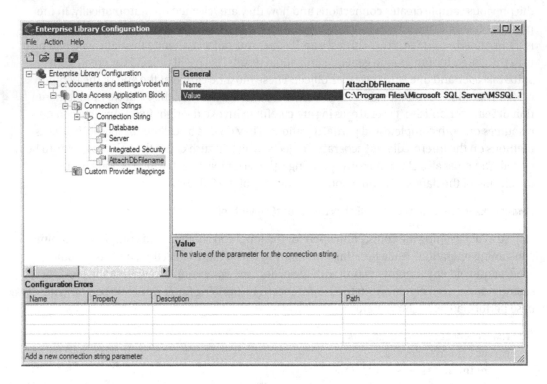

Figure 9-1. *The enterprise library configuration console*

EntLib simplifies data access by allowing you to create an instance of the Database class that is based on the connection string and provider configured in the <connectionStrings> section in the .config file. This Database class then allows you to execute queries against the database with minimal effort. Further, because you don't directly create the ADO.NET objects, you can change which type of provider you want to use just by changing the configuration file. I'll discuss how this works in the section "ADO.NET Extensions" later in the chapter.

The following example shows how to use EntLib to execute a stored procedure, "uspGetBillOfMaterials", against the configured AdventureWorks database:

```
#light
#r "Microsoft.Practices.EnterpriseLibrary.Data.dll";;
open System
open Microsoft.Practices.EnterpriseLibrary.Data

let database = DatabaseFactory.CreateDatabase()
```

```
let reader = database.ExecuteReader(
    "uspGetBillOfMaterials",
    [| box 316; box (new DateTime(2006,1,1)) |])

while reader.Read() do
    for x = 0 to (reader.FieldCount - 1) do
        printfn "%s = %O"
            (reader.GetName(x))
            (reader.Item(x))
```

The results are as follows:

```
ProductAssemblyID = 316
ComponentID = 486
ComponentDesc = Metal Sheet 5
TotalQuantity = 1,00
StandardCost = 0,0000
ListPrice = 0,0000
BOMLevel = 4
RecursionLevel = 0
```

In my experience, EntLib can help you reduce the amount of data access code you need to write and assist you in changing between the types of databases you are using.

Data Binding

Data binding is the process of mapping a value or set of values to a user interface control. The data does not particularly need to be from a relational database, but it is generally from some system external to the program, and the process of accessing this data and transforming it into a state where it can be bound is more complicated than the binding itself, which is straightforward. This is why I cover this topic in this chapter rather than in Chapter 8. The next example shows how to bind data from a database table to a combo box:

```
#light
#r "Microsoft.Practices.EnterpriseLibrary.Data.dll";;
open System
open System.Collections.Generic
open System.Data
open System.Windows.Forms
open Microsoft.Practices.EnterpriseLibrary.Data

let opener commandString =
    let database = DatabaseFactory.CreateDatabase()
    database.ExecuteReader(CommandType.Text, commandString)
```

```
let generator (reader : IDataReader) =
    if reader.Read() then
        let dict = new Dictionary<string, obj>()
        for x = 0 to (reader.FieldCount - 1) do
            dict.Add(reader.GetName(x), reader.Item(x))
        Some(dict)
    else
        None

let execCommand (commandString : string) =
    Seq.generate_using
        (fun () -> opener commandString)
        (fun r -> generator r)

let contactsTable =
    execCommand
        "select top 10 * from Person.Contact"

let contacts =
    [| for row in contactsTable ->
            Printf.sprintf "%O %O"
                (row.Item("FirstName"))
                (row.Item("LastName")) |]

let form =
    let temp = new Form()
    let combo = new ComboBox(Top=8, Left=8, DataSource=contacts)
    temp.Controls.Add(combo)
    temp

Application.Run(form)
```

Figure 9-2 shows the resulting form.

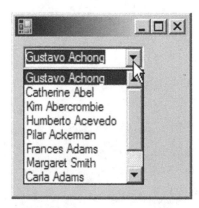

Figure 9-2. *A data-bound combo box*

If you break the previous example down a bit, first you execute the query:

```
let contactsTable =
    execCommand
        "select top 10 * from Person.Contact"
```

You then need to turn the resulting IEnumerable collection into something suitable to be bound to the combo box; you do this by first grabbing the important members, then mapping them into a string collection, and finally converting it to an array. Then you must bind the collection to the control that will display it; you do this by setting the control's DataSource property:

```
combo.DataSource <- contacts
```

Although you've looked only at the ComboBox class, most Windows and web controls can be data bound in a similar way. These include the ListBox and CheckListBox classes. Next, you'll look at binding data to a more complicated control, the DataGridView class.

Data Binding and the DataGridView

The DataGridView control, unlike the controls you saw in the previous section, can display more than one column; the data must be formatted in such a way that the data grid knows which columns to display. You can achieve this in two ways. One is to bind the DataGridView to a DataTable. The other is to bind the grid to a list of objects that have properties; the various properties will become the grid's columns.

Binding to a DataSet is the simpler solution, as in the next example:

```
#light
#r "Microsoft.Practices.EnterpriseLibrary.Data.dll";;
open System
open System.Collections.Generic
open System.Data
open System.Windows.Forms
open Microsoft.Practices.EnterpriseLibrary.Data

let database = DatabaseFactory.CreateDatabase()

let dataSet = database.ExecuteDataSet
                (CommandType.Text,
                  "select top 10 * from Person.Contact")
let form =
    let temp = new Form()
    let grid = new DataGridView(Dock = DockStyle.Fill)
    temp.Controls.Add(grid)
    grid.DataSource <- dataSet.Tables.Item(0)
    temp

Application.Run(form)
```

Figure 9-3 shows the results from this example.

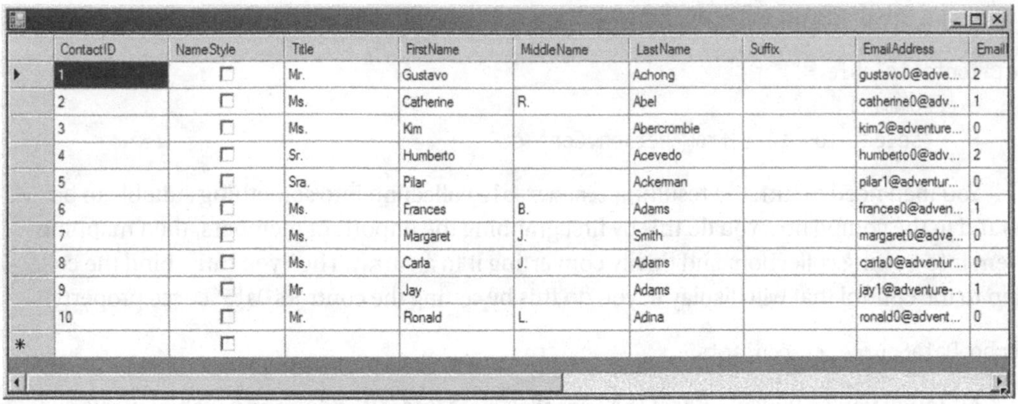

ContactID	NameStyle	Title	FirstName	MiddleName	LastName	Suffix	EmailAddress	Email
1		Mr.	Gustavo		Achong		gustavo0@adve...	2
2		Ms.	Catherine	R.	Abel		catherine0@adv...	1
3		Ms.	Kim		Abercrombie		kim2@adventure...	0
4		Sr.	Humberto		Acevedo		humberto0@adv...	2
5		Sra.	Pilar		Ackerman		pilar1@adventur...	0
6		Ms.	Frances	B.	Adams		frances0@adven...	1
7		Ms.	Margaret	J.	Smith		margaret0@adve...	0
8		Ms.	Carla	J.	Adams		carla0@adventur...	0
9		Mr.	Jay		Adams		jay1@adventure-...	1
10		Mr.	Ronald	L.	Adina		ronald0@advent...	0

Figure 9-3. *A data-bound data grid*

An alternative to using a `DataSet` is to use an F# record type; to do this, you would generally create a generic function that uses reflection to create and populate your strongly typed collection. Here's an example of such a function:

```
#light
#r "Microsoft.Practices.EnterpriseLibrary.Data.dll";;

open System
open System.Collections.Generic
open System.Data
open System.Windows.Forms
open Microsoft.Practices.EnterpriseLibrary.Data

let execCommand<'a> commandString : seq<'a> =
    let opener() =
        let database = DatabaseFactory.CreateDatabase()
        database.ExecuteReader(CommandType.Text, commandString)

    let generator (reader : IDataReader) =
        if reader.Read() then
            let t = (type 'a)
            let props = t.GetProperties()
            let types =
                props
                |> Seq.map (fun x -> x.PropertyType)
                |> Seq.to_array
            let cstr = t.GetConstructor(types)
            let values = Array.create reader.FieldCount (new obj())
            reader.GetValues(values) |> ignore
```

```
        let values =
            values
            |> Array.map
                (fun x -> match x with | :? DBNull -> null | _ -> x)
        Some (cstr.Invoke(values) :?> 'a)
    else
        None

Seq.generate_using
    opener
    generator
```

The first line of the sample uses a technique that you have not met before. Here you explicitly declare your function's type parameter:

```
let execCommand<'a> commandString : seq<'a>
```

You do this so you can explicitly give the generic argument 'a. This is used later in the function to create a type object that you then reflect over:

```
let t = (type 'a)
```

The function is designed to work with an F# record type, whose fields exactly match the fields resulting from the query. If this precondition is not met, then the code will fail, but such preconditions are typical in applications that use reflection in this way.

The function execCommand you have defined is generic and can be used with any query and matching record type. The following example shows how to apply it:

```
type Contact =
  {
    ContactID : Nullable<int> ;
    NameStyle : Nullable<bool> ;
    Title : string ;
    FirstName : string ;
    MiddleName : string ;
    LastName : string ;
    Suffix : string ;
    EmailAddress : string ;
    EmailPromotion : Nullable<int> ;
    Phone: string ;
    PasswordHash : string ;
    PasswordSalt : string ;
    AdditionalContactInfo : string ;
    rowguid : Nullable<Guid> ;
    ModifiedDate : Nullable<DateTime> ;
  }
```

```
let form =
    let temp = new Form()
    let grid = new DataGridView(Dock = DockStyle.Fill)
    temp.Controls.Add(grid)

    let contacts =
        execCommand<Contact> "select top 10 * from Person.Contact"
    let contactsArray = contacts |> Seq.to_array
    grid.DataSource <- contactsArray
    temp

Application.Run(form)
```

The most important point is as follows:

```
let contacts =
    execCommand<Contact> "select top 10 * from Person.Contact"
```

Here you have explicitly declared the type parameter for the generic function execCommand. The results from this example are the same as the previous example and are shown in Figure 9-3.

ADO.NET Extensions

ADO.NET has been successful at providing a set of bases classes and interfaces that others have been able to implement to provide access to their relational database, so most relational databases can be accessed from F# with little effort. You have already met most of these classes, or at least classes that implement the functionality they are intended to provide, and Table 9-2 summarizes the key ones.

Table 9-2. *The Key Classes in ADO.NET*

Class	Description
System.Data.Common.DbConnection	Represents a connection to a particular instance of a relational database; you use classes derived from this class to specify on which database you want the query to be executed.
System.Data.Common.DbCommand	You use classes derived from this base class to configure what query you want to execute against the database, whether it be an actual SQL query or a stored procedure.
System.Data.Common.DbParameter	This class represents the parameters of a query; typically, queries that are parameterized promote reuse in the relational database so execute more efficiently.
System.Data.Common.DbDataReader	Classes derived from this class allow access to the results of a query in a linear manner; use this class for fast access to your results.

Class	Description
System.Data.Common.DbDataAdapter	This class is used to fill a DataSet class with data from a relational database.
System.Data.DataSet	An in-memory representation of a database that can contain tables and relationships between them; unlike the other class in this table, this class is concrete and can be used directly.

The classes in Table 9-2, with the exception of System.Data.DataSet, are all abstract, so you must use concrete implementations of them. For example, here you create an instance of System.Data.SqlClient.SqlConnection, which is an implementation of System.Data.Common. DbConnection, which gives access to a SQL Server database:

```
using (new SqlConnection(connectionString))
```

If you wanted to access an Oracle database, you would simply replace the SqlConnection class with the OracleConnection class. Table 9-3 summarizes some of the most popular libraries and namespaces that implement these classes, although this table is incomplete because the range of providers is large.

Table 9-3. *Database Providers for .NET*

Namespace	DLL	Description
System.Data.Odbc	System.Data.dll	This namespaces allows you to connect to any database that provides drives that support the Open Database Connectivity standard. Most databases provide drivers that support this standard, but they should generally be avoided in favor of a more specific driver, which will probably be more efficient.
System.Data.OleDb	System.Data.dll	OleDb is a COM-based standard for database drivers; again, a huge number of relational databases provide drivers that support this standard, but where possible you should use something more specific. This namespace is often used to connect to Access databases or Excel spreadsheets, which do not have .NET drivers of their own.
System.Data. SqlClient	System.Data.dll	This is the native .NET Microsoft SQL Server driver. It will work with all supported versions of SQL Server and is the de facto choice when working with SQL Server. This has been the namespace used by the examples in this book.
System.Data. OracleClient	System.Data. OracleClient.dll	This is the native .NET provider for the Oracle database created by Microsoft; it is distributed with the .NET Framework.

continued

Table 9-3. *Continued*

Namespace	DLL	Description
Oracle.DataAccess.Client	Oracle.DataAccess.Client.dll	The Oracle data provider for .NET (ODP.NET) is a database provider for .NET developed by Oracle; it is available from www.oracle.com/technology/software/tech/windows/odpnet.
IBM.Data.DB2	IBM.Data.DB2.dll	This is the native .NET provider developed by IBM; it is provided with the distribution of the database.
MySql.Data.MySqlClient	MySql.Data.dll	This is the open source native .NET provider created by the MySQL team. You can download it from dev.mysql.com/downloads/connector/net.
FirebirdSql.Data.FirebirdClient	FirebirdSql.Data.FirebirdClient.dll	This is the native provider for the open source database Firebird; you can download it from www.firebirdsql.org/index.php?op=files&id=netprovider.

To demonstrate how to use the other .NET providers, I will now show an example of connecting to the Firebird employee sample database. To run this sample, you will need to install the Firebird database engine and Firebird .NET provider components from http://www.firebirdsql.org and be running the Firebird database service on your local machine.

```
#light
#I @"C:\Program Files\FirebirdClient";;
#r @"FirebirdSql.Data.FirebirdClient.dll";;
open System.Configuration
open System.Collections.Generic
open System.Data
open FirebirdSql.Data.FirebirdClient;
open System.Data.Common
open System

let connectionString =
    @"Database=C:\Program Files\Firebird\" +
    @"Firebird_2_0\examples\empbuild\EMPLOYEE.FDB;" +
    @"User=SYSDBA;" + "Password=masterkey;" +
    @"Dialect=3;" + "Server=localhost";

let openFBConnection() =
    let connection = new FbConnection (connectionString)
    connection.Open();
    connection
```

```
let openConnectionReader cmdString =
    let conn = openFBConnection()
    let cmd = conn.CreateCommand(CommandText=cmdString,
                                 CommandType = CommandType.Text)
    let reader = cmd.ExecuteReader(CommandBehavior.CloseConnection)
    reader

let readOneRow (reader: #DbDataReader) =
    if reader.Read() then
        let dict = new Dictionary<string, obj>()
        for x = 0 to (reader.FieldCount - 1) do
            dict.Add(reader.GetName(x), reader.Item(x))
        Some(dict)
    else
        None

let execCommand  (cmdString : string) =
    Seq.generate_using
            // This function gets called to open a conn and create a reader
            (fun () -> openConnectionReader cmdString)
            // This function gets called to read a single item in
            // the enumerable for a reader/conn pair
            (fun reader -> readOneRow(reader))

let employeeTable =
    execCommand
        "select * from Employee"

for row in employeeTable do
    for col in row.Keys do
        printfn "%s = %O " col (row.Item(col))
```

The results of this example are as follows:

```
...
EMP_NO = 145

FIRST_NAME = Mark

LAST_NAME = Guckenheimer

PHONE_EXT = 221
```

```
HIRE_DATE = 02/05/1994 00:00:00

DEPT_NO = 622

JOB_CODE = Eng

JOB_GRADE = 5

JOB_COUNTRY = USA

SALARY = 32000

FULL_NAME = Guckenheimer, Mark
```

You will observe that very little changes were needed to convert the SQL Server Adventure-Works contact table example given earlier in the chapter to an example that executed a query against the Firebird employee example database.

Introducing LINQ

Language-Integrated Query (LINQ) is the next generation of .NET data access technology. It borrows heavily from functional programming, so it fits very nicely with F#.

■**Note** All examples in this section and other sections about LINQ are based on the Community Technology Preview of May 2006, the Microsoft .NET LINQ Preview (May 2006), and the F# LINQ bindings that match this release. If you use the examples with later versions of LINQ, you will have to make changes to the code.

At its heart, LINQ is a set of libraries for manipulating collections that implement the IEnumerable<T> interface, a lot like F#'s Seq module, which was discussed in Chapter 7. The idea is that you can use this library to query any in-memory collection, whether the data comes from a database, an XML file, or just objects returned from another API.

Although the concepts implemented in the LINQ library will be familiar to you by now, they follow a slightly different naming convention that is based on SQL. For instance, the equivalent of Seq.map is called Sequence.Select, and the equivalent Seq.filter is called Sequence.Where. The next example shows how to use this library. The first step is to import the methods exposed by the LINQ library into a more usable form; this is how to do that:

```
#light
#I "C:\Program Files\LINQ Preview\Bin";;
#r "System.Query.dll";;
open System.Query
open System.Reflection
```

```
// define easier access to LINQ methods
let select f s =  Sequence.Select(s, new Func<_,_>(f))
let where f s =  Sequence.Where(s, new Func<_,_>(f))
let groupBy f s =  Sequence.GroupBy(s, new Func<_,_>(f))
let orderBy f s =  Sequence.OrderBy(s, new Func<_,_>(f))
let count s =  Sequence.Count(s)
```

Once these functions have been imported, they can easily be applied, typically using the pipe forward operator. The following example demonstrates this. It uses the LINQ library to query the string class and group the overloads of its nonstatic methods together.

```
// query string methods using functions
let namesByFunction =
    (type string).GetMethods()
    |> where (fun m -> not m.IsStatic)
    |> groupBy (fun m -> m.Name)
    |> select (fun m -> m.Key, count m)
    |> orderBy (fun (_, m) -> m)

namesByFunction
|> Seq.iter (fun (name, count) -> printfn "%s - %i" name count)
```

The results are as follows:

```
ToLowerInvariant - 1
TrimEnd - 1
GetHashCode - 1
TrimStart - 1
GetEnumerator - 1
GetType - 1
GetTypeCode - 1
ToUpperInvariant - 1
Clone - 1
CopyTo - 1
get_Length - 1
Insert - 1
get_Chars - 1
PadLeft - 2
CompareTo - 2
PadRight - 2
ToUpper - 2
ToLower - 2
ToString - 2
Trim - 2
Remove - 2
ToCharArray - 2
Substring - 2
IsNormalized - 2
```

```
Normalize - 2
Replace - 2
IndexOfAny - 3
EndsWith - 3
Equals - 3
StartsWith - 3
LastIndexOfAny - 3
Split - 6
LastIndexOf - 9
IndexOf - 9
```

Using LINQ to XML

The goal of LINQ to XML is to provide an XML object model that works well with LINQ's functional style of programming. Table 9-4 summarizes the important classes within this namespace.

Table 9-4. *A Summary of the Classes Provided by LINQ to XML*

Class Name	Parent Class	Description
XNode		This class provides the basic functionality that is applicable to all nodes in an XML document.
XContainer	XNode	This class provides the functionality for XML nodes that can contain other nodes.
XDocument	XContainer	This class represents the XML document as a whole.
XElement	XContainer	This class represents an element in the XML document, that is, a regular XML node that can be a tag, <myTag />, or can possibly contain other tags or an attribute, such as myAttribute="myVal".
XDocumentType	XNode	This class represents a document type tag.
XProcessInstruction	XNode	This class represents a processing instruction, which is a tag of the form <? name instruction ?>.
XText	XNode	This class represents text contained within the XML document.
XName		This class represents the name of a tag or an attribute.

To show how to use this object model, you can revise the example from the previous section to output XML instead of plain text. LINQ to XML makes this easy to do; first you modify the select statement to return an XElement instead of a tuple:

```
|> select (fun m -> new XElement(XName.Get(m.Key), count m))
```

This gives an array of XElements that you can then use to initialize another XElement, which provides the root of the document. It is then just a matter of calling the root XElement's ToString method, which will provide the XML in the form of a string.

```
#light
#I "C:\Program Files\LINQ Preview\Bin";;
#r "System.Query.dll";;
#r "System.Xml.XLinq.dll";;
open System.Query
open System.Reflection
open System.Xml.XLinq

// define easier access to LINQ methods
let select f s =  Sequence.Select(s, new Func<_,_>(f))
let where f s =  Sequence.Where(s, new Func<_,_>(f))
let groupBy f s =  Sequence.GroupBy(s, new Func<_,_>(f))
let orderBy f s =  Sequence.OrderBy(s, new Func<_,_>(f))
let count s =  Sequence.Count(s)

// query string methods using functions
let namesByFunction =
    (type string).GetMethods()
    |> where (fun m -> not m.IsStatic)
    |> groupBy (fun m -> m.Name)
    |> select (fun m -> new XElement(XName.Get(m.Key), count m))
    |> orderBy (fun e -> int_of_string e.Value)

let overloadsXml =
    new XElement(XName.Get("MethodOverloads"), namesByFunction)

print_endline (overloadsXml.ToString())
```

The results of this code, when compiled and executed, are as follows:

```
<MethodOverloads>
  <Contains>1</Contains>
  <ToLowerInvariant>1</ToLowerInvariant>
  <TrimEnd>1</TrimEnd>
  <GetHashCode>1</GetHashCode>
  <TrimStart>1</TrimStart>
  <GetEnumerator>1</GetEnumerator>
  <GetType>1</GetType>
  <GetTypeCode>1</GetTypeCode>
  <ToUpperInvariant>1</ToUpperInvariant>
  <Clone>1</Clone>
  <CopyTo>1</CopyTo>
  <get_Length>1</get_Length>
  <Insert>1</Insert>
  <get_Chars>1</get_Chars>
  <PadLeft>2</PadLeft>
  <CompareTo>2</CompareTo>
  <PadRight>2</PadRight>
```

```
    <ToUpper>2</ToUpper>
    <ToLower>2</ToLower>
    <ToString>2</ToString>
    <Trim>2</Trim>
    <Remove>2</Remove>
    <ToCharArray>2</ToCharArray>
    <Substring>2</Substring>
    <IsNormalized>2</IsNormalized>
    <Normalize>2</Normalize>
    <Replace>2</Replace>
    <IndexOfAny>3</IndexOfAny>
    <EndsWith>3</EndsWith>
    <Equals>3</Equals>
    <StartsWith>3</StartsWith>
    <LastIndexOfAny>3</LastIndexOfAny>
    <Split>6</Split>
    <LastIndexOf>9</LastIndexOf>
    <IndexOf>9</IndexOf>
</MethodOverloads>
```

Using LINQ to SQL

LINQ to SQL is designed to allow data access to relational databases. It does this through a combination of code generation and the ability to quote code. For the code generation, LINQ to SQL provides a tool called SqlMetal.exe, which will generate a code version of your relational database; this code version of your database is an object model where the tables become classes with properties representing their columns. Quoting code means the ability to have the compile transform a section of code into data structure called an *expression tree*; you first came across this technique in Chapter 6, but this is the first time you will see it put into real use. The quoted code will be transformed into SQL that can then be executed on the database.

The first step in working with LINQ to ADO.NET is to generate a code version of your database. To do this, you would use the following command line, which generates a code version of the AdventureWorks database that is running on the local version of SQL Server Express:

```
SqlMetal.exe /server:.\SQLEXPRESS /database:AdventureWorks /code:AdWorks.cs
/language:csharp
```

The C# classes that represent the database's objects are generated, but you do not need to know C# to work with it, because you only ever use a compiled version of the code, just like using any other .NET library.

This example relies on an example LINQ library distributed with F# that you can find in the \samples\fsharp\FLinq directory of the distribution. This library also provides useful functions that your DLINQ library requires; first it imports the .NET methods, and then it transforms them into F# methods. The other function it provides is to transform the F# expression trees into the trees used by DLINQ. The library is distributed as a sample, rather than being integrated into the

F# libraries, because the F# team did not want to introduce a binary dependency onto something as experimental as LINQ. Once LINQ is released and part of the .NET Framework, the functionalities provided by this sample library will be migrated into the F# libraries.

The following example shows how to use DLINQ in F#. It shows two powerful features of DLINQ: the ability to have your F# code transformed into a SQL query and the ability to create instances of rows without having to use reflection, like you did for the data binding example earlier in the chapter:

```
#light
#r "Microsoft.Practices.EnterpriseLibrary.Data.dll";;
#r "flinq.dll";;
#r "AdventureWorks.dll";;
#r "System.Data.DLinq.dll";;
#r "System.Query.dll";;

open System.Windows.Forms
open Microsoft.FSharp.Quotations.Typed
open Microsoft.FSharp.Bindings.DLinq.Query
open Microsoft.Practices.EnterpriseLibrary.Data

module sOps = Microsoft.FSharp.Bindings.Linq.SequenceOps

let database = DatabaseFactory.CreateDatabase()
let adventureWorks = new AdventureWorks(database.CreateConnection())

type Person =
    { Title : string ;
      FirstName : string ;
      LastName : string ; }

let contacts =
    adventureWorks.Person.Contact
    |> where « fun c -> c.FirstName = "Robert" »
    |> sOps.select
        (fun c ->
            { Title = c.Title ;
              FirstName = c.FirstName;
              LastName = c.LastName })
    |> Seq.to_array

let form =
    let temp = new Form()
    let grid = new DataGridView(Dock = DockStyle.Fill)
    temp.Controls.Add(grid)
    grid.DataSource <- contacts
    temp

Application.Run(form)
```

■**Caution** If you want to use guillemets in your code, as in the expression « `fun c -> c.FirstName =` `"Robert"` », then you must save the file as UTF-8.

Figure 9-4 shows that the results from both examples are the same.

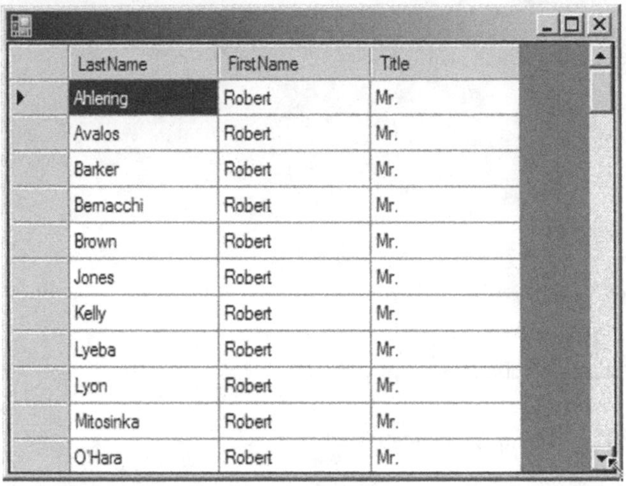

Figure 9-4. *Data grid containing the results of a DLINQ query*

Summary

This chapter has looked at the options for data access in F#. It has shown that the combination of F# with .NET libraries is powerful yet straightforward, no matter what your data source is. The next chapter will look at the related topic of how applications exchange data to become *distributed applications*.

CHAPTER 10

■ ■ ■

Distributed Applications

Applications that use networks, called *distributed applications*, become more important every day. Fortunately, the .NET BCL and other libraries offer many constructs that make communicating over a network easy, so creating distributed applications in F# is straightforward.

Networking Overview

Several types of distributed applications exist; they're generally classified into either *client-server* applications, in which clients make requests to a central server, or *peer-to-peer* applications, in which computers exchange data among themselves. In this chapter, you'll focus on building client-server applications, since these are currently more common. Whichever type of distributed application you want to build, the way computers exchange data is controlled by a protocol. A *protocol* is a standard that defines the rules for communication over a network.

Building a network-enabled application is generally considered one of the most challenging tasks a programmer can perform, with good reason. When building a network application, you must consider three important requirements:

Scalability: The application must remain responsive when used by many users concurrently; typically this means extensive testing and profiling of your server code to check that it performs when a high load is placed on it. You can find more information about profiling code in Chapter 12.

Fault tolerance: Networks are inherently unreliable, and you shouldn't write code that assumes that the network will always be there. If you do, your applications will be very frustrating to end users. Every application should go to lengths to ensure communication failures are handled smoothly, which means giving the user appropriate feedback, displaying error messages, and perhaps offering diagnostic or retry facilities. Do not let your application crash because of a network failure. You should also consider data consistency (that is, can you be sure that all updates necessary to keep data consistent reached the target computer?). Using transactions and a relational database as a data store can help with this. Depending on the type of application, you might also want to consider building an offline mode where the user is offered access to locally stored data and network requests are queued up until the network comes back online. A good example of this kind of facility is the offline mode that most email clients offer.

Security: Although security should be a concern for every application you write, it becomes a hugely important issue in network programming. This is because when you expose your application to a network, you open it up to attack from any other user of the network; therefore, if you expose your application to the Internet, you might be opening it up to thousands or even millions of potential attackers. Typically you need to think about whether data traveling across the network needs to be secured, either signed to guarantee it has not been tampered with or encrypted to guarantee only the appropriate people can read it. You also need to ensure that the people connecting to your application are who they say they are and are authorized to do what they are requesting to do.

Fortunately, modern programmers don't have to tackle these problems on their own; network protocols can help you tackle these problems. For example, if it is important that no one else on the network reads the data you are sending, you should not attempt to encrypt the data yourself. Instead, you should use a network protocol that offers this facility. These protocols are exposed though components from libraries that implement them for you. The type of protocol, and the library used, is dictated by the requirements of the applications. Some protocols offer encryption and authentication, and others don't. Some are suitable for client-server applications, and others are suitable for peer-to-peer applications. You'll look at the following components and libraries, along with the protocols they implement, in this chapter:

TCP/IP sockets: Provide a great deal of control over what passes over a network for either client-server or peer-to-peer applications

HTTP/HTTPS requests: Support requests from web pages to servers, typically only for client-server applications

Web services: Expose applications so other applications can request services, typically used only for client-server applications

Windows Communication Foundation: Extends web services to support many features required by modern programmers including, but not limited to, security, transactions, and support for either client-server or peer-to-peer applications

A simple way of providing a user interface over a network is to develop a web application. Web applications are not covered here, but you can refer to the ASP.NET sections in Chapter 8.

Using TCP/IP Sockets

TCP/IP sockets provide a low level of control over what crosses over a network. A TCP/IP socket is a logical connection between two computers through which either computer can send or receive data at any time. This connection remains open until it is explicitly closed by either of the computers involved. This provides a high degree of flexibility but raises various issues that you'll examine in this chapter, so unless you really need a very high degree of control, you're better off using the more abstract network protocols you'll look at later in this chapter.

The classes you need in order to work with TCP/IP sockets are contained in the namespace `System.Net`, as summarized in Table 10-1.

Table 10-1. *Classes Required for Working with TCP/IP Sockets*

Class	Description
System.Net.Sockets.TcpListener	This class is used by the server to listen for incoming requests.
System.Net.Sockets.TcpClient	This class is used by both the client and the server to control how data is sent over a network.
System.Net.Sockets.NetworkStream	This class can be used to both send and receive data over a network. It sends bytes over a network, so it is typically wrapped in another stream type to send text.
System.IO.StreamReader	This class can be used to wrap the NetworkStream class in order to read text from it. The StreamReader provides the methods ReadLine and ReadToEnd, which both return a string of the data contained in the stream. Various different text encodings can be used by supplying an instance of the System.Text.Encoding class when the StreamWriter is created.
System.IO.StreamWriter	This class can be used to wrap the NetworkStream class in order to write text to it. The StreamWriter provides the methods Write and WriteLine, which both take a string of the data to be written to the stream. Various different text encodings can be used by supplying an instance of the System.Text.Encoding class when the StreamWriter is created.

In this chapter's first example, you'll build a chat application, consisting of a chat server (shown in Listing 10-1) and a client (shown in Listing 10-2). It is the chat server's job to wait and listen for clients that connect. Once a client connects, it must ask the client to provide a username, and then it must constantly listen for incoming messages from all clients. Once it receives an incoming message, it must push that message out to all clients. It is the job of the client to connect to the server and provide an interface to allow the user to read the messages received and to write messages to send to the other users. The TCP/IP connection works well for this type of application because the connection is always available, and this allows the server to push any incoming messages directly to the client without polling from the client.

Listing 10-1. *A Chat Server*

```
#light
open System
open System.IO
open System.Net
open System.Net.Sockets
open System.Threading
open System.Collections.Generic

type ClientTable() = class
    let clients = new Dictionary<string,StreamWriter>()
```

```fsharp
    /// Add a client and its stream writer
    member t.Add(name,sw:StreamWriter) =
        lock clients (fun () ->
            if clients.ContainsKey(name) then
                sw.WriteLine("ERROR - Name in use already!")
                sw.Close()
            else
                clients.Add(name,sw))

    /// Remove a client and close it, if no one else has done that first
    member t.Remove(name) =
        lock clients (fun () -> clients.Remove(name) |> ignore)

    /// Grab a copy of the current list of clients
    member t.Current =
        lock clients (fun () -> clients.Values |> Seq.to_array)

    /// Check whether a client exists
    member t.ClientExists(name) =
        lock clients (fun () -> clients.ContainsKey(name) |> ignore)


end

type Server() = class

    let clients = new ClientTable()

    let sendMessage name message =
        let combinedMessage =
            Printf.sprintf "%s: %s" name message
        for sw in clients.Current do
            try
                lock sw (fun () ->
                    sw.WriteLine(combinedMessage)
                    sw.Flush())
            with
            | _ -> () // Some clients may fail

    let emptyString s = (s = null || s = "")

    let handleClient (connection : TcpClient) =
        let stream = connection.GetStream()
        let sr = new StreamReader(stream)
        let sw = new StreamWriter(stream)
        let rec requestAndReadName() =
            sw.WriteLine("What is your name? ");
            sw.Flush()
```

```fsharp
        let rec readName() =
            let name = sr.ReadLine()
            if emptyString(name) then
                readName()
            else
                name
        let name = readName()
        if clients.ClientExists(name) then
            sw.WriteLine("ERROR - Name in use already!")
            sw.Flush()
            requestAndReadName()
        else
            name
    let name = requestAndReadName()
    clients.Add(name,sw)

    let rec listen() =
        let text = try Some(sr.ReadLine()) with _ -> None
        match text with
        | Some text ->
            if not (emptyString(text)) then
                sendMessage name text
            Thread.Sleep(1)
            listen()
        | None ->
            clients.Remove name
            sw.Close()

    listen()

let server = new TcpListener(IPAddress.Loopback, 4242)

let rec handleConnections() =
    server.Start()
    if (server.Pending()) then
        let connection = server.AcceptTcpClient()
        printf "New Connection"
        let t = new Thread(fun () -> handleClient connection)
        t.Start()
    Thread.Sleep(1);
    handleConnections()

member server.Start() = handleConnections()
end
(new Server()).Start()
```

Let's work our way through Listing 10-1 starting at the top and working down. The first step is to define a class to help you manage the clients connected to the server. The members Add, Remove, Current, and ClientExists share a mutable dictionary, defined by the binding:

```
let clients = new Dictionary<string,StreamWriter>()
```

This contains a mapping from client names to connections, hidden from other functions in the program. The Current member copies the entries in the map into an array to ensure there is no danger of the list changing while you are enumerating it, which would cause an error. You can still update the collection of clients using Add and Remove, and the updates will become available the next time Current is called. Because the code is multithreaded, the implementation of Add and Remove lock the client collection to ensure no changes to the collection are lost through multiple threads trying to update it at once.

The next function you define, sendMessage, uses the Current member to get the map of clients and enumerates it using a list comprehension, sending the message to each client as you go through the collection. Note here how you lock the StreamWriter class before you write to it:

```
lock sw (fun () ->
    sw.WriteLine(message)
    sw.Flush())
```

This is to stop multiple threads writing to it at once, which would cause the text to appear in a jumbled order on the client's screen.

After defining the emptyString function, which is a useful little function that wraps up some predicate that you use repeatedly, you define the handleClient function, which does the work of handling a client's new connection and is broken down into a series of inner functions. The handleClient function is called by the final function you will define, handleConnections, and will be called on a new thread that has been assigned specifically to handle the open connection. The first thing handleClient does is get the stream that represents the network connection and wrap it in both a StreamReader and a StreamWriter:

```
let stream = connection.GetStream()
let sr = new StreamReader(stream)
let sw = new StreamWriter(stream)
```

Having a separate way to read and write from the stream is useful because the functions that will read and write to the stream are actually quite separate. You have already met the sendMessage function, which is the way messages are sent to clients, and you will later see that a new thread is allocated specifically to read from the client.

The inner function requestAndReadName that you define next in handleClient is fairly straightforward; you just repeatedly ask the user for a name until you find a name that is not an empty or null string and is not already in use. Once you have the client name, you use the addClient function to add it to the collection of clients:

```
let name = requestAndReadName()
addClient name sw
```

The final part of handleConnection is defining the listen function, which is responsible for listening to messages incoming from the client. Here you read some text from the stream, wrapped in a try expression using the option type's Some/None values to indicate whether text was read:

```
let text = try Some(sr.ReadLine()) with _ -> None
```

You then use pattern matching to decide what to do next. If the text was successfully read, then you use the sendMessage function to send that message to all the other clients; otherwise, you remove yourself from the collection of clients and allow the function to exit, which will in turn mean that the thread handling the connections will exit.

■**Note** Although the listen function is recursive and could potentially be called many times, there is no danger of the stack overflowing. This is because the function is tail recursive, meaning that the compiler emits a special tail instruction that tells the .NET runtime that the function should be called without using the stack to store parameters and local variables. Any recursive function defined in F# that has the recursive call as the last thing that happens in the function is tail recursive.

Next you create an instance of the TcpListener class. This is the class that actually does the work of listening to the incoming connections. You normally initialize this with the IP address and the port number on which the server will listen. When you start the listener, you tell it to listen on the IPAddress.Any address so that the listener will listen for all traffic on any of the IP addresses associated with the computer's network adapters; however, because this is just a demonstration application, you tell the TcpListener class to listen to IPAddress.Loopback, meaning it will pick up the request only from the local computer. The port number is how you tell that the network traffic is for your application and not another. Using the TcpListener class, it is possible for only one listener to listen to a port at once. The number you choose is somewhat arbitrary, but you should choose a number greater than 1023, because the port numbers from 0 to 1023 are reserved for specific applications. So, to create a listener on port 4242 that you code, you use the TcpListener instance in the final function you define, handleConnections:

```
let server = new TcpListener(IPAddress.Loopback, 4242)
```

This function is an infinite loop that listens for new clients connecting and creates a new thread to handle them. It's the following code that, once you have a connection, you use to retrieve an instance of the connection and start the new thread to handle it:

```
let connection = server.AcceptTcpClient()
print_endline "New Connection"
let t = new Thread(fun () -> handleClient connection)
t.Start()
```

Now that you understand how the server works, let's take a look at the client, which is in many ways a good deal simpler than the server. Listing 10-2 shows the full code for the client, which is followed by a discussion of how the code works.

Listing 10-2. *A Chat Client*

```
#light
open System
open System.ComponentModel
open System.IO
```

```fsharp
open System.Net.Sockets
open System.Threading
open System.Windows.Forms

let form =
    let temp = new Form()
    temp.Text <- "F# Talk Client"

    temp.Closing.Add(fun e ->
        Application.Exit()
        Environment.Exit(0))

    let output =
        new TextBox(Dock = DockStyle.Fill,
                    ReadOnly = true,
                    Multiline = true)
    temp.Controls.Add(output)

    let input = new TextBox(Dock = DockStyle.Bottom, Multiline = true)
    temp.Controls.Add(input)

    let tc = new TcpClient()
    tc.Connect("localhost", 4242)

    let load() =
        let run() =
            let sr = new StreamReader(tc.GetStream())
            while(true) do
                let text = sr.ReadLine()
                if text <> null && text <> "" then
                    temp.Invoke(new MethodInvoker(fun () ->
                        output.AppendText(text + Environment.NewLine)
                        output.SelectionStart <- output.Text.Length))
                    |> ignore
        let t = new Thread(new ThreadStart(run))
        t.Start()

    temp.Load.Add(fun _ -> load())

    let sw = new StreamWriter(tc.GetStream())
    let keyUp _ =
        if(input.Lines.Length > 1) then
            let text = input.Text
            if (text <> null && text <> "") then
```

```
            begin
                try
                    sw.WriteLine(text)
                    sw.Flush()
                with err ->
                    MessageBox.Show(sprintf "Server error\n\n%O" err)
                    |> ignore
            end;
            input.Text <- ""

    input.KeyUp.Add(fun _ -> keyUp e)
    temp

[<STAThread>]
do Application.Run(form)
```

Figure 10-1 shows the resulting client-server application.

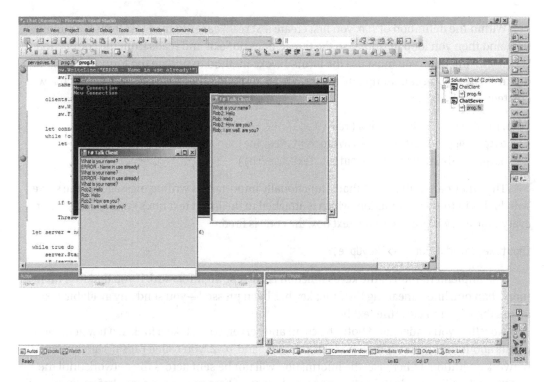

Figure 10-1. *The chat client-server application*

Now you'll look at how the client in Listing 10-2 works. The first portion of code in the client is taken up initializing various aspects of the form; this is not of interest to you at the moment, though you can find details of how WinForms applications work in Chapter 8. The first part of Listing 10-2 that is relevant to TCP/IP sockets programming is when you connect to the server. You do this by creating a new instance of the TcpClient class and calling its Connect method:

```
let tc = new TcpClient()
tc.Connect("localhost", 4242)
```

In this example, you specify localhost, which is the local computer, and port 4242, which is the same port on which the server is listening. In a more realistic example, you'd probably give the DNS name of the server or allow the user to give the DNS name, but localhost is good because it allows you to easily run the sample on one computer.

The function that drives the reading of data from the server is the load function. You attach this to the form's Load event; to ensure this executes after the form is loaded and initialized properly, you need to interact with the form's controls:

```
temp.Load.Add(fun _ -> load())
```

To ensure that you read all data coming from the server in a timely manner, you create a new thread to read all incoming requests. To do this, you define the function run, which is then used to start a new thread:

```
let t = new Thread(new ThreadStart(run))
t.Start()
```

Within the definition of run, you first create a StreamReader to read text from the connection, and then you loop infinitely, so the thread does not exit and reads from the connection. When you find data, you must use the form's Invoke method to update the form; you need to do this because you cannot update the form from a thread other than the one on which it was created:

```
temp.Invoke(new MethodInvoker(fun () ->
    output.AppendText(text + Environment.NewLine)
    output.SelectionStart <- output.Text.Length))
```

The other part of the client that is functionally important is writing messages to the server. You do this in the keyUp function, which is attached to the input text box's KeyUp event so that every time a key is pressed in the text box, the code is fired:

```
input.KeyUp.Add(fun _ -> keyUp e)
```

The implementation of the keyUp function is fairly straightforward: if you find that there is more than one line—meaning the Enter key has been pressed—you send any available text across the wire and clear the text box.

Now that you understand both the client and server, you'll take a look at a few general points about the application. In both Listings 10-1 and 10-2, you called Flush() after each network operation. Otherwise, the information will not be sent across the network until the stream cache fills up, which leads to one user having to type many messages before they appear on the other user's screen.

This approach has several problems, particularly on the server side. Allocating a thread for each incoming client ensures a good response to each client, but as the number of client connections grows, so will the amount of context switching needed for the threads, and the overall performance of the server will be reduced. Also, since each client requires its own thread, the maximum number of clients is limited by the maximum number of threads a process can contain. Although these problems can be solved, it's often easier to simply use one of the more abstract protocols discussed next.

Using HTTP

The Web uses Hypertext Transfer Protocol (HTTP) to communicate, typically with web browsers, but you might want to make web requests from a script or a program for several reasons, for example, to aggregate site content through RSS or Atom feeds.

To make an HTTP request, you use the static method Create from the System.Net. WebRequest class. This creates a WebRequest object that represents a request to the uniform resource locator (URL, an address used to uniquely address a resource on a network) that was passed to the Create method. You then use the GetResponse method to get the server's response to your request, represented by the System.Net.WebResponse class.

The following example (Listing 10-3) illustrates calling an RSS on the BBC's website. The core of the example is the function getUrlAsXml, which does the work of retrieving the data from the URL and loading the data into an XmlDocument. The rest of the example illustrates the kind of post-processing you might want to do on the data, in this case displaying the title of each item on the console and allowing users to choose which item to display.

Listing 10-3. *Using HTTP*

```
#light
open System.Diagnostics
open System.Net
open System.Xml

let getUrlAsXml (url : string) =
    let request = WebRequest.Create(url)
    let response = request.GetResponse()
    let stream = response.GetResponseStream()
    let xml = new XmlDocument()
    xml.Load(new XmlTextReader(stream))
    xml

let url = "http://newsrss.bbc.co.uk/rss/newsonline_uk_edition/sci/tech/rss.xml"
let xml = getUrlAsXml url

let mutable i = 1
for node in xml.SelectNodes("/rss/channel/item/title") do
    printf "%i. %s\r\n" i node.InnerText
    i <- i + 1

let item = read_int()

let newUrl =
    let xpath = sprintf "/rss/channel/item[%i]/link" item
    let node = xml.SelectSingleNode(xpath)
    node.InnerText

let proc = new Process()
```

```
proc.StartInfo.UseShellExecute <- true
proc.StartInfo.FileName <- newUrl
proc.Start()
```

The results of this example at the time of writing (your results will vary) were as follows:

1. Five-step check for nano safety
2. Neanderthal DNA secrets unlocked
3. Stem cells 'treat muscle disease'
4. World Cup site threat to swallows
5. Clues to pandemic bird flu found
6. Mice star as Olympic food tasters
7. Climate bill sets carbon target
8. Physics promises wireless power
9. Heart 'can carry out own repairs'
10. Average European 'is overweight'
11. Contact lost with Mars spacecraft
12. Air guitar T-shirt rocks for real
13. Chocolate 'cuts blood clot risk'
14. Case for trawl ban 'overwhelming'
15. UN chief issues climate warning
16. Japanese begin annual whale hunt
17. Roman ship thrills archaeologists
18. Study hopeful for world's forests

Calling Web Services

Web services are based on standards (typically SOAP) that allow applications to exchange data using HTTP. Web services consist of web methods, that is, methods that have been exposed for execution over a network. You can think of this as somewhat similar to F# functions, since a web method has a name, can have parameters, and returns a result. The parameters and results are described in metadata that the web services also exposes, so clients know how to call it.

You can call a web service in F# in two ways. You can use the HttpRequest class and generate the XML you need to send, or you can use the wsdl.exe tool that comes with the .NET Framework SDK to generate a proxy for you. Generally, most people prefer using an automatically generated proxy, because it is much easier, but some like to generate the XML themselves since they think it's easier to handle changes to a web service this way. You'll look at both options, starting with generating the XML yourself.

The example in Listing 10-4 calls the Microsoft Developers Network (MSDN) web service. (MSDN is a vast library containing details about all the APIs and other software aimed at developers that Microsoft provides.) The call to the web service will retrieve details about a class or method in the BCL. The listing first defines a generic function, getWebService, to call the web service. This is slightly more complicated than the getUrlAsXml function in Listing 10-4, because you need to send extra data to the server; that is, you need to send the name of the web method you are calling and the request body—the data that makes up the request's parameters.

You need to use the HTTP POST protocol, rather than the default HTTP GET protocol, so you set this in the Method property of the WebRequest class. You also need to set the content type to "text/xml":

```
webRequest.Method <- "POST"
webRequest.ContentType <- "text/xml"
```

Then you add the web method name to the HTTP header:

```
webRequest.Headers.Add("Web-Method", methodName)
```

And finally you use the GetRequestStream method to get a stream of data into which you write requestBody, the data that makes up the parameters of the request:

```
using (new StreamWriter(webRequest.GetRequestStream()))
    (fun s -> s.Write(requestBody))
```

You then go on to define a more specific function, queryMsdn, just to query MSDN using the web service it exposes. This function calls the web service using a template of the request bound to the identifier requestTemplate. The rest of queryMsdn uses XPath to determine whether any results are available and if so writes them to the console. Listing 10-4 shows the full example.

Listing 10-4. *Calling the MSDN Web Service*

```
 #light
open System
open System.IO
open System.Net
open System.Windows.Forms
open System.Xml

let getWebService (url : string) (methodName : string) (requestBody : string) =
    let webRequest =
        WebRequest.Create(url, Method = "POST", ContentType = "text/xml")
    webRequest.Headers.Add("Web-Method", methodName)
    using (new StreamWriter(webRequest.GetRequestStream()))
        (fun s -> s.Write(requestBody))
    let webResponse = webRequest.GetResponse()
    let stream = webResponse.GetResponseStream()
    let xml = new XmlDocument()
    xml.Load(new XmlTextReader(stream))
    xml

let (requestTemplate : Printf.string_format<_>) =
    @"<soap:Envelope xmlns:soap=""http://schemas.xmlsoap.org/soap/envelope/""
    xmlns:xsi=""http://www.w3.org/2001/XMLSchema-instance""
    xmlns:xsd=""http://www.w3.org/2001/XMLSchema"">
  <soap:Body>
    <getContentRequest xmlns=""urn:msdn-com:public content-syndication"">
      <contentIdentifier>%s</contentIdentifier>
```

```
        <locale xmlns=""urn:mtpg-com:mtps/2004/1/key"">en-us</locale>
        <version xmlns=""urn:mtpg-com:mtps/2004/1/key"">VS.80</version>
        <requestedDocuments>
          <requestedDocument type=""common"" selector=""Mtps.Search"" />
          <requestedDocument type=""primary"" selector=""Mtps.Xhtml"" />
        </requestedDocuments>
      </getContentRequest>
    </soap:Body>
</soap:Envelope>"

let url = "http://services.msdn.microsoft.com" +
            "/ContentServices/ContentService.asmx"
let xpath = "/soap:Envelope/soap:Body/c:getContentResponse/" +
            "mtps:primaryDocuments/p:primary"

let queryMsdn item =
    let request = Printf.sprintf requestTemplate item
    let xml = getWebService url "GetContent" request
    let namespaceManage =
        let temp = new XmlNamespaceManager(xml.NameTable)
        temp.AddNamespace("soap", "http://schemas.xmlsoap.org/soap/envelope/")
        temp.AddNamespace("mtps", "urn:msdn-com:public-content-syndication")
        temp.AddNamespace("c", "urn:msdn-com:public-content-syndication")
        temp.AddNamespace("p", "urn:mtpg-com:mtps/2004/1/primary")
        temp

    match xml.SelectSingleNode(xpath, namespaceManage) with
    | null -> print_endline "Not found"
    | html -> print_endline html.InnerText

queryMsdn "System.IO.StreamWriter"
```

Running the code in Listing 10-4 queries MSDN to find out about the System.IO.StreamWriter class. Figure 10-2 shows the results of such a query, which is run inside F# interactive hosted in Visual Studio. It's easy to define other queries to the web service—just call queryMsdn, passing it a different string parameter.

Although the results of this web service can appear poorly formatted, since the body text you grab is HTML and you simply strip the formatting tags, I often find this is the quickest way to search for information on MSDN. If I know that I'm going to be searching MSDN a lot, I load this script into fsi hosted in Visual Studio, and then I can query MSDN just by typing queryMsdn, which can be much quicker than loading a browser.

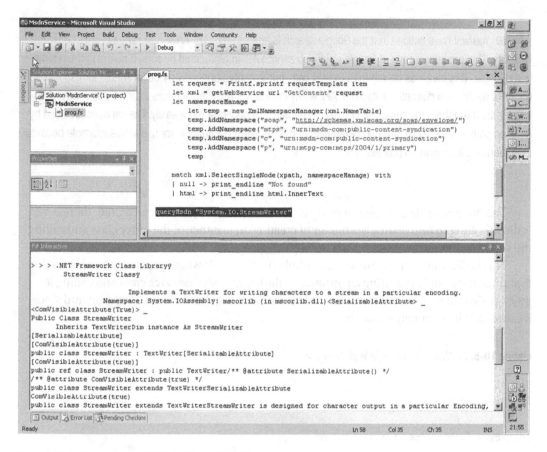

Figure 10-2. *Querying MSDN in Visual Studio*

This method of calling web services has its advocates who claim it's more resistant to changes in the service interface than generated proxies. However, this example is flawed for at least two reasons. It's not typically a good idea to place a large quantity of string data in source code, as you did with the `requestTemplate` identifier in Listing 10-4, and it's often easier to work with strongly typed objects rather than querying an XML document.

To explore the alternatives, let's look at an example that queries Google's web service using a generated proxy.

First, you need to generate the proxy; you do this using the `wsdl.exe` tool. Using `wsdl.exe` is straightforward. Just pass it the URL of the service you want to use, and `wsdl.exe` will generate a proxy. So, to create the Google proxy, use the command line `wsdl.exe` `http://strangelights.com/` `EvilAPI/GoogleSearch.wsdl`. This creates a C# proxy class that can easily be compiled into a .NET assembly and used in F#.

Note You will have noticed that the Google search is hosted on http://www.strangelights.com, my web site. This provides a copy of Google's old web service API implemented by screen scraping the results from Google. This idea was copied from EvilAPI.com, implemented originally by Collin Winter, in response to Google's decision to discontinue its SOAP API. Many companies use web services internally as a way of letting teams throughout the company, or partner companies, cooperate more easily. The services provided by Amazon.com and eBay.com are good examples of this but were not suitable for use in this example because they require a long sign-up process.

The huge advantage of using a proxy is that once the proxy has been created, there is very little plumbing to do. It's simply a matter of creating an instance of the proxy class and calling the service's methods.

This is illustrated in the following example (Listing 10-5) where you query Google for the first three pages of F#. Creating an instance of the GoogleSearchService class and calling its doGoogleSearch method is straightforward, and processing the result is straightforward since it's available in a strongly typed class.

Listing 10-5. *Calling the Google Web Service*

```
#light
#r "Proxy.dll";;

let key = "xxxx xxxx xxxx xxxx"

  let google =
    new GoogleSearchService(Url = "http://strangelights.com/EvilAPI/google.asmx")

let result =
    google.doGoogleSearch(key=key,
                          q="FSharp",
                          start=0,
                          maxResults=3,
                          filter=false,
                          restrict="",
                          safeSearch=false,
                          lr="",
                          ie="",
                          oe="")
```

```
result.resultElements
|> Array.iteri
    (fun i result ->
        printf "%i. %s\r\n%s\r\n%s\r\n\r\n"
            i
            result.title
            result.URL
            result.snippet)

read_line() |> ignore
```

The results of this example, when executed (on the day of this writing), are as follows:

```
0. <b>F#</b>
http://research.microsoft.com/fsharp/fsharp.aspx
A .NET variant of ML with a core language similar to that of the OCaml programmi
ng <br> language.

1. <b>f#</b> language
http://research.microsoft.com/fsharp/fsharp.aspx
<b>F#</b> is a programming language that provides the much sought-after <b>...</
b> The only <br>  language to provide a combination like this is <b>F#</b> (pron
ounced FSharp) - a <b>...</b>

2. F Sharp programming language - Wikipedia, the free encyclopedia
http://en.wikipedia.org/wiki/F_Sharp
The correct title of this article is <b>F#</b> programming language. <b>...</b>
NET components <br>  in <b>F#</b>. Consequently, the main <b>F#</b> libraries ar
e the . <b>...</b>
```

Creating Web Services

In addition to calling web services, you can create web services in F#, and this is also very straightforward. In fact, when creating a web service, the main problem is probably exposing code through a web server. Web servers receive requests for files, in the form of a URL; you must tell the web server to which .NET class this request will map. Typically you use an .asmx file to run a specific F# class that will responded to the web service request if the web server gets a request for the .asmx file. The exact way of doing this varies depending on your development environment and the web server on which you host your services.

Visual Studio 2005 comes with a built-in web server, so creating a new web site is just a matter of selecting File ➤ New ➤ Web Site and then choosing the location for the website.

This site will run only those pages written in C# or Visual Basic .NET, so you need to add an F# project to the solution and then manually alter the solution file so that it lives inside the website directory. This is easier than it sounds. You just need to copy the .fsharpp file to the website directory, open the .sln file in Notepad, and alter the path to the .fsharpp file. After this, you just need to configure the project file to output a library and write this to a bin subdirectory. This might seem like a lot of effort, but afterward you will just be able to press F5, and your project will compile and run.

If you don't have Visual Studio 2005, then the next best thing to do is to host the site in Internet Information Services (IIS, Microsoft's own web server for Windows). In some ways, this is easier than hosting in Visual Studio, but it doesn't have the convenience of just being able to execute your code once coding is completed. To host your code in IIS, you need to create an IIS virtual directory with a subdirectory called bin. You then need to copy your .asmx pages and your web.config file to the virtual directory.

Note Getting ASP.NET to work with F# and Apache is possible, but it is more difficult than the situation either with or without Visual Studio 2005; see the following page for more details: http://strangelights.com/FSharp/Foundations/default.aspx/FSharpFoundations.HostingWebServices.

The service itself is straightforward. The service should be a class that derives from System.Web.Service.WebService and has a parameterless constructor. It should also be marked with System.Web.Service.WebServiceAttribute. If you intend to expose your web service publicly, you must set the attribute's Namespace. The default is http://tempuri.org, and even if you don't intend to expose your service publicly, setting this attribute will lead to more manageable web services. The members of the class can then become web methods by simply marking them with System.Web.Service.WebServiceAttribute. This too has a number of useful properties; it's particularly worth setting the Description property so clients of your service know what they're getting.

Listing 10-6 shows the definition of a simple web service. You create a type Service with one member, Addition, that must have its parameters in the tuple style.

Listing 10-6. *Creating a Simple Web Service*

```
#light
namespace Strangelights.WebServices

open System.Web.Services

[<WebService(Namespace =
    "http://strangelights.com/FSharp/Foundations/WebServices")>]
type Service = class
    inherit WebService
    new() = {}
    [<WebMethod(Description = "Performs integer addition")>]
    member x.Addition (x : int, y : int) = x + y
end
```

To allow the web service to be found by the web server, you need to create an `.asmx` file. An example `.asmx` file is as follows; the most important thing for you is to set the `Class` attribute to the name of the class that is your service. When the server receives a request for this file, it invokes the appropriate service.

```
<%@ WebService Class="Strangelights.WebServices.Service" %>
```

If you're running the service locally, you can test the service by simply opening it in a browser. In a browser, you'll see the interface shown in Figure 10-3, which allows you to give values for the web service's parameters and then invoke the service.

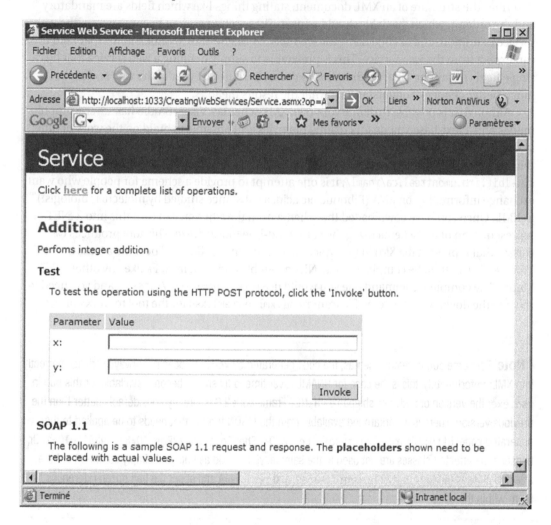

Figure 10-3. *Invoking a local web service*

Invoking this service with the arguments 46 and 28 produces the following XML:

```
<?xml version="1.0" encoding="utf-8" ?>
<int xmlns="http://strangelights.com/FSharp/Foundations/WebServices">74</int>
```

It is generally not efficient to send small amounts of data across the network, since there is a certain amount of metadata that must be sent with each request. In general, it is better to build applications that are not "chatty," that is, applications that make one big request rather than repeatedly making lots of small ones.

A web service will attempt to serialize any .NET object that is returned from one for its methods to XML; however, the results can be a little unpredictable, and the resulting XML data might not contain all the fields you expect it to and might be difficult to work with from other programming languages. To avoid this, it's best to use XSD schemas to define the objects that you want to pass across the web service. An XSD schema is a type of XML document that describes the structure of an XML document, stating things like which fields are mandatory and the order in which the fields should appear. These schemes then become part of the web service definition, and anyone using the web service will be able to understand what field they can expect from the web service. This is preferable to simply defining a web service that has a single field containing binary or hexadecimal data because the user of the web service has a much better chance of understanding what the results mean.

Although it is possible to define your own XML schemas, Visual Studio has several graphic modes and a text-based mode for creating them; it's also possible to build on the work of others in this field—many predefined schemas are available for download on the Web. For instance, the example you are going to look at next uses RNAML, a schema you can find at http://www-lbit.iro.umontreal.ca/rnaml/; it is one attempt to provide a schema for people who want exchange information on RNA (Ribonucleic acid, a substance studied by molecular biologist) in XML. Once you have downloaded the schema from the site, you can turn this into a .NET representation of the schema using the command-line tool xsd.exe. This tool produces C# classes that represent the XML data; typically, each tag in the XML will become a class in .NET. This C# file can then be compiled into a .NET assembly and used from F# like any other .NET library. The complete command line you would use is xsd rnaml.xsd /classes, and you need to rename the downloaded schema file from rnaml.xml to rnaml.xsd for the tool to work correctly.

Note For some complicated schemas, the code generated by xsd.exe does not always serialize perfectly into XML; unfortunately, this is the case for RNAML. Over time, a fix should become available for this bug in xsd.exe; the version of xsd.exe shipped with .NET Framework 2.0 is already considerably better than the previous version. There is a workaround available from the MSDN forums that needs to be applied to the generated code: http://forums.microsoft.com/MSDN/ShowPost.aspx?PostID=87289&SiteID=1. Or, because the affected classes are not used in the sample, you can do as I did and simply comment out the affected classes (numberingtable, coordinates, and revision) and about the half dozen references to them within the code.

The following example shows how to create a web service that returns the structure of a yeast RNA molecule. This is an abridged version of the sequence sample available from the RNAML website (http://www-lbit.iro.umontreal.ca/rnaml/). As before, you need an .asmx file to link the file requested to the .NET type that will handle the request; here it is:

```
<%@ WebService Class="Strangelights.WebServices.DnaWebService" %>
```

Listing 10-7 shows the web service; you will notice how the basic components of the service are the same as our simple web service. You have a class definition as before, marked with the WebService attribute. The code that actually does the work is the method definition GetYeastMolecule; here you create and populate various objects that are defined in the library you created from the rnaml.xsd file, such as a molecule object and a sequence object.

Listing 10-7. *Creating a Web Service Returning the Definition of RNA Molecule*

```
#light
namespace Strangelights.WebServices

open System.Web.Services

[<WebService(Namespace =
    "http://strangelights.com/FSharp/Foundations/DnaWebService")>]
type DnaWebService = class
    inherit WebService
    new() = {}
    [<WebMethod(Description = "Gets a representation of a yeast molecule")>]
    member x.GetYeastMolecule () =
        let yeast = new molecule(id = "Yeast-tRNA-Phe")
        let id = new identity(name = "Saccharomyces cerevisiae tRNA-Phe")
        let tax = new taxonomy(domain = "Eukaryota", kingdom = "Fungi",
                               phylum = "Ascomycota", ``class`` = "Saccharomycetes",
                               order = "Saccharomycetales",
                               family = "Saccharomycetaceae",
                               genus = "Saccharomyces",
                               species = "Saccharomyces cerevisiae")
        let numRange1 = new numberingrange(start = "1", Item = "10")
        let numRange2 = new numberingrange(start = "11", Item = "66")
        let numSys = new numberingsystem(id="natural", usedinfile=true)
        numSys.Items <- [|box numRange1; box numRange2|]
        let seqData = new seqdata()
        seqData.Value <- "GCGGAUUUAG CUCAGUUGGG AGAGCGCCAG ACUGAAGAUC
        UGGAGGUCCU GUGUUCGAUC CACAGAAUUC GCACCA"
        let seq = new sequence()
        seq.numberingsystem <- [|numSys|]
        seq.seqdata <- seqData
        id.taxonomy <- tax
        yeast.identity <- id
        yeast.sequence <- [|seq|]
        yeast
end
```

Again, the same simple web-based testing option is available, and the resulting XML is as follows:

```xml
<?xml version="1.0" encoding="utf-8"?>
<molecule xmlns:xsi="http://www.w3.org/2001/XMLSchema-instance"
  xmlns:xsd="http://www.w3.org/2001/XMLSchema" id="Yeast-tRNA-Phe">
  <identity>
    <name>Saccharomyces cerevisiae tRNA-Phe</name>
    <taxonomy>
      <domain>Eukaryota</domain>
      <kingdom>Fungi</kingdom>
      <phylum>Ascomycota</phylum>
      <class>Saccharomycetes</class>
      <order>Saccharomycetales</order>
      <family>Saccharomycetaceae</family>
      <genus>Saccharomyces</genus>
      <species>Saccharomyces cerevisiae</species>
    </taxonomy>
  </identity>
  <sequence>
    <numbering-system id="natural" used-in-file="true">
      <numbering-range>
        <start>1</start>
        <end>10</end>
      </numbering-range>
      <numbering-range>
        <start>11</start>
        <end>66</end>
      </numbering-range>
    </numbering-system>
    <seq-data>GCGGAUUUAG CUCAGUUGGG AGAGCGCCAG ACUGAAGAUC
        UGGAGGUCCU GUGUUCGAUC CACAGAAUUC GCACCA</seq-data>
  </sequence>
</molecule>
```

Although this example, just returning a static unchanging XML document, is not particularly realistic, it is easy to see the potential of this sort of application. Instead of a GetYeastMolecule method, you'd more realistically provide a GetMolecule method that took a name of a molecule, looked the details of the molecule up in a database, and returned the resulting molecule data. The advantage is that a program running on almost any platform can work with the resulting data; in this case, the example site already provides an API for working with the data in C++ and Java, and as you have seen, working with this kind of data in F# is already very straightforward. Of course, this technology is not limited to molecular biology; there are XML schemas becoming available for almost every field of science, engineering, math, and finance.

Web services such as these can be secured so that they can be accessed only by a subset of users or so that the information traveling over the network is encrypted or signed, via several methods. One option is to upgrade to Windows Communication Foundation (WCF), which is similar to web services but offers more flexibility in this area, discussed in the next section. The other is to configure your web server to handle these security requirements for you. I'll discuss these options as well as several troubleshooting options in the section "IIS Configuration and Troubleshooting Guide."

Windows Communication Foundation

It is the goal of the Windows Communication Framework (WCF) to provide a unified model for creating distributed applications. The idea is that you create a service, something very similar to a web service, containing the functionality you want to expose. This service can then be exposed in a variety of different ways. For example, web services always pass XML messages, but WCF services can be configured to pass binary data or XML messages. Further, WFC services can be hosted in any process, rather than just on a web server. This means you could create a desktop application that listens for incoming messages without having to install a web server on the desktop.

■**Note** WCF is part of the .NET Framework 3, a group of APIs that were released at the same time as Windows Vista and come already installed on that operating system. They can also be downloaded from `http://www.microsoft.com` and installed on Windows XP and Windows Server 2003 (`http://www.` `microsoft.com/downloads/details.aspx?FamilyId=10CC340B-F857-4A14-83F5-` `25634C3BF043&displaylang=en`). The protocols that WCF uses are based on a group of specifications that extend web services and are sometimes referred to as the WS-* protocols because each protocol is generally given a name prefixed by WS-, such as WS-Security or WS-Reliability. Each of these protocols either has been standardized or is currently being put forward for standardization. To develop with WCF, you need to download the .NET Framework 3 SDK from `http://www.microsoft.com/downloads`.

In the first example, shown in Listing 10-8, you'll build a simple WCF service that is hosted on a web server and looks rather like a simple web service. You'll refine this service to show off some of the interesting features of WCF. To create a WCF service hosted in a web server, you follow the same steps discussed in the "Creating Web Services" section, except that hosting in Apache on Linux is not possible because WCF relies on some features that are specific to Windows.

Listing 10-8. *Creating a Simple WCF Service*

```
#light
namespace Strangelights.Services
open System.ServiceModel

[<ServiceContract
    (Namespace =
        "http://strangelights.com/FSharp/Foundations/WCFServices")>]
type IGreetingService = interface
    [<OperationContract>]
    abstract Greet : name:string -> string
end
```

```
type GreetingService() = class
    interface IGreetingService with
        member x.Greet(name)  = "Hello: " + name
    end
end
```

This service is defined in two parts, an interface that describes the service contract and an implementation of that contract. All WCF services are defined this way. This interface is named IGreetingService and exposes one function, named Greet. To make it a valid WCF contract, mark the interface with System.ServiceModel.ServiceContractAttribute, which should contain a namespace for the service. Use OperationContractAttribute to mark each function within the interface that the service will expose. It is important that each parameter has a name. It's possible to create interfaces in F# where the parameters don't have names but are simply defined by their types. An interface acting as a WCF contract whose functions do not have parameters will compile, but you'll receive an error when you invoke the service since the parameter names are used (via reflection) in the WCF framework to create the data that is sent across the wire. The class GreetingService provides the implementation of the contract. You simply offer a greeting by appending "hello: " to whatever name is passed.

To integrate the service with the web server, you need to create a .svc file, which plays a similar role to the web service's .asmx file, telling the web server what type should be used to handle the service request. An example of an .svc that goes with the service is as follows; the complete file is shown—they are typically only one line long. The most important attribute in the .svc file is the Service attribute that tells the web server which type it should use:

```
<% @ServiceHost Debug="true" Service="Strangelights.Services.GreetingService" %>
```

Finally, you must configure the service. Since WCF offers a choice of protocols, you use the configuration file to tell it which one to use. The configuration file in Listing 10-9 shows a configuration file that could be used to configure your service. The service element defines two endpoints; these are the protocols that a client can use to talk to this service. One of the endpoints is a standard web service HTTP binding, and the other is a metadata exchange binding; this allows the service to expose metadata about itself that will tell any potential client how it should talk to the service. This is the endpoint you'll use when you create the client proxy.

Listing 10-9. *The Configuration File for a WCF Service*

```
<configuration xmlns="http://schemas.microsoft.com/.NetConfiguration/v2.0">
  <system.serviceModel>
    <services>
      <service
        name="Strangelights.Services.GreetingService"
        behaviorConfiguration="MyServiceTypeBehaviors">
        <endpoint
          contract="Strangelights.Services.IGreetingService"
          binding="wsHttpBinding"/>
```

```
      <endpoint
        contract="Strangelights.Services.IGreetingService"
        binding="mexHttpBinding" address="mex"/>
    </service>
  </services>
  <behaviors>
    <serviceBehaviors>
      <behavior name="MyServiceTypeBehaviors" >
        <serviceDebug includeExceptionDetailInFaults="true" />
        <serviceMetadata httpGetEnabled="true" />
      </behavior>
    </serviceBehaviors>
  </behaviors>
</system.serviceModel>

<system.web>
  <compilation debug="true"/>
</system.web>

</configuration>
```

To create a client for the service, you use the utility SvcUtil.exe, which has a similar purpose to the utility wsdl.exe that I discussed in the "Creating Web Services" section. To use SvcUtil.exe to create a proxy for your service, you need to use the following command line, taking care to adapt the URL appropriately:

```
svcutil.exe http://localhost:1033/WCFService/Service.svc?wsdl
```

This will generate a C# proxy file that can then be compiled into a .NET assembly that can be used from F#. It will also generate a .config file, which can be used to configure any client application.

Using the proxy is straightforward, once you've added a reference to the proxy .dll file. Simply create an instance of the proxy, and call its Greet method with the appropriate arguments. Listing 10-10 shows an example of a proxy; because it is important to call the proxy's Dispose method, I have created it wrapped in the using function.

Listing 10-10. *Invoking the WCF Service*

```
using (new GreetingServiceClient())
    (fun client ->
        print_endline (client.Greet("Rob"))
        read_line() |> ignore)
```

Listing 10-11 is an example of a generated configuration file that has had certain things removed from it to make the sample run more smoothly. The security settings have been removed, because these can cause the example to fail if it is run on a computer disconnected from its domain controller (a common case for programmers on the move!). Also, one of the two generated endpoints has been removed so there is no need to specify an endpoint in the code.

Listing 10-11. *The Configuration File for Invoking the WCF Service*

```xml
<configuration>
    <system.serviceModel>
        <bindings>
            <wsHttpBinding>
                <binding name="WSHttpBinding_IGreetingService"
                    closeTimeout="00:01:00" openTimeout="00:01:00"
                    receiveTimeout="00:10:00" sendTimeout="00:01:00"
                    bypassProxyOnLocal="false" transactionFlow="false"
                    hostNameComparisonMode="StrongWildcard"
                    maxBufferPoolSize="524288"
                    maxReceivedMessageSize="65536" messageEncoding="Text"
                    textEncoding="utf-8" useDefaultWebProxy="true"
                    allowCookies="false">
                    <readerQuotas maxDepth="32"
                        maxStringContentLength="8192"
                        maxArrayLength="16384"
                        maxBytesPerRead="4096"
                        maxNameTableCharCount="16384" />
                    <reliableSession ordered="true"
                        inactivityTimeout="00:10:00"
                        enabled="false" />
                </binding>
            </wsHttpBinding>
        </bindings>
        <client>
            <endpoint address="http://localhost:8080/service"
                binding="wsHttpBinding"
                bindingConfiguration="WSHttpBinding_IGreetingService"
                contract="IGreetingService"
                name="WSHttpBinding_IGreetingService">
            </endpoint>
        </client>
    </system.serviceModel>
</configuration>
```

The results of executing Listing 10-10 are as follows:

```
Hello: Rob
```

■**Caution** Although removing security settings is great for getting examples to run smoothly, security is an important aspect that you should consider carefully throughout the development life cycle. If you are involved in serious WCF development, I strongly recommend that you look at the appropriate security settings for your application (for example, what kind of authentication do you want your users to provide?) as soon as possible. For further information about WCF security, please see http://strangelights.com/FSharp/ Foundations/default.aspx/FSharpFoundations.WCFSecurity.

Hosting WCF Services

To me, the most exciting aspect of WCF is the ability to host a service in any program without the need for a web server. One possibility this opens up is the ability to create services whose implementation can be changed dynamically because they are hosted in fsi.exe. Although it is necessary to make some modifications to the previous sample to get it running in fsi.exe, these modification are surprisingly straightforward.

Listing 10-12 shows a modified version of the previous example, Listing 10-8, designed to run in fsi.exe.

Listing 10-12. *A Service Designed to be Hosted in F# Interactive*

```
#light
#I @"C:\Program Files\Reference Assemblies\Microsoft\Framework\v3.0";;
#r "System.ServiceModel.dll";;
open System
open System.ServiceModel
open System.Runtime.Serialization

let mutable f = (fun x -> "Hello: " + x)
f <- (fun x -> "Bonjour: " + x)
f <- (fun x -> "Goedendag: " + x)

[<ServiceContract
    (Namespace =
        "http://strangelights.com/FSharp/Foundations/WCFServices")>]
type IGreetingService = interface
    [<OperationContract>]
    abstract Greet : name:string -> string
end
```

```
type GreetingService() = class
    interface IGreetingService with
        member x.Greet( name ) = f name
    end
end

let myServiceHost =
    let baseAddress = new Uri("http://localhost:8080/service")

    let temp = new ServiceHost((type GreetingService), [|baseAddress|])

    let binding =
        let temp =
            new WSHttpBinding(Name = "binding1",
                              HostNameComparisonMode =
                                 HostNameComparisonMode.StrongWildcard,
                              TransactionFlow = false)
        temp.Security.Mode <- SecurityMode.Message
        temp.ReliableSession.Enabled <- false
        temp

    temp.AddServiceEndpoint((type IGreetingService), binding, baseAddress)
    |> ignore
    temp

myServiceHost.Open()
```

Notice that in Listing 10-12 the IGreetingService and GreetingService types are pretty much unchanged from Listing 10-8, except that the GreetingService type has been modified to use a mutable function so you can manipulate what it does at runtime. You then need to create a service host to do what the web server and web.config did in the previous example. The web.config is shown in Listing 10-9, and the service itself is shown in Listing 10-8. Note that myServiceHost contains a baseAddress, which the service will listen for a request on, and a binding, which controls which protocols are used. Finally, you call the myServiceHost's Open method to set the service listening.

Then you make an alteration to the client to call the service repeatedly, shown in Listing 10-13, so you can see the service results change overtime.

Listing 10-13. *A Client to Access the Service Hosted in F# Interactive*

```
#light
using (new GreetingServiceClient()) (fun client ->
        while true do
            print_endline (client.Greet("Rob"))
            read_line() |> ignore)
```

You also need to alter the client's .config file to point to the correct address:

```
<endpoint address="http://localhost:8080/service"
```

The service is changed dynamically, as shown in Figure 10-4.

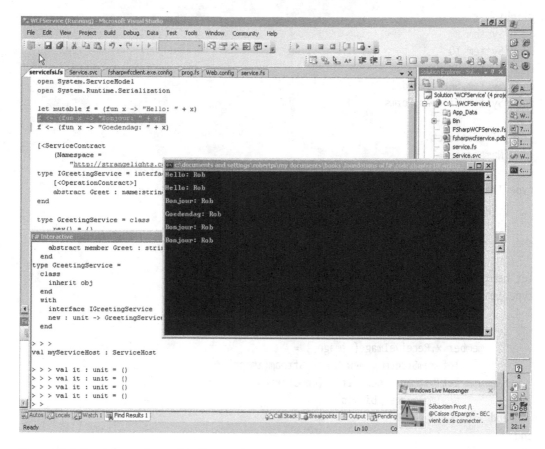

Figure 10-4. *Invoking a dynamic WCF service*

Another interesting reason to host services in a program is to create desktop applications that can listen for updates for some kind of central server. Traditionally, these kinds of applications have been to poll central server, which can lead to a large amount of unnecessary network traffic if polling is too frequent.

Listing 10-14 demonstrates how to do this. It shows a blank form that hosts a service that will listen to updates from a client; in this case, the update will be a background image to display. The service defines one function, ReceiveImage, which receives that binary data that makes up an image. The implementation of the service raises an event, newImgEvent, every time an image is received; this is so that the form can be updated every time a new image is received. Hooking the form up to the event is straightforward:

```
newImgEvent.Add(fun img -> form.BackgroundImage <- img)
```

You just need to call the event's Add method and pass it a function that updates the form. You will notice that the code required to host the service (that is, the code that defines myServiceHost) is unchanged from the previous example.

Listing 10-14. *A Windows Form with a Service Built In*

```
#light
open System
open System.IO
open System.Drawing
open System.ServiceModel
open System.Windows.Forms

[<ServiceContract
    (Namespace =
        "http://strangelights.com/FSharp/Foundations/WCFImageService")>]
type IImageService = interface
    [<OperationContract>]
    abstract ReceiveImage : image:array<Byte> -> unit
end

let newImgTrigger, newImgEvent = IEvent.create<Bitmap>()
type ImageService() = class

    interface IImageService with
        member x.ReceiveImage( image ) =
            let memStream = new MemoryStream(image)
            let bitmap = new Bitmap(memStream)
            newImgTrigger bitmap
    end
end

let myServiceHost =
    let baseAddress = new Uri("http://localhost:8080/service")

    let temp = new ServiceHost((type ImageService), [|baseAddress|])

    let binding =
        let temp =
            new WSHttpBinding(Name = "binding1",
                             HostNameComparisonMode =
                                HostNameComparisonMode.StrongWildcard,
                             TransactionFlow = false)
        temp.Security.Mode <- SecurityMode.Message
        temp.ReliableSession.Enabled <- false
        temp

    temp.AddServiceEndpoint((type IImageService), binding, baseAddress)
    |> ignore
    temp

myServiceHost.Open()
```

```
let form = new Form()

newImgEvent.Add(fun img ->
                  form.BackgroundImage <- img)

[<STAThread>]
do Application.Run(form)
```

To create the client, you must first create a proxy, using the same technique that you used in the example given in Listing 10-10. The utility SvcUtil.exe is run passing it the URL of the service, and this creates a proxy in C# that can be compiled into a .NET assembly and used from F#. In this case, the proxy is named ImageServiceClient. The definition of the client in Listing 10-15 might look a little complicated, but a lot of the code just lays out the form's controls or opens the image files. The really interesting code comes right at the end, where you add a function to the Send button's click event. This code reads an image from disk and loads it into a byte array. This byte array is then passed to the proxy's ReceiveImage method.

Listing 10-15. *A Client That Sends Images to Its Server*

```
#light
open System
open System.IO
open System.Windows.Forms

let form =
    let temp = new Form(Width=272, Height=64)

    let imagePath = new TextBox(Top=8, Left=8, Width=128)

    let browse = new Button(Top=8, Width=32, Left=8+imagePath.Right, Text = "...")
    browse.Click.Add(fun _ ->
        let dialog = new OpenFileDialog()
        if dialog.ShowDialog() = DialogResult.OK then
            imagePath.Text <- dialog.FileName)

    let send = new Button(Top=8, Left=8+browse.Right, Text = "Send")
    send.Click.Add(fun _ ->
        let buffer = File.ReadAllBytes(imagePath.Text)
        let service = new ImageServiceClient()
        service.ReceiveImage(buffer))

    temp.Controls.Add(imagePath)
    temp.Controls.Add(browse)
    temp.Controls.Add(send)
    temp

[<STAThread>]
do Application.Run(form)
```

Figure 10-5 shows the example being executed. The user is about to select an image to send to the client.

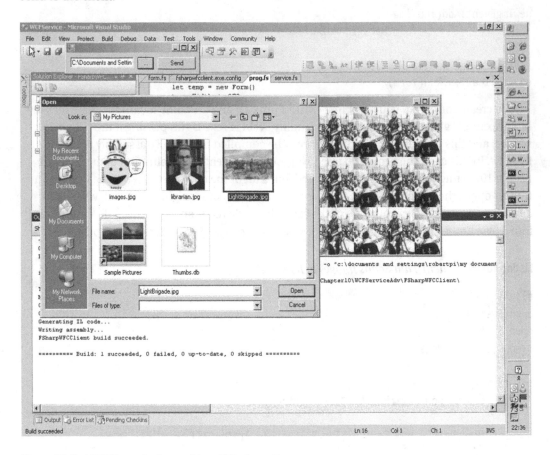

Figure 10-5. *A WCF service hosted in a Windows form*

This is not quite the whole story for a desktop application that listens for updates. The "client" that sends out updates needs to know the services and desktop applications to which it should send updates. In the services, you do this very simply—by hard-coding the address of the service. In the real world, you'd need to implement a service in the other direction as well. This service would tell the central "client" that a service was listening for updates and alert the central "client" when a service stops. Then the central "client" would need to loop through all services that were listening for updates and push the data out to each one of them.

Summary

This chapter covered the main options for creating distributed applications in F#. It showed that combining F# with .NET libraries allows the programmer to concentrate on the key technical challenges of creating distributed applications and allows them to use the features of F# to help control the complexity of these applications. In the next chapter, you will look at language-oriented programming, a technique that has been tried and trusted by functional programmers for years and can really make a programmer's life simpler.

CHAPTER 11

■ ■ ■

Language-Oriented Programming

In this chapter, you will first take a look at what I mean by *language-oriented programming*, a term that has been used by many people to mean different things. I'll also briefly discuss its advantages and disadvantages. You'll then look at several different approaches to language-oriented programming in F#. These techniques include using F# literals to create "little languages," using F# quotations, and creating a parser using `fslex.exe` and `fsyacc.exe`, which are themselves little languages.

What Is Language-Oriented Programming?

Although people use the term *language-oriented programming* to describe many different programming techniques, the techniques they refer to generally share a common theme. It's quite common for programmers to have to implement a predefined language; often this is because of a need to extract structured data from information stored or received as string or XML data that conforms to this predefined language. The techniques introduced in this chapter will help you do this more reliably. Related to this is the idea of little languages, or *domain-specific languages* (DSLs); you can create a DSL when the best way to solve a problem is to create a specialist language to describe the problem and then use this language to solve the problem. Functional programming has always had a strong relationship with language-oriented programming, because functional programming languages generally have features that are well suited to creating parsers and compilers.

Data Structures As Little Languages

Language-oriented development doesn't necessarily mean you need to write your own parser or compiler, although you'll examine this possibility later in this chapter. You can accomplish a lot by creating data structures that describe *what* you want to do and then creating functions or modules that define *how* the structure should be interpreted.

You can create data structures that represent a program in just about any language, but F# lends itself well to this approach. F#'s literal lists and arrays are easy to define and require no bulky type annotations. Its union types allow the programmer to create structures that express related concepts yet do not necessarily contain the same types of data, something that is useful when creating languages. Finally, since functions can be treated as values, you can easily embed functions within data structures so F# expressions can become part of your language, usually as an action in response to some particular condition of the language.

You've already seen a great example of this style of programming in Chapter 7. There you looked at a module that provides a simple way to create a command-line argument processor. It is simple because it allows the user to specify a data structure, such as the one shown here, that describes what the arguments should be without really having to think about how they will be parsed:

```
let argList =
    [ ("-set", Arg.Set myFlag, "Sets the value myFlag");
      ("-clear", Arg.Clear myFlag, "Clears the value myFlag");
      ("-str_val", Arg.String(fun x -> myString := x), "Sets the value myString");
      ("-int_val", Arg.Int(fun x -> myInt := x), "Sets the value myInt");
      ("-float_val", Arg.Float(fun x -> myFloat := x), "Sets the value myFloat") ]
```

I am particularly fond of this kind of DSL because I think it makes it really clear what arguments the program is expecting and what processing should take place if that argument is received. The fact that the help text is also stored in the structure serves a double purpose; it allows the function processing command-line arguments to automatically print out a help message if anything goes wrong, and it also reminds the programmer what the argument is in case they forget. I also like this method of creating a command-line interpreter because I have written several command-line interpreters in imperative languages, and it is not a satisfying experience—you end up having to write lots of code to detail how your command line should be broken up. If you are writing it in .NET, then you usually spend way too much time calling the string type's IndexOf and Substring methods.

A Data Structure–Based Language Implementation

Creating any DSL should start with defining what problem you need to solve; in this case, you will design a language to describe lines to be drawn on a graph. This is something of an obvious choice for F#, because its lambda functions lend themselves well to describing equations to produce lines on graphs. I'll walk you through the various elements for implementing this language. (Listing 11-1 later in this chapter lists the full program.)

The first step is to design the types to describe the graph. The first type you need to create is LineDefinition, which you use to describe the path of a line that will be plotted on the graph. You want to allow three types of line: one defined by a list of *x* and *y* coordinates, one defined by a function, and one defined by a combination of functions and a list of points. Languages are usually described formally by listing the valid constructs of the language, that is, the valid syntactic ways of constructing phrases in the language. F#-discriminated unions provide a perfect way to model the list of different possibilities, and thus a direct transcription from the formal definition of the language into code is often possible. In this case, you define a type LineDefinition that consists of three possibilities—the three possible phrases in the language. The first phrase is Points, an array of type Point. The second is Function, which consists of a function that takes a float and returns a float. The third is Combination, which consists of a list of tuples made up of float and LineDefinitions; remember, type definitions can be recursive. float gives a weight to the line, allowing the programmer to specify how much of this section should appear. LineDefinitions allows the user to specify sections that consist of a list of points or sections that consist of functions. The definition of the type is as follows:

```
type LineDefinition =
|   Points of Point array
|   Function of (float -> float)
|   Combination of (float * LineDefinition) list
```

Simply knowing the path of a line doesn't give you enough information to be able to draw it. You also need to know the color, the width, and other attributes. Fortunately, a simple way to provide this sort of information is the System.Drawing.Pen class, which lets you specify the color, specify the width, and add effects such as making the line a dashed one.

To group this information, you create the LineDetail record type. This has two fields: one field of Pen type and one of LineDefinition type.

```
type LineDetails =
    { pen : Pen
      definition : LineDefinition }
```

Of course, you could add more fields to this record, perhaps for a description to be added to the graph's legend, but I'll leave it at these two fields to keep the example simple. You'll then group instances of this LineDetail type together in a list that is used to describe all the lines that should be drawn on the graph. An example of such a list is as follows:

```
let wiggle = PointList [ (0.1,0.6); (0.3,-0.3); (0.5,0.8); (0.7,-0.2) ]
let straight = Function (fun x -> x + 0.1)
let square = Function (fun x -> x * x)
let strange = Combination [ (0.2, square); (0.4, wiggle); (0.4, straight) ]

let lines =
    [{ pen = new Pen(Color.Blue) ;
       definition = wiggle };
     { pen = new Pen(Color.Orange) ;
       definition = straight };
     { pen = new Pen(Color.Red) ;
       definition = square };
     { pen = new Pen(Color.Green) ;
       definition = strange } ]
```

The last function that is critical to this example is the sample function. This allows you to specify a range of x values for a line definition and then calculate a list of points consisting of x, y values. This function actually does the work of turning the definition in your language into points that you can use to draw a graph.

The sample function definition is shown next. The first two cases are fairly straightforward. If you have a list of points for each x value, you use an interpolate function you have defined to calculate the appropriate y value. The interpolate function uses some straightforward geometry to calculate the intermediate points between the points that the user of the language has defined as a line definition and therefore work out the most appropriate y value. The case for a function is even simpler for each x value: you simply use the function that the user has defined to calculate the y value. The final case, where you have a combination, is a little more complicated mainly because you have to weigh the value of each section of the combination. You do this by creating a vector of all the weights and binding this to the identifier weights; then you create a list of points that lists all the line definitions that have been defined using the language by recursive function calls to the sample function. The resulting list from the recursive sample function call is bound to the identifier ptsl. Then you do the work of calculating the real *y* values; you extract all the *y* values from the list of points within the list ptsl and create a vector of these lists of *y* values using the combinel function you have defined and the Vector.of_list function. Then you use the Vectors module's dot function to scale each of the resulting vectors by the vector weights. After this, it is just a matter of combining the resulting *y* values with the original *x* values to create a list of points.

```
// Sample the line at the given sequence of X values
let rec sample xs line  =
    match line with
    | Points(pts) ->
        { for x in xs -> interpolate pts x }

    | Function(f) ->
        { for x in xs -> {X=x;Y=f x} }

    | Combination wlines ->
        let weights = wlines |> List.map fst |> Vector.of_list
        // Sample each of the lines
        let ptsl    = wlines |> List.map snd |> List.map (sample xs)
        // Extract the vector for each sample and combine by weight
        let ys = ptsl |> List.map (Seq.map (fun p -> p.Y))
                      |> combinel
                      |> Seq.map Vector.of_list
                      |> Seq.map (Vector.dot weights)
        // Make the results
        Seq.map2 (fun x y -> { X=x;Y=y }) xs ys
```

Listing 11-1 shows the full program.

Listing 11-1. *A Graph Control, Based on Language-Oriented Programming Techniques*

```
#light
open System
open System.Drawing
open System.Windows.Forms
open Microsoft.FSharp.Math

type Point = { X : float; Y : float }

type LineDefinition =
    |   Points of Point array
    |   Function of (float -> float)
    |   Combination of (float * LineDefinition) list

// Derived construction function
```

```
let PointList pts =
    Points(pts |> Array.of_list |> Array.map (fun (x,y) -> {X=x;Y=y}))

module LineFunctions = begin

    // Helper function to take a list of sequences and return a sequence of lists
    // where the sequences are iterated in lockstep.
    let combinel (seqs : list< #seq<'a> >) : seq< list<'a> > =
        Seq.generate
            (fun () -> seqs |> List.map (fun s -> s.GetEnumerator()) )
            (fun ies ->
                let more = ies |> List.for_all (fun ie -> ie.MoveNext())
                if more then Some(ies |> List.map (fun ie -> ie.Current))
                else None)
            (fun ies -> ies |> List.iter (fun ie -> ie.Dispose()))

    // Interoplate the given points to find a Y value for the given X
    let interpolate pts x =
        let best p z = Array.fold_right (fun x y -> if p x y then x else y) pts z
        let l = best (fun p1 p2 -> p1.X > p2.X && p1.X <= x) pts.[0]
        let r = best (fun p1 p2 -> p1.X < p2.X && p1.X >= x) pts.[pts.Length-1]
        let y = (if l.X = r.X then (l.Y+r.Y)/2.0
                    else l.Y + (r.Y-l.Y)*(x-l.X)/(r.X-l.X))
        { X=x; Y=y }

    // Sample the line at the given sequence of X values
    let rec sample xs line  =
        match line with
        | Points(pts) ->
            { for x in xs -> interpolate pts x }

        | Function(f) ->
            { for x in xs -> {X=x;Y=f x} }

        | Combination wlines ->
            let weights = wlines |> List.map fst |> Vector.of_list
            // Sample each of the lines
            let ptsl    = wlines |> List.map snd |> List.map (sample xs)
            // Extract the vector for each sample and combine by weight
            let ys = ptsl |> List.map (Seq.map (fun p -> p.Y))
                        |> combinel
                        |> Seq.map Vector.of_list
                        |> Seq.map (Vector.dot weights)
            // Make the results
            Seq.map2 (fun x y -> { X=x;Y=y }) xs ys

end
```

```
type LineDetails =
    { pen : Pen
      definition : LineDefinition }

let f32 x = Float32.of_float x
let f64 x = Float.of_float32 x

type Graph = class
    inherit Control
    val mutable maxX : float
    val mutable maxY : float
    val mutable minX : float
    val mutable minY : float
    val mutable lines : LineDetails list
    new () as x =
      { maxX = 1.0;
        maxY = 1.0;
        minX = -1.0;
        minY = -1.0;
        lines = [] }
      then
        x.Paint.Add(fun e -> x.DrawGraph(e.Graphics))
        x.Resize.Add(fun _ -> x.Invalidate())

    member f.DrawGraph(graphics : Graphics) =
        let height = Convert.ToSingle(f.Height)
        let width = Convert.ToSingle(f.Width)
        let widthF = f32 f.maxY - f32 f.minY
        let heightF = f32 f.maxX - f32 f.minX
        let stepY = height / heightF
        let stepX =  width / widthF
        let orginY = (0.0f - f32 f.minY) * stepY
        let orginX = (0.0f - f32 f.minX) * stepX
        let black = new Pen(Color.Black)
        graphics.DrawLine(black, 0.0f, orginY, width, orginY)
        graphics.DrawLine(black, orginX, 0.0f, orginX, height)

        let mapPoint pt =
            new PointF(orginX + (f32 pt.X * stepX),
                       height - (orginY + (f32 pt.Y * stepY)))
```

```
        let xs = { f.minX .. (1.0 / f64 stepX) .. f.maxX }
        f.lines
        |> List.iter
            (fun line -> LineFunctions.sample xs line.definition
                         |> Seq.map mapPoint
                         |> Seq.to_array
                         |> (fun pts -> graphics.DrawLines(line.pen, pts)))
end

module GraphTest = begin

    let wiggle = PointList [ (0.1,0.6); (0.3,-0.3); (0.5,0.8); (0.7,-0.2) ]
    let straight = Function (fun x -> x + 0.1)
    let square = Function (fun x -> x * x)
    let strange = Combination [ (0.2, square); (0.4, wiggle); (0.4, straight) ]

    let lines =
        [{ pen = new Pen(Color.Blue) ;
           definition = wiggle };
         { pen = new Pen(Color.Orange,
                         DashStyle = DashStyle.Dot,
                         Width = 2.0f) ;
           definition = straight };
         { pen = new Pen(Color.Red,
                         DashStyle = DashStyle.Dash,
                         Width = 2.0f) ;
           definition = square };
         { pen = new Pen(Color.Green, Width = 2.0f) ;
           definition = strange } ]

    let form =
        let temp = new Form(Visible=true,TopMost=true)
        let g = new Graph(Dock = DockStyle.Fill)
        g.lines <- lines
        temp.Controls.Add(g)
        temp

    [<STAThread>]
    do Application.Run(form)
end
```

This example produces the graph in Figure 11-1.

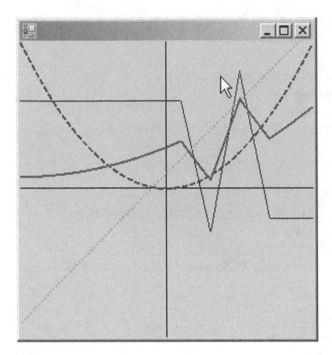

Figure 11-1. *Drawing lines with a DSL*

Metaprogramming with Quotations

In Chapter 6 you used quotations; these are quoted sections of F# code where the quote operator instructs the compiler to generate data structures representing the code rather than IL representing the code. This means instead of code that can be executed, you have a data structure that represents the code that was coded, and you're free to do what you want with it. You can either interpret it, performing the actions you require as you go along, or compile it into another language. Or you can simply ignore it if you want. You could, for example, take a section of quoted code and compile it for another runtime, such as the Java virtual machine (JVM). Or, like the LINQ example in Chapter 9, you could turn it into SQL and execute it against a database.

In the next example, you'll write an interpreter for integer-based arithmetic expressions in F#. This might be useful for learning how stack-based calculations work. Here, your language is already designed for you; it is the syntax available in F#. You'll work exclusively with arithmetic expressions of the form « (2 * (2 - 1)) / 2 ». This means you need to generate an error whenever you come across syntax that is neither an integer nor an operation. When working with quotations, you have to query the expression that you receive to see whether it is a specific type of expression. For example, here you query an expression to see whether it is an integer, and if it is, you push it onto the stack:

```
match uexp with
| Raw.Int32(x) ->
    printf "Push: %i\r\n" x
    operandsStack.Push(x)
| _ ->
```

If it isn't an integer, you check whether it is of several other types. Listing 11-2 shows the full example.

Listing 11-2. *Stack-Based Evaluation of F# Quoted Arithmetic Expressions*

```
#light
open System.Collections.Generic
open Microsoft.FSharp.Quotations
open Microsoft.FSharp.Quotations.Typed

let interpret exp =
    let uexp = to_raw exp
    let operandsStack = new Stack<int>()
    let rec interpretInner uexp =
        match uexp with
        | Raw.Apps(op, args) when args.Length > 0 ->
            args |> List.iter (fun x -> interpretInner x)
            interpretInner op
        | _ ->
        match uexp with
        | Raw.Int32 x ->
            printf "Push: %i\r\n" x
            operandsStack.Push(x)
        | Raw.AnyTopDefnUse(def, types) ->
            let preformOp f name =
                let x, y = operandsStack.Pop(), operandsStack.Pop()
                printf "%s %i, %i\r\n" name x y
                let result = f x y
                operandsStack.Push(result)
            let _,name = def.Path
            match name with
            | "op_Addition" ->
                let f x y = x + y
                preformOp f "Add"
            | "op_Subtraction" ->
                let f x y = y - x
                preformOp f "Sub"
            | "op_Multiply" ->
                let f x y = y * x
                preformOp f "Multi"
            | "op_Division" ->
                let f x y = y / x
                preformOp f "Div"
            | _ -> failwith "not a valid op"
        | _ -> failwith "not a valid op"
    interpretInner uexp
    printfn "Result: %i" (operandsStack.Pop())
```

```
interpret « (2 * (2 - 1)) / 2 »
read_line()
```

The results of this example are as follows:

```
Push: 2
Push: 2
Push: 1
Sub 1, 2
Multi 1, 2
Push: 2
Div 2, 2
Result: 1
```

When you use quotations, you are always working with F# syntax, which is both an advantage and a disadvantage. The advantage is that you can produce powerful libraries based on this technique that integrate very well with F# code, without having to create a parser. The disadvantage is that it is difficult to produce tools suitable for end users based on this technique; however, libraries that consume or transform F# quotations can still be used from other .NET languages because the F# libraries include functions and samples to convert between F# quotations and other common metaprogramming formats such as LINQ quotations.

You'll code a parser for a small arithmetic language in the next section. Although the results are much more flexible, more design work is potentially involved if you are creating a new language rather than implementing an existing one; in addition, there is always more programming work because you need to create a parser—although the tools F# provides help simplify the creation of a parser.

An Arithmetic-Language Implementation

Another approach to language-oriented programming is to create your own language represented in a textual format. This doesn't necessarily have to be a complicated process—if your language is quite simple, then you will find it straightforward to implement. Whether creating a simple language to be embedded into an application or full-fledged DSLs, the approach is similar. It's just that the more constructs you add to your language, the more work it will be to implement it.

You'll spend the remainder of this chapter looking at how to implement a really simple arithmetic language consisting of floating-point literals; floating-point identifiers; the operators +, -, *, and /; and parentheses for the disambiguation of expressions. Although this language is probably too simple to be of much benefit, it's easy to see how with a few simple extensions it could be a useful tool to embed into many financial or mathematical applications.

Creating the language can be broken down into two steps: parsing the user input and then acting on the input.

Parsing the language can itself be broken down into three steps: defining the *abstract syntax tree* (AST), creating the grammar, and tokenizing the text. When creating the parser, you can implement these steps in any order, and in fact you would probably design your grammar in small, repeated iterations of all three steps. You will look at the steps separately, in the sections "The Abstract Syntax Tree," "Tokenizing the Text: Fslex," and "Generating a Parser: Fsyacc."

There are two distinct modes of acting on the results of the parser: compiling the results and interpreting them. Compiling simply means changing the AST into some other format that is faster or easier for a machine to execute. Originally this nearly always meant native code, but these days it's more likely to be something a little more abstract, such as IL, F#, or even C#. Interpreting the results means acting on the results straightaway without any transformation of the AST. You'll look briefly at both topics in the sections "Interpreting the AST" and "Compiling the AST"; then you'll compare the two approaches to get some idea of when to use each one in the section "Compilation vs. Interpretation."

The Abstract Syntax Tree

An AST is a representation of the construct that makes up the program that is meant to be easy for the programmer to use. One reason F# is good for this kind of development is its union type. Because you can use this type to represent items that are related yet do not share the same structure, it is great for representing languages. The following example shows the abstract syntax tree:

```
type Expr =
  | Ident of string
  | Val of System.Double
  | Multi of Expr * Expr
  | Div of Expr * Expr
  | Plus of Expr * Expr
  | Minus of Expr * Expr
```

The tree consists of just one type because it is quite simple. A complicated tree would contain many more types, but all will be generally based around this pattern. Here you can see that the tree, the type `Expr`, will consist of either identifiers (the `Ident` type), the names of the identifiers represented by a string, or values (the `Val` type), with their values represented by a `System.Double`. The type `Expr` consists of four more types (`Multi`, `Div`, `Plus`, and `Minus`), which represent the arithmetic operations and use recursion so are composed of other expressions.

Tokenizing the Text: Fslex

Tokenizing the text (sometimes called *lexical analysis* or *lexing*) basically means breaking up the text into manageable lumps, or *tokens*. To do this, you use the tool `fslex.exe`, which is itself a DSL for creating *lexers* (sometimes called *scanners*), programs, or modules for tokenizing text. The program `fslex.exe` is a command-line application that takes a text file representing the lexer and turns into an F# file that implements the lexer.

An `fslex.exe` file has the extension `.fsl`. The file can have an optional header, which is placed between braces ({}) and is pure F# code, generally used to open modules or possibly to define helper functions. The rest is used to define the regular expressions that make up the lexer. You can bind a regular expression to an identifier using the `let` keyword, like this:

```
let digit = ['0'-'9']
```

or you can define a regular expression as part of a rule. A *rule* is a collection of regular expressions that are in competition to match sections of the text. A rule is defined with the keyword rule and followed by a name for the rule and then an equals sign and the keyword parse. Next come the definitions of the regular expressions, which should be followed by an action, which is an F# expression surrounded by braces. Each rule is separated by a vertical bar (|). Each rule will become a function that is capable of matching against a stream of text. If a match is found, then the rule fires, and the F# expression is executed. If several regular expressions match the rule, then the longest match is used. The value returned by the function is the value returned by the action. This means that each action must be of the same type. If no match is found, then an exception is raised.

Note The regular expressions used in the lexer are not the same as the ones used with the .NET BCL Regex class. You can find more details about the syntax at http://strangelights.com/FSharp/Foundations/default.aspx/FSharpFoundations.FSLexRegEx.

Although the actions can be any valid F# expressions, it's normal to return the token declarations that you will make in the fsyacc file. See the next section, "Generating a Parser: Fsyacc," for more information about this. If you want to use the lexer on its own, you will place whatever logic you want to happen here, such as writing the token to the console or storing the token found in a list.

The following example shows a file that is capable of tokenizing your little language. You usually do one of two things in the actions. If you're interested in the match, you return a token that has been defined in the parser file. These are the identifiers in block capitals like RPAREN or MULTI. If you're not interested, you call token with the special lexbuf value function to start the parsing again. The lexbuf value is automatically placed in your parser definition and represents the text stream being processed. It is of type Microsoft.FSharp.Tools.FsLex.LexBuffer. Also notice how, in places where you're actually interested in the value found rather than just the fact a value was found, you use a function lexeme from the module Microsoft.FSharp.Compatibility.OCaml.Lexing to get the string representing the match from the lexbuf. Table 11-1 summarizes other useful functions from this module.

```
{
open System
open Pars
open Lexing
}

let digit = ['0'-'9']
let whitespace = [' ' '\t' ]
let newline = ('\n' | '\r' '\n')

rule token = parse
| whitespace        { token lexbuf }
| newline           { token lexbuf }
| "("               { LPAREN }
| ")"               { RPAREN }
```

```
| "*"                { MULTI }
| "/"                { DIV }
| "+"                { PLUS }
| "-"                { MINUS }
| '['['^']']'+']'    { ID(lexeme lexbuf) }
| ['-']?digit+('.'digit+)?(['e''E']digit+)?
                     { FLOAT (Double.Parse(lexeme lexbuf)) }
| eof                { EOF }
```

Table 11-1. *Useful Functions from the Lexing Module*

Function	Description
lexeme	Gets the current lexeme from the lexbuf as a string
lexeme_bytes	Gets the current lexeme from the lexbuf as a byte array
lexeme_char	Takes an integer and returns the character at this index from the current lexeme in the lexbuf as a char from the lexbuf as a string
lexeme_end	Gets the absolute position of the lexeme, which is useful when trying to provide error information to the user
from_text_reader	Creates a lexbuf from a text reader, which is useful when using the lexer from F# code
from_string	Creates a lexbuf from a string, which is useful when using the lexer from F# code

A lexer can contain several rules; any further rules are separated from each other by the keyword and, then a name for the rule, then an equals sign, and then the keyword parse. After this come the definitions of the regular expressions that make up this rule. This is often useful if you want to implement comments in your language. Comments often produce false positives in lexers, since they can contain any text. To deal with this, when a start-comment token is detected, it is customary to switch to another rule that looks only for an end-comment token and ignores all other input.

The following example shows a simple parser that either finds strings that are like F# identifiers or discards C#-style multiline comments. Notice how when you find the start of a comment, you call the comment function to hop into the comment rule, and to find the end of it, you return unit to hop out of it.

```
{
open Lexing
}

rule token = parse
| "/*"          { comment lexbuf; token lexbuf }
| ['_''a'-'z''A'-'Z']['_''a'-'z''A'-'Z''0'-'9']*
                { lexeme lexbuf }
and comment = parse
| "*/" | eof    { () }
| _             { comment lexbuf }
```

This has been quite a rapid overview of `fslex.exe`; you can find more information about it at `http://strangelights.com/FSharp/Foundations/default.aspx/FSharpFoundations.FSLex`.

Generating a Parser: Fsyacc

A *scanner* is a program or module that breaks a text stream into pieces. You can think of a parser as the thing that reorganizes the text into something more meaningful. The aim of the parser is usually to produce an AST, and this is done by defining rules that determine the order in which the tokens should appear. The tool `fsyacc.exe` can generate parsers that are look-ahead left-to-right parsers, more commonly called LALR(1). This is an algorithm for parsing grammars. Not all grammars can be parsed by this algorithm, but grammars that can't are quite rare. For more information about how the LALR(1) algorithm works, please see `http://strangelights.com/FSharp/Foundations/default.aspx/FSharpFoundations.LALR`.

■Note The YACC part of the name `fsyacc.exe` is an acronym for Yet Another Compiler Compiler.

The tool `fsyacc.exe` works with text files with the extension `.fsy`. These files have three distinct parts. First is the header, which is a section of pure F# code surrounded by percentage signs and braces (%{ for opening and %} for closing). This section is typically used to open your AST module and to define short helper functions for creating the AST. Next comes the declarations, defining the terminals of your language. A *terminal* is something concrete in your grammar such as an identifier name or a symbol. Typically these are found by the lexer. Declarations have several different forms that are summarized in Table 11-2. The third section contains the rules that make up the grammar; these are described in the next paragraph.

Table 11-2. *Declarations of Terminals in an* `fsyacc.exe` *File*

Declaration	Description
`%token`	This declares the given symbol as the token in the language.
`%token<type>`	This declares the given symbol as a token, like `%token`, but with arguments of the given type; this is useful for things such as identifiers and literals when you need to store information about them.
`%start`	This declares the rule at which the parser should start parsing.
`%type<type>`	This declares the type of a particular rule; it is mandatory for the start rule but optional for all other rules.
`%left`	This declares a token as left-associative, which can help resolve ambiguity in the grammar.
`%right`	This declares a token as right-associative, which can help resolve ambiguity in the grammar.
`%nonassoc`	This declares a token as nonassociative, which can help resolve ambiguity in the grammar.

The declarations are separated from the rules by two percentage signs, which make up the last section of the file. Rules are the nonterminals of the grammar. A *nonterminal* defines something that can be made up of several terminals. So, each rule must have a name, which is followed by a colon and then the definition of all the items that make up the rule, which are separated by vertical bar. The items that make up rule are either the names of tokens you have defined or the names of rules; this must always be followed by an action that is F# code surrounded by braces. Here is a snippet of a rule:

```
Expression: ID { Ident($1) }
    | FLOAT {  Val($1)  }
```

Expession is the rule name, and ID and FLOAT are two rules made up of just terminals. The sections { Ident($1) } and { Ident($1) } are the rule actions. Within these actions, you can grab the data associated with the terminal or nonterminal using a dollar sign and then the number representing the position of the item in which you are interested. The result of the action will itself become associated with the rule. All the actions of a rule must be of the same type, since a rule will be implemented as an F# function with the actions making up the items that it returns. Any comments within the rules should use the C-style comment markers, /* */.

The following example shows a simple parser definition for your language. Note how all the actions associated with rules are simple, just creating instances of types from the AST, and that all the languages terminals are in block capitals.

```
%{

open Strangelights.ExpressionParser.Ast

%}

%start Expression
%token <string> ID
%token <System.Double> FLOAT
%token LPAREN RPAREN EOF MULTI DIV PLUS MINUS
%type < Strangelights.ExpressionParser.Ast.Expr > Expression

%left MULTI
%left DIV
%left PLUS
%left MINUS

%%

Expression: ID { Ident($1) }
    | FLOAT {  Val($1)  }
    | LPAREN Expression RPAREN {  $2  }
    | Expression MULTI Expression {  Multi($1, $3)  }
    | Expression DIV Expression {  Div($1, $3)  }
    | Expression PLUS Expression {  Plus($1, $3)  }
    | Expression MINUS Expression {  Minus($1, $3)  }
```

Let's take a closer look at the items that make up your rule. The simplest rule item you have consists of one terminal, ID, in this case an identifier:

```
ID { Ident($1) }
```

In the rule item's action, the string that represents the identifier is used to create an instance of the Ident constructor from the AST. A slightly more complex rule is one that involves both terminals and nonterminals:

```
| Expression MULTI Expression {  Multi($1, $3)  }
```

This rule item recognizes the case where you have a valid expression followed by a multiplication sign and then a valid expression. These expressions are then loaded into the constructor Multi from your AST. These expressions could be terminals in your language, such as an identifier or a literal, or they might be an expression composed of several terminals, such as a multiplication operation.

The hardest thing about creating a grammar is making sure it is not ambiguous. A grammar is ambiguous when two or more rules could be matched by the same input. Fortunately, fsyacc.exe can spot this automatically and warns you when this has occurred. It is only a warning, because the parser can still function; it just has some rules that will not be matched so is probably incorrect in some way.

Note For more information about debugging grammars, see http://strangelights.com/FSharp/ Foundations/default.aspx/FSharpFoundations.FsYaccAmbigous. This has been quite a rapid overview of fsyacc.exe. You can find more information about it at http://strangelights.com/ FSharp/Foundations/default.aspx/FSharpFoundations.FsYacc.

Using the Parser

Using the parser is very straightforward. You can use a lexer on its own, but a parser generated with fsyacc.exe always requires a lexer to work. You'll look at how to use your lexer on its own and combined with a parser in this section.

Caution Remember, .fsl and .fsy files cannot be used directly by the F# compiler. You need to compile them using fslex.exe and fsyacc.exe and then use the generated .fs files.

To use your lexer, you first need to create a LexBuffer that represents the text to be processed. The easiest way to do this is to create the LexBuffer from a string using the function Lexing.from_string, although it is not difficult to create one from a file using the Lexing.from_text_reader function. You can then pass this buffer to a function created by a rule in your lexer, and it will pull off the first token.

The following example shows your lexer in action. You've compiled the lexer into a module, Lex, and you use the token function to find the first, and in this case the only, token in the string.

```
#light
let lexbuf = Lexing.from_string "1"
let token = Lex.token lexbuf
print_any token
```

The result of this example is as follows:

FLOAT 1.0

Just grabbing the first token from the buffer is rarely of much value, so if you use the lexer in stand-alone mode, it is much more common to create a loop that repeatedly grabs all tokens from the buffer. The next example demonstrates how to do this, printing the tokens found as you go:

```
#light
let lexbuf2 = Lexing.from_string "(1 * 1) + 2"
while not lexbuf2.IsPastEndOfStream do
    let token = Lex.token lexbuf2
    printf "%s\r\n" (any_to_string token)
```

The results of this example are as follows:

```
LPAREN
FLOAT 1.0
MULTI
FLOAT 1.0
RPAREN
PLUS
FLOAT 2.0
EOF
```

It is much more common for a lexer to be used in conjunction with a parser module. The functions generated by the parser expect their first parameter to be a function that takes a LexBuffer and transforms it into a token (LexBuffer<'a,'cty> -> Pars.token in this case). Fortunately, this is the signature that your lexer's token function has. The next example shows how you would implement this:

```
#light
let lexbuf3 = Lexing.from_string "(1 * 1) + 2"
let e = Pars.Expression Lex.token lexbuf3
print_any e
```

The result of this example is as follows:

Plus (Multi (Val 1.0,Val 1.0),Val 2.0)

And that's it! Once you have your AST, you have a nice abstract form of your grammar, so now it is up to you to create a program that acts on this tree.

Interpreting the AST

When you have created your AST, you have two choices; you can either interpret it or compile it. Interpreting it simply means walking the tree and performing actions as you go. Compiling it means changing it into some other form that is easier, or more typically faster, for the machine to execute. This section will examine interpreting the results, and the next will look at the options for compiling them; finally, you will look at when you should use interpretation and when you should use compilation.

The following example shows a short interpreter for your program. The main work of interpreting the AST is done by the function `interpret`, which walks the tree performing the necessary action as it goes. The logic is quite simple. If you find a literal value or an identifier, you simply return the appropriate value.

```
| Ident (s) -> variableDict.[s]
| Val (v) -> v
```

If you find an operand, you recursively evaluate the expressions it contains to obtain their values and then perform the operation:

```
| Multi (e1, e2) -> (interpretInner e1) * (interpretInner e2)
```

Listing 11-3 gives the full interpreter.

Listing 11-3. *Interpreting an AST Generated from Command-Line Input*

```
#light
open System.Collections.Generic
open Strangelights.ExpressionParser.Ast

// requesting a value for variable from the user
let getVariableValues e =
    let rec getVariableValuesInner input (variables : Map<string, float>) =
        match input with
        | Ident (s) ->
            match variables.TryFind(s) with
            | Some _ -> variables
            | None ->
                printf "%s: " s
                let v = read_float()
                variables.Add(s,v)
        | Multi (e1, e2) ->
            variables
            |> getVariableValuesInner e1
            |> getVariableValuesInner e2
        | Div (e1, e2) ->
            variables
            |> getVariableValuesInner e1
            |> getVariableValuesInner e2
```

```
        | Plus (e1, e2) ->
            variables
                |> getVariableValuesInner e1
                |> getVariableValuesInner e2
        | Minus (e1, e2) ->
            variables
                |> getVariableValuesInner e1
                |> getVariableValuesInner e2
        | _ -> variables
    getVariableValuesInner e (Map.Empty())

// function to handle the interpretation
let interpret input (variableDict : Map<string,float>) =
    let rec interpretInner input =
        match input with
        | Ident (s) -> variableDict.[s]
        | Val (v) -> v
        | Multi (e1, e2) -> (interpretInner e1) * (interpretInner e2)
        | Div (e1, e2) -> (interpretInner e1) / (interpretInner e2)
        | Plus (e1, e2) -> (interpretInner e1) + (interpretInner e2)
        | Minus (e1, e2) -> (interpretInner e1) - (interpretInner e2)
    interpretInner input

// request input from user and interpret it
printf "input expression: "
let lexbuf = Lexing.from_string (read_line())
let e = Pars.Expression Lex.token lexbuf
let args = getVariableValues e
let v = interpret e args
printf "result: %f" v
read_line()
```

The results of this example, when compiled and executed, are as follows:

```
input expression: (1 + 3) * [my var]
[my var]: 12
result: 48.000000
```

Compiling the AST

To many, compilation means generating native code, so it has a reputation for being difficult. But it doesn't have to mean generating native code, and for a DSL you typically generate some other more general-purpose programming language. The .NET Framework provides several features for compiling an AST into a program.

Your choice of technology depends on several factors. For example, if you're targeting your language at developers, it might be enough to generate a text file containing F#, some other language, or a compiled assembly that can then used within an application. However, if you're targeting end users, you will almost certainly have to compile and then execute it on the fly. Table 11-3 summarizes the various options available.

Table 11-3. *.NET Code-Generation Technologies*

Technology	Description
Microsoft.CSharp. CSharpCodeProvider	This class supports compilation of a C# file that has been created on the fly, either by using simple string concatenation or by using the System.CodeDom namespace. Once the code has been compiled into an assembly, it can be loaded dynamically into memory and executed via reflection. This operation is relatively expensive, because it requires writing to the disk and using reflection to execute methods.
System.CodeDom	This is a set of classes aimed at abstracting between operations available in different languages. The idea is that you describe your operations using the classes available in this namespace and then use a provider to compile them into the language of your choice. .NET ships with a provider for both C# and Visual Basic. Providers for other languages are available for download. They are often the results of community projects.
System.Reflection.Emit	This namespace allows you to build up assemblies using IL. Since IL offers more features than either F#, C#, or System.CodeDom, it provides more flexibility; however, it is lower level so requires more patience and will probably take more time to get right.
AbstractIL	This is a library written in F# for manipulating IL. It provides roughly the same functionality as System.Reflection.Emit, but F# programmers might find it is more suited to their style of programming than the options available in System.Reflection.Emit.

Note If you want to use System.CodeDom, you could consider compiling these into F# code rather than C# code using the code DOM provider written by Tomas Petricek, which is available from http://www.codeplex.com/fscodedom.

You'll use the System.Reflection.Emit.DynamicMethod class, not particularly because you need the flexibility of IL, but since IL has built-in instructions for floating-point arithmetic, it's well suited to implement the little language. The DynamicMethod also provides a fast and easy way to let you call into the resulting program.

The method createDynamicMethod actually compiles the AST by walking the AST and generating code. First, it creates an instance of the DynamicMethod class to hold the IL you define to represent the method:

```
let temp = new DynamicMethod("", (type float), paramsTypes, meth.Module)
```

Then createDynamicMethod starts walking the tree. When you encounter an identifier, you emit some code to load an argument of your dynamic method:

```
| Ident name ->
    il.Emit(OpCodes.Ldarg, paramNames.IndexOf(name))
```

When you encounter a literal, you emit the IL code to load the literal value:

```
| Val x -> il.Emit(OpCodes.Ldc_R8, x)
```

When you encounter an operation, you must recursively evaluate both expressions and then emit the instruction that represents the required operation:

```
| Multi (e1 , e2) ->
    generateIlInner e1
    generateIlInner e2
    il.Emit(OpCodes.Mul)
```

Note how the operation is emitted last, after both expressions have been recursively evaluated. This is because IL is stack based, so data from the other operations must have been pushed onto the stack before the operator is evaluated.

Note It is beyond the scope of this book to give you a full overview of IL; however, you can find more details at http://strangelights.com/FSharp/Foundations/default.aspx/FSharpFoundations.IL.

Listing 11-4 gives the full compiler.

Listing 11-4. *Compiling an AST Generated from Command-Line Input*

```
#light
open System.Collections.Generic
open System.Reflection
open System.Reflection.Emit
open Strangelights.ExpressionParser.Ast

// get a list of all the parameter names
let rec getParamList e =
    let rec getParamListInner e names =
        match e with
        | Ident name ->
            if not (List.exists (fun s -> s = name) names) then
                name :: names
            else
                names
        | Multi (e1 , e2) ->
            names
            |> getParamListInner e1
            |> getParamListInner e2
```

```
        | Div (e1 , e2) ->
            names
            |> getParamListInner e1
            |> getParamListInner e2
        | Plus (e1 , e2) ->
            names
            |> getParamListInner e1
            |> getParamListInner e2
        | Minus (e1 , e2) ->
            names
            |> getParamListInner e1
            |> getParamListInner e2
        | _ -> names
    getParamListInner e []

// create the dynamic method
let createDynamicMethod e (paramNames: string list) =
    let generateIl e (il : ILGenerator) =
        let rec generateIlInner e  =
            match e with
            | Ident name ->
                let index = List.find_index (fun s -> s = name) paramNames
                il.Emit(OpCodes.Ldarg, index)
            | Val x -> il.Emit(OpCodes.Ldc_R8, x)
            | Multi (e1 , e2) ->
                generateIlInner e1
                generateIlInner e2
                il.Emit(OpCodes.Mul)
            | Div (e1 , e2) ->
                generateIlInner e1
                generateIlInner e2
                il.Emit(OpCodes.Div)
            | Plus (e1 , e2) ->
                generateIlInner e1
                generateIlInner e2
                il.Emit(OpCodes.Add)
            | Minus (e1 , e2) ->
                generateIlInner e1
                generateIlInner e2
                il.Emit(OpCodes.Sub)
        generateIlInner e
        il.Emit(OpCodes.Ret)
```

```
    let paramsTypes = Array.create paramNames.Length (type float)
    let meth = MethodInfo.GetCurrentMethod()
    let temp = new DynamicMethod("", (type float), paramsTypes, meth.Module)
    let il = temp.GetILGenerator()
    generateIl e il
    temp

let collectArgs (paramNames : string list) =
    paramNames
    |> IEnumerable.map
        (fun n ->
            printf "%s: " n
            box (read_float()))
    |> Array.of_seq

printf "input expression: "
let lexbuf = Lexing.from_string (read_line())
let e = Pars.Expression Lex.token lexbuf
let paramNames = getParamList e
let dm = createDynamicMethod e paramNames
let args = collectArgs paramNames
printf "result: %O" (dm.Invoke(null, args))
read_line()
```

The results of this example are as follows:

```
input expression: 5 * ([my var] + 2)
[my var]: 4
result: 30
```

This has been a brief overview of code generation and compilation. You can find more information at http://strangelights.com/FSharp/Foundations/default.aspx/ FSharpFoundations.Compilation.

Compilation vs. Interpretation

So, when should you use compilation, and when should you use interpretation? Because the final result is pretty much the same, the answer generally comes down to the raw speed of the final generated code, though memory usage and start-up times are also key concerns. If you need your code to execute more quickly, then compilation will generally give you better results, with some activities.

The test harness in Listing 11-5 enables you to execute the interpret function results of createDynamicMethod repeatedly and time how long this takes. It also tests an important variation on dynamic methods; that is where you also generate a new .NET delegate value to act as the handle by which you invoke the generated code. As you will see, it turns out that this is by far the fastest technique. Remember, you're timing how long it takes to evaluate the AST either directly or in a compiled form; you're not measuring the parse time or compilation time.

Listing 11-5. *A Test Harness for Comparing*

```
#light
open System.Diagnostics

printf "input expression: "
let input = read_line()
printf "Interpret/Compile/Compile Through Delegate [i/c/cd]: "
let interpertFlag = read_line()
printf "reps: "
let reps = read_int()

type Df0 = delegate of unit -> float
type Df1 = delegate of float -> float
type Df2 = delegate of float * float -> float
type Df3 = delegate of float * float * float -> float
type Df4 = delegate of float * float * float * float -> float

match interpertFlag with
| "i" ->
    let lexbuf = Lexing.from_string input
    let e = Pars.Expression Lex.token lexbuf
    let args = Interpret.getVariableValues e
    let clock = new Stopwatch()
    clock.Start()
    for i = 1 to reps do
        Interpret.interpret e args |> ignore
    clock.Stop()
    printf "%Li" clock.ElapsedTicks
| "c" ->
    let lexbuf = Lexing.from_string input
    let e = Pars.Expression Lex.token lexbuf
    let paramNames = Compile.getParamList e
    let dm = Compile.createDynamicMethod e paramNames
    let args = Compile.collectArgs paramNames
    let clock = new Stopwatch()
    clock.Start()
    for i = 1 to reps do
        dm.Invoke(null, args) |> ignore
    clock.Stop()
    printf "%Li" clock.ElapsedTicks
| "cd" ->
    let lexbuf = Lexing.from_string input
    let e = Pars.Expression Lex.token lexbuf
    let paramNames = Compile.getParamList e
```

```
let dm = Compile.createDynamicMethod e paramNames
let args = Compile.collectArgs paramNames
let args = args |> Array.map (fun f -> f :?> float)
let d =
    match args.Length with
    | 0 -> dm.CreateDelegate(type Df0)
    | 1 -> dm.CreateDelegate(type Df1)
    | 2 -> dm.CreateDelegate(type Df2)
    | 3 -> dm.CreateDelegate(type Df3)
    | 4 -> dm.CreateDelegate(type Df4)
    | _ -> failwith "too many parameters"
let clock = new Stopwatch()
clock.Start()
for i = 1 to reps do
    match d with
    | :? Df0 as d -> d.Invoke() |> ignore
    | :? Df1 as d -> d.Invoke(args.(0)) |> ignore
    | :? Df2 as d -> d.Invoke(args.(0), args.(1)) |> ignore
    | :? Df3 as d -> d.Invoke(args.(0), args.(1), args.(2)) |> ignore
    | :? Df4 as d -> d.Invoke(args.(0), args.(1), args.(2), args.(4)) |> ignore
    | _ -> failwith "too many parameters"
clock.Stop()
printf "%Li" clock.ElapsedTicks
| _ -> failwith "not an option"
```

Table 11-4 summarizes the results of this program, when executed on the expression 1 + 1.

Table 11-4. *Summary of Processing the Expression 1 + 1 for Various Numbers of Repetitions*

Repetitions	1	10	100	1,000	10,000	100,000	1,000,000
Interpreted	6,890	6,979	6,932	7,608	14,835	84,823	799,788
Compiled via delegate	8,65	856	854	1,007	2,369	15,871	151,602
Compiled	1,112	1,409	2,463	16,895	151,135	1,500,437	14,869,692

From Table 11-4 and Figure 11-2, you can see that "Compiled" and "Compiled via delegate" are much faster over a small number of repetitions. But notice that over 1, 10, and 100 repetitions, the amount of time required grows negligibly. This is because over these small numbers of repetitions, the time taken for each repetition is insignificant. It is the time that the JIT compiler takes to compile the IL code into native code that is significant. This is why the "Compiled" and "Compiled via delegate" times are so close. They both have a similar amount of code to JIT compile. The "Interpreted" time takes longer because you must JIT compile more code, specifically the interpreter. But JIT is a one-off cost because you need to JIT each method only once; therefore, as the number of repetitions go up, this one-off cost is paid for, and you begin to see a truer picture of the relative performance cost.

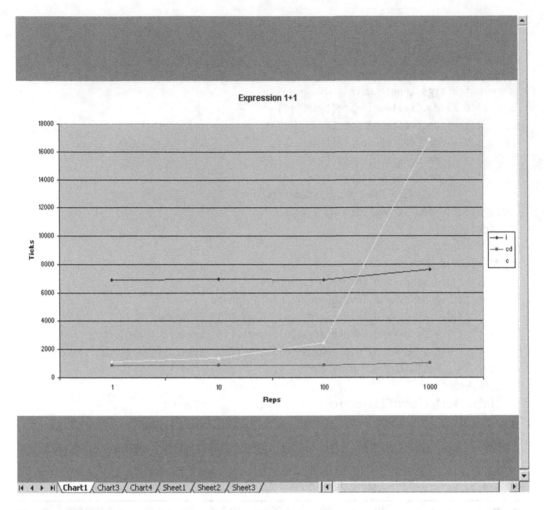

Figure 11-2. *The evaluation time in machine ticks of the expression 1 + 1 against the number of evaluations of the express*

You can see clearly from Figure 11-2 that as the number of repetitions goes up, the cost of "Compiled" goes up steeply. This is because accessing the compiled DynamicMethod through its Invoke method is expensive, and you incur this cost on every repetition, so the time taken for a "Compiled" method increases at the same rate as the number of repetitions. However, the problem lies not with compilation but with how you are invoking the compiled code. It turns out that calling a DynamicMethod through a delegate rather than the Invoke member on the dynamic delegate allows you to pay only once for the cost of binding to the method, so executing a DynamicMethod this way is much more efficient if you intend to evaluate the expression multiple times. So from the results, compilation with invocation via a delegate is the best option in terms of speed.

This analysis shows the importance of measurement: don't assume that compilation has given you the expected performance gains until you actually see the benefits on realistic data sets and have used all the available techniques to ensure no unnecessary overhead is lurking. However, in reality, many other factors can affect this. For example, if your expressions change often, your interpreter will need to be JIT compiled only once, but each compiled expression will need to be to JIT compiled, so you'll need to run your compiled code many times if you want to see any performance gains. Given that interpretation is usually easier to implement and that compiled code provides only significant performance gains in certain situations, interpretation is often a better choice.

When dealing with situations that require code to perform as quickly as possible, it's generally best to try a few different approaches and then profile your application to see which one gives better results. You can find more information about performance profiling in Chapter 12.

Summary

In this chapter, you looked at the main features and techniques for language-oriented programming in F#. You have seen various techniques; some use data structures as little languages or work with quotations, which involve working with the existing F# syntax to change or extend it. Others, such as implementing a parser, enable you to work with just about any language that is text based, whether this language is of your own design or perhaps more commonly a preexisting language. All these techniques when used correctly can lead to big productivity gains.

The next chapter will look at the tools available to help you to program in F#, not only the tools that are distributed with F# but also the various tools available for .NET that are useful for F# programming.

CHAPTER 12

■ ■ ■

The F# Tool Suite and .NET Programming Tools

This chapter will be a little different from most of the chapters in this book; instead of focusing on examples of F# programs, it'll focus on how to use various programming tools, both those that are distributed with F# and those that target .NET in general.

The F# distribution includes two versions of the compiler and a number of other tools. These are all available in the distribution's \bin directory. You can find the F# compiler, at the time of writing, in c:\Program Files\FSharp<version>\bin where <version> is the version number of F# that you have installed. This chapter will give a quick tour of the useful tools in this directory.

Specifically, I'll cover the following:

fsc.exe: The F# compiler

fsi.exe: F# interactive, which is an interactive version of the compiler

fslex.exe: A tool for creating lexical analyzers

fsyacc.exe: A tool for creating parsers

resxc.exe: A resource file compiler

First, you'll take a closer look at the various command-line switches for fsc.exe. Next, you'll examine various ways you can use fsi.exe more effectively.

Using Useful fsc.exe Command-Line Switches

You can view the basic F# command-line options using the -help switch; I describe them in the section "Basic Compiler Switches." F# also has a large number of advanced command-line switches; you can view them using the --full-help command-line flag. You don't need to know all of them for your everyday F# programming. A lot of them are just for using the compiler in experimental ways, so I won't document them here. Don't think this means you shouldn't use the switches that aren't documented, but if you do use them, then carefully test any resulting assembly before it is released. I've grouped the nonexperimental switches by functional area, and I'll describe them in the rest of this chapter.

Basic Compiler Switches

F# offers a number of basic command-line switches that do everything you'd expected a compiler to be able to do. I summarize them in Table 12-1.

Table 12-1. *Basic F# Compiler Switches*

Switch	Description
-o <string>	This controls the name of the assembly that will be produced.
-a	This produces an archive, a .dll, rather than an executable. You can use the advanced command-line options that start with --target to get more fined-grained control over this.
-r <string>	This is the filename of a .NET assembly to reference so types and methods can be used from the assembly. If a full file path is given, then this is used as is; if just the filename or a relative path that is given, then the current directory, the F# binaries directory (usually c:\Program Files\FSharp-<version>\bin), and the framework directory (usually c:\WINDOWS\Microsoft.NET\Framework\v<version>) are searched for the assembly. You can add directories to this search path by using the -I switch described in this table. If no assembly is found matching the given name, an error is raised, whether the input source files are valid or not.
-R <string>	This is the same as -r, except that the assembly being referenced is copied locally. This is useful because it means the .NET loader will be able to find the assembly when it is run.
-I <string>	This specifics a directory that will be used in the search for assemblies when they are referenced with the -r or -R flag.
-g	This produces a symbol file, a .pdb, that will allow you to set breakpoints and step through the source line by line in a debugger. This also turns off all optimizations, unless you give one of the optimizations flags (flags that begin with -O).
--define <string>	This defines a symbol for conditional compilation, a technique that you can use to exclude source code from compilation. I discuss this technique further in Chapter 6.
-i	This prints the inferred interface of a file to the console so that you can see what types have been inferred by the compiler for your values. This is useful for creating signature files, which I discuss further in Chapter 6.
-doc <string>	This writes the doc comments for the assembly to the given file. *Doc comments* are a special type of comment and are intended to create documentation for programmers who will use the finished assembly. I discuss them further in Chapter 6.

Compiler Optimization Switches

The compiler optimization switches are listed among the basic command-line options when you use the -help command-line option. I recommend that you compile code using the optimization switches when you compile your code for release, because compiler optimizations can significantly increase the performance of your code. Table 12-2 summarizes the optimization switches.

Table 12-2. *Optimization F# Compiler Switches*

Switch	Description
-Ooff	This turns off all optimizations including those performed by the .NET Framework's JIT compiler.
-O0	This enables optimizations by the JIT compiler but turns off all optimizations by the F# compiler.
-O1	This enables optimizations by the JIT compiler and optimizations that are local to an F# module.
-O	This is the same as -O2; it is the default unless you specify that debugging symbols should be produced (by using the -g flag).
-O2	This is the same as -O1 except that optimizations between F# modules are also allowed.
-O3	This is the same as -O2 but with increased inlining and lambda lifting.

I took the OCaml "Spectral Norm" benchmark from the Computer Language Shootout Benchmarks site (http://shootout.alioth.debian.org/) and ported it to F#. You can find information about what a spectral norm is at http://mathworld.wolfram.com/SpectralNorm.html. Here's the code used to do the benchmark:

```
#light
let evalA i j = 1.0 / float((i+j)*(i+j+1)/2+i+1)

let evalATimesU u v =
    let n = Array.length v - 1
    for i = 0 to  n do
        v.(i) <- 0.0
        for j = 0 to n do
            v.(i) <- v.(i) + evalA i j * u.(j)

let evalAtTimesU u v =
    let n = Array.length v -1 in
    for i = 0 to n do
        v.(i) <- 0.0
        for j = 0 to n do
            v.(i) <- v.(i) + evalA j i * u.(j)

let evalAtATimesU u v =
    let w = Array.create (Array.length u) 0.0
    evalATimesU u w
    evalAtTimesU w v

let main() =
    let n =
        try
            int_ot_string(Sys.argv.(1))
        with _ -> 2000
```

```
let u = Array.create n 1.0
let v = Array.create n 0.0
for i = 0 to 9 do
    evalAtATimesU u v
    evalAtATimesU v u

let vv = ref 0.0
let vBv = ref 0.0
for i=0 to n-1 do
    vv := !vv + v.(i) * v.(i)
    vBv := !vBv + u.(i) * v.(i)

Printf.printf "%0.9f\n" (sqrt(!vBv / !vv))
```

main()

I then compiled this into a number of different executables, differing only by optimization level, and I timed the execution of these programs using ntimer.exe, which is available with the Windows Server 2003 Resource Kit. The times shown in Table 12-3 are all in seconds, and the "Percentage Diff" number is the percentage change from the unoptimized time.

Table 12-3. *Times from the Spectral Norm Benchmark*

Optimization Level	Command Line	Kernel	User	Total	Percentage Diff
-Ooff	ntimer spectral-Ooff.exe 2000	00.090	03.535	03.715	0
-O0	ntimer spectral-O0.exe 2000	00.080	03.525	03.725	−0.27
-O1	ntimer spectral-O1.exe 2000	00.080	02.954	03.174	17.0
-O2	ntimer spectral-O2.exe 2000	00.030	02.984	03.154	17.9
-O3	ntimer spectral-O3.exe 2000	00.050	03.214	03.394	9.5

Although the time difference might look relatively small, there is actually a 17.9 percent difference between the fastest time and the unoptimized time. Although it's difficult to predict what effect these flags would have on other programs, and particularly on user perception of response time, a 17.9 percent increase in execution speed is not insignificant, and it's worth using these switches since they can give performance gains for such little effort.

Compiler Warning Switches

The compiler generates warnings to let you know when it thinks you've done something you didn't mean to, such as initializing a private identifier or not using it within the module in which it's defined. Unlike errors that cause the compilation to fail, when the compiler produces only warnings, it will still compile the code. Table 12-4 summarizes the warning switches.

Table 12-4. *Warning F# Compiler Switches*

Switch	Description
--all-warnings	This flag means the compiler will print all the warnings it finds with the source code.
--no-warnings	This means the compiler will not print any warnings; it is generally not advisable to use this flag.
--all-warnings-as-errors	This means that any warning will be treated as an error, meaning that an assembly will not be produced. This is useful to stop yourself from getting lazy and ignoring warnings; if left unchecked, warnings can quickly get out of control on large projects, especially if they are shared between many programmers.
--warn-as-error <int>	This is a lesser form of the --all-warnings-as-errors flag, allowing you to treat a specific warning as an error.
--warn <int>	This informs the compiler to warn you when it finds a specific warning; this is useful in conjunction with the --no-warnings flag.
--no-warn <int>	This informs the compiler to not warn you about a specific warning; this is useful when there are mitigating circumstances for a warning appearing in your code; however, you should not use it without careful consideration.

Compiler Target Switches

These flags give you fine-grained control over what the compiler produces. These are most useful when producing a WinForms application that does not need to write to the console. Table 12-5 summarizes the target switches.

Table 12-5. *Target F# Compiler Switches*

Switch	Description
--target-exe	This produces an executable assembly designed to execute within the window's console; if you execute it outside the console, it will pop up its own console, even if the application uses WinForms components.
--target-winexe	This produces an executable assembly that does not have a console associated with it; usually you will use this flag when you create WinForm applications in F#.
--target-dll	This produces a .dll file.
--target-module	This produces a binary file that is a module rather than an assembly; several modules can be composed into a multifile assembly using tools distributed with the .NET SDK. However, this functionality is not used very often.

Signing and Versioning Switches

Assemblies must be cryptographically signed and have a version number before they can be installed in the GAC. Assemblies are signed with keys produced by the sn.exe tool, distributed with the .NET SDK. Signing an assembly also gives you some level of confidence that the assembly has not been tampered with after it left its creator; since anyone can create a strong name key, this does not tell you anything about who the creator was. Adding a version number of an assembly is most useful for the producers of libraries, because it allows the users of your library to better track changes to it and to decide which of their applications will upgrade to the new version when it is released. Table 12-6 summarizes the signing switches.

Table 12-6. *Signing F# Compiler Switches*

Switch	Description
--keyfile <string>	This tells the compiler to sign the assembly with the key that it finds in the given key file.
--public-keyfile <string>	This tells the compiler to sign the assembly with a key file that contains only a public key. This is a process known as *delayed signing*; by signing with the public key, it allows many developers to work on an assembly while keeping the private key safe, limited to a privileged few. The assemblies produced will run a machine only where the CLR has been told to skip verification for the specific key. This can be achieved using the sn.exe tool.
--version <string>	This sets the version number of an assembly; the format of the string is <major version>.<minor version>.<build number>.<revision number>, resulting in a string like 2.1.53.3. If this flag is not set, then it defaults to 0.0.0.0.
--version-file <string>	This sets the version number the same way as the --version flag does, but it takes the version number for a text file. This is useful if you intended to increment your file number for each build, keeping track of it via a file under source control.

■**Note** You can find more information about the sn.exe tool, which is used to create the key files, at http://msdn2.microsoft.com/en-us/library/k5b5tt23(VS.80).aspx.

Printing the Interface Switches

The -ifile <string> flag prints the inferred interface of an assembly the same way that -i does, but it prints it to a file rather than to the console.

Adding Resources Switches

A *resource* is something that is embedded in an assembly. It can be one of several different things. It might be a string that will be displayed to the user, or it might be an image, icon, video, music file, or any sort of binary data. Resources can help make application deployment easier. For example, if your application needs to display an image to the user, embedding it in the assembly as a resource will mean that it is always there when your code needs to use it, and you do not need to worry about deploying it along with your assembly.

Resources can be divided into two groups, Win32 resources and .NET resources. Win32 resources are created using the resource compiler (http://msdn2.microsoft.com/en-us/library/aa381042.aspx), which allows the user to define resources in a C++-like language that is stored in a text file with the extension .rc. Although you can use these resource files to define lots of different types of resources, it is generally best to use them just for storing icons, because it is generally easier to store and access your resources using .NET resource files. However, you can use embedded Win32 icons to control what the resulting assembly files look like in Windows Explorer. .NET resources are either text files that have the normal .txt extension or XML files that have the extension .resx. The latter can be included on the F# command line directly or can alternatively be converted into a binary .resource format by using the .NET resources generator, resgen.exe (http://msdn2.microsoft.com/en-us/library/ccec7sz1(VS.80).aspx), or the resxc.exe tool distributed with F#. .NET resource files have a number of advantages over Win32 resource files. The .NET file format is much easier to understand and work with, and also Visual Studio provides some nice resource management tools. It is also much easier to localize your applications, making them available in different languages, with .NET resource files. Table 12-7 summarizes the resource switches.

Table 12-7. *Resource F# Compiler Switches*

Switch	Description
--win32res <string>	This specifies a file that should be embedded into the assembly as a Win32 resource.
--resource <string>	This embeds the specified .NET .resource file in the assembly. A .resource file is created using the tool resgen.exe distributed with the .NET SDK or the tool resxc.exe distributed with F#. Note that you can also give a .resx file directly as a source input to the F# compiler, and it will invoke resxc.exe for you.
--link-resource <string>	This is the same as the --resource flag but gives control over the name of the embedded resource file and whether it is public or private. The format of the string passed to this flag is <filename>,<resource name>,<public | private>. The <resource name> and <public | private> fields are optional strings such as res.resource,AssemblyResources or res.resource,AssemblyResources,private.

■**Note** You can find more information about the format of .resx files, which are used to produce managed .resource files, at http://msdn2.microsoft.com/en-us/library/ekyft91f.aspx.

Generating HTML Switches

You can use the compiler's -doc switch to place doc comments, described in Chapter 6, into an XML file. Tools such as NDoc or Microsoft's Sandcastle can then turn these into different documentation formats. Although F# ultimately produces .NET code, its type system is, practically speaking, more expressive than the .NET type system and uses .NET constructs in powerful ways; therefore, under some circumstances, these tools do not always do a good job producing documentation for F# assemblies. That is why the compiler provides a set of switches to produce HTML documents directly. Table 12-8 summarizes the HTML documentation switches.

Table 12-8. *HTML Documentation F# Compiler Switches*

Switch	Description
`--generate-html`	This flag will make the compiler output HTML documentation for the assembly.
`--html-output-directory <string>`	This flag allows you to specify the directory to which the HTML documentation is output.
`--html-css <string>`	This flag allows the user to specify a path to a CSS file that will be automatically embedded into the headers of each resulting documentation file.
`--html-namespace-file <string>`	This allows the user to specify the name of a file that the namespaces within the assembly should summarize, creating an index of all the types and modules within the assembly.
`--html-namespace-file-append`	This specifies that the summary of the namespace in an assembly should be appended to a file, rather than overwriting it. This is useful if you are aiming to produce a set of two or more libraries.

The choice about whether you should use these flags to document your code or whether you should use a tool that targets .NET is usually dictated by the type of library you produce. If you want a library that can be easily used only from F#, then you should use these command-line tools. If your aim is to produce a library that can be used easily from any language, then you'll probably get better results using Sandcastle or NDoc. You can find a more detailed explanation of why these two types of libraries exist and how you can create them in Chapter 13.

CLI Version Switches

Because the .NET Framework has multiple versions, it's highly likely that you will have multiple versions installed on your machine; typically, most users will have versions 1.1 and 2.0 installed. The story can be even more complicated because various implementations of the CLI standard exist, such as Mono and SSCLI (Rotor), meaning these versions of the CLI (or even customized builds of these versions) could also be installed.

These two flags allow you to control exactly which version of the CLI is used; this is important because there are variations in the types and methods that exist in the different versions. This means a program that will compile one version may not compile with another. It is therefore important that the programmer has control over which version is used. Table 12-9 summarizes the CLI version switches.

Table 12-9. *CLI Version F# Compiler Switches*

Switch	Description
`--cli-version <string>`	This flag controls the version number of the CLI that is used. It can take the values `1.0`, `1.1`, and `2.0` and custom build tags such as `v2.0.x86chk`. You may need to use the flag `--clr-root` to direct the compiler to the right version of the CLI; typically you need to use this when you are using a custom-built CLR.
`--clr-root <string>`	This directs the compiler to the framework directory, where the libraries for that particular version of the framework can be found.

Compilation Details Switches

The --progress flag shows the progress of the compiler to let you know a little about what is going on inside the compiler.

Statically Linking Switches

Static linking is the process where methods and types from referenced assemblies are copied and embedded directly into an assembly. This removes the dependency on the referenced assembly. Table 12-10 summarizes the linking switches.

Table 12-10. *Linking F# Compiler Switches*

Switch	Description
--standalone	This will place all the types and values from any F# library DLL, or any referenced DLL that transitively depends on an F# library DLL, into the assembly being produced. For this process to work effectively, the program being compiled must not expose any F# types on its interface; for example, this means a public function should not return a tuple because this is an F# type.
--static-link <string>	This will statically link any assembly referenced, not just F# library DLLs. The given string should be the name of the assembly without its extension, so it's MyLib, not MyLib.dll.

Using fsi.exe Effectively

The interactive version of F#, fsi.exe, allows you to execute code as you type it into the console. The following sections will look at the commands that were added to F# to aid users working with the console, cover the command-line switches it supports, and give some general tips for working with F# interactive.

fsi.exe Commands

Because of fsi.exe's dynamic nature, you need to perform some tasks with special commands that you would ordinarily use command-line switches for with the fsc.exe compiler. There are also some features, such as automatically timing program execution and quitting the compiler, that just aren't relevant to the command-line compiler. Table 12-11 describes the fsi.exe commands.

Table 12-11. *The F# Interactive Commands*

Command	Description
#r "<assembly file>";;	This allows an assembly to be referenced by fsi.exe, meaning that programs created within the console can use their types and values. It has the same meaning as the compiler's -r flag.
#I "<file path>";;	This adds a directory to the list of directories that are searched when looking for referenced assemblies. If a filename, or a relative file path, is used when using the #r command, then this list of directories will be searched for the assembly.

continued

Table 12-11. *Continued*

Command	Description
#use "\<source file>";;	This loads, compiles, and runs a single F# source file as if it had been typed into the console directly.
#load "\<source file>" ... "\<source file>";;	This loads and compiles a series of F# source files, as if they were to form a single assembly file. Commands from the sources are not executed immediately, but the types and values they contain are available in the console session.
#time;;	This toggles on and off the timing mode of F# interactive.
#types;;	This is used to control whether types are displayed.
#quit;;	This exits F# interactive; it has a short form of #q;;.

■ **Note** The Ctrl+C combination cannot be used to quit F# interactive because Ctrl+C is used to abort long-running computations.

Controlling the fsi.exe Environment

One of the most useful features of fsi.exe is its ability to print values, meaning that you can more easily see the contents of lists, arrays, or any IEnumerable collection. For example, you might want to see the assemblies that are currently in memory, and you could do that by typing the following program into fsi.exe:

```
> open System;;
```

```
> AppDomain.CurrentDomain.GetAssemblies();;
```

When entered, the program will start with the following output and carry on for many hundreds of lines:

```
val it : Assembly []
= [|mscorlib, Version=2.0.0.0, Culture=neutral, PublicKeyToken=b77a5c561934e089
    {CodeBase = "file:///C:/WINDOWS/Microsoft.NET/Framework/v2.0.50727/mscorlib.dll";
    EntryPoint = null;
...
```

So much information is shown because fsi.exe automatically prints the values of any properties it finds too. Although this can be useful sometimes, it can be undesirable because it can lead to too much information being shown, as demonstrated with the previous program. To give the user fine-grained control over what actually should be shown, fsi.exe provides the special value fsi of type InteractiveSession, which can be used to control the fsi.exe environment. The easiest way to see what you can do with the fsi values is simply to type fsi;; into the F# interactive console, which gives the following output:

```
val it : InteractiveSession
    = Microsoft.FSharp.Compiler.Interactive.InteractiveSession
        {EventLoop = Microsoft.FSharp.Compiler.Interactive.Shell+main@1283;
         FloatingPointFormat = "g10";
         FormatProvider = ;
         PrintDepth = 100;
         PrintIntercepts = null;
         PrintLength = 100;
         PrintWidth = 78;
         ShowIEnumerable = true;
         ShowProperties = true;}
```

All the properties of fsi are mutable so can be set to control the environment. In the previous example, too much information was shown because the properties of each value were printed; you could correct this by using the following command:

```
> fsi.ShowProperties <- false;;
```

So, rerunning the previous example would now result in the following output, a much more manageable amount of information:

```
val it : Assembly []
= [|mscorlib, Version=2.0.0.0, Culture=neutral, PublicKeyToken=b77a5c561934e089;
   fsi, Version=1.1.13.8, Culture=neutral, PublicKeyToken=null;
   fslib, Version=1.1.13.8, Culture=neutral, PublicKeyToken=a19089b1c74d0809;
   System, Version=2.0.0.0, Culture=neutral, PublicKeyToken=b77a5c561934e089;
   mllib, Version=1.1.13.8, Culture=neutral, PublicKeyToken=a19089b1c74d0809;
   FSharp.Compiler, Version=1.1.13.8, Culture=neutral,
       PublicKeyToken=a19089b1c74d0809;
   System.Windows.Forms, Version=2.0.0.0, Culture=neutral,
       PublicKeyToken=b77a5c561934e089;
   System.Drawing, Version=2.0.0.0, Culture=neutral,
       PublicKeyToken=b03f5f7f11d50a3a;
   FSI-ASSEMBLY, Version=0.0.0.0, Culture=neutral, PublicKeyToken=null;
   FSharp.Interactive.Settings, Version=1.1.13.8, Culture=neutral,
       PublicKeyToken=a19089b1c74d0809|]
```

Table 12-12 summarizes the members of the fsi value.

Table 12-12. *The Properties of the F# Interactive Command's* fsi *Value*

Property	Description
EventLoop	This gives access to F# interactive's event loop, which is the thread that takes care of any forms that are currently shown.
FloatingPointFormat	This is a string that controls the format in which floating-point numbers are printed.
FormatProvider	This an instance of the standard .NET interface System.IFormatProvider.
PrintDepth	This is the number of levels of inner lists or properties that will be printed.
PrintIntercepts	This is a list of functions that will be executed on items that are printed, before they are printed. This gives the user very fine-grained control over what is printed. See the functions AddPrinterTransformer and AddPrinter for more details.
PrintLength	The number of items in any collection type that will be printed.
PrintWidth	The number of characters that will be printed on each line before automatically wrapping.
ShowIEnumerable	This controls whether IEnumerable collections will be printed.
ShowProperties	This controls whether properties should be shown.
AddPrintTransformer	This adds a print transformer, which is a function that will be called on an object to transform it before it is printed. This function takes a function of type 'a -> obj; the function is executed only on types that match the type of the parameter of the function.
AddPrinter	This adds a printer, which is a function that will be called to get the output that should be printed for an object. It differs from a print transformer because the function is directly responsible for creating text that will be printed, whereas a printer transformer transforms the object to be printed into something more relevant to be printed. This function takes a function of type 'a -> string, and the function is executed only on types that match the type of the parameter of the function.

fsi.exe Command-Line Switches

Table 12-13 summarizes the command-line switches that you can use with fsi.exe.

Table 12-13. *The F# Interactive Command-Line Switches*

Switch	Description
--gui	This creates a GUI loop so that the fsi.exe user can open WinForms windows. There is a script, load-wpf.fsx, available as part of the samples in the F# distribution that shows how to replace the WinForms event loop with WPF so WPF applications will run correctly interactively. You can find more information about WPF in Chapter 8.
--no-gui	This turns off the GUI loop required for a WinForms application.

Switch	Description
`--exec`	This causes `fsi.exe` to exit after running the scripts given on the command line, which is useful for using F# to execute finished scripts.
`--no-logo`	This stops the splash text being shown on start-up.
`--no-banner`	This is the same as `--no-logo`.
`--no-readline`	This stops attempts to process individual keystrokes from the console.

Using the Source Directory Macro

The source directory macro is a #define macro with the name `__SOURCE_DIRECTORY__`
automatically set to the directory for each file being processed by `fsi.exe` and to the current
directory for a script fragment being loaded into `fsi.exe` (including fragments loaded interactively using Visual Studio). You could use this to access image files that are required for the
script and are stored in the same directory as the script.

You can use the identifier `__SOURCE_DIRECTORY__` as if it were a string inside any F# `fsi.exe`
script. The following example shows it being used to create a `DirectoryInfo` object that could
then be used to find out what files that directory contains:

```
#light
open System.IO
let dir = new DirectoryInfo(__SOURCE_DIRECTORY__);;
```

Writing NUnit Tests

NUnit is an open-source framework for creating NUnit tests for .NET code. The idea is loosely
based on JUnit, a Java open source framework. The idea has been popular amongst the .NET
development community, and a similar framework is now also included in the Team Editions
of Visual Studio 2005.

The idea behind NUnit is simple; you create a .NET class that is a suite of unit tests for
your code. Ideally each test will call the functions that you have created with a number of different parameters, asserting that each function returns the expected result. The class and class
members are then marked with attributes that show they represent a test. NUnit then provides
a framework for running your tests, either through a GUI so programs can easily see the
results of their test and drill down on any that are failing or through a command-line tool so
the test can be automated as part of a build process.

The following example shows a small library and a unit test suite associated with it. Notice
how the test suite, the class `TestCases`, is marked with the custom attribute `TestFixture`, and all
its members are marked with the custom attribute `Test`. These custom attributes are both
defined in the assembly `NUnit.Framework.dll`. This is so NUnit knows that this class is a test
suite. The assembly can contain other types that are test suites, and equally the class

TestCases can contain other members that are not directly test cases but are, for example, helper functions. It would be more natural to separate the code for the test cases from the code being tested into separate files and even separate assembles, but for simplicity I'll show them both together.

Each test case typically calls the function it is testing and then uses the Assert class to check the result. This is not true for the TestDiv02 case; here you know that calling div with a second argument of 0 will cause the function to raise an exception, so you mark the method with the ExpectedException attribute instead of making an assertion.

```
#light
open System

let add x y = x + y
let div x y = x / y

open NUnit.Framework

[<TestFixture>]
type TestCases = class
    new() = {}
    [<Test>]
    member x.TestAdd01() =
        Assert.AreEqual(3, add 1 2)
    [<Test>]
    member x.TestAdd02() =
        Assert.AreEqual(4, add 2 2)
    [<Test>]
    member x.TestDiv01() =
        Assert.AreEqual(1, div 2 2)
    [<Test; ExpectedException(type DivideByZeroException)>]
    member x.TestDiv02() =
        div 1 0 |> ignore
end
```

You could load this test case into the NUnit GUI, allowing you to call each test individually or all the tests together. Figure 12-1 shows the NUnit GUI in action, with the TestDiv01 case being run.

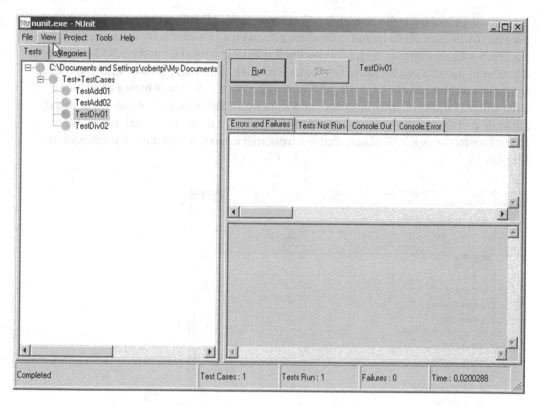

Figure 12-1. *The NUnit GUI*

Using Assembly Browsers

Because of all the metadata built into .NET assemblies, it is a fairly easy task to reflect over an assembly to determine its contents. Several class browsers are available that take advantage of this to let developers see the contents of an assembly. The .NET Framework SDK includes a tool called ildasm.exe that lets you browse the contents of an assembly and even look at the IL bytecodes that make up the method bodies. Visual Studio also ships with a .NET class browser that allows you to browse classes and view the signatures of their methods.

However, the best class browser in my opinion is Reflector, which is shown in Figure 12-2 and available for download from http://www.aisto.com/roeder/dotnet/. Reflector lets you browse a number of different assembles at once and provides an easy way to navigate between related types. It also allows you to view the method signatures, and even the code itself, in a variety of different languages. At the time of this writing, IL, C#, VB .NET, and Delphi were supported by default with the option to add others through a plug-in system; currently, a plug-in to view code in F# is in the early stages of development.

Although looking at the code that makes up an assembly is fun, there are some serious uses for the F# user. If you intend to produce a library that is suitable for use from other languages, it is likely that your target audience will consist of a lot of C# and VB .NET developers. If you want them to be able to use the library easily, it is important to know what the method signatures will look like in C# or VB .NET. Although after a while you'll have a good idea of what will play nicely in other languages and what won't, Reflector can help shortcut this by allowing you to view the method signature and check that it looks OK. You can find more about how to create a .NET library that will work well when used from other languages in Chapter 13.

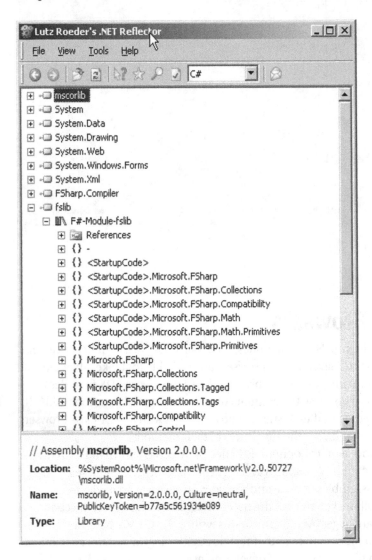

Figure 12-2. *Reflector, a class browser*

Using Debugging Tools

Visual Studio provides a graphical debugger that is easy and intuitive to use. If you have F# integration installed, then debugging is simply a matter of setting a breakpoint and pressing F5. However, not everybody uses Visual Studio; if you don't, several other debugging options are available.

The .NET Framework SDK comes with two command-line debuggers, mdbg.exe and cordbg.exe, but personally I find command-line debuggers too difficult to use. Fortunately, it also comes with a graphical debugger. The debugger is located by default in SDK\v2.0\ GuiDebug, under the install root of the SDK. This debugger, shown in Figure 12-3, is also simple to use. You generally open a source file, set breakpoints within it, and then use the Tools ➤ Attach to Process menu option to choose the program you want to debug. If the program has debugging symbols (generated by the -g option) and the debugger can find them, then your breakpoints will be hit, and you can step through the code. A good way to check whether symbols are loaded is through the Modules windows (Debug ➤ Windows ➤ Modules). This shows all the DLLs that are currently loaded into the process and whether they have debugging symbols associated with them. If no symbols are associated with a particular DLL, then you can try to load some by right-clicking and searching for the correct symbols on the disk.

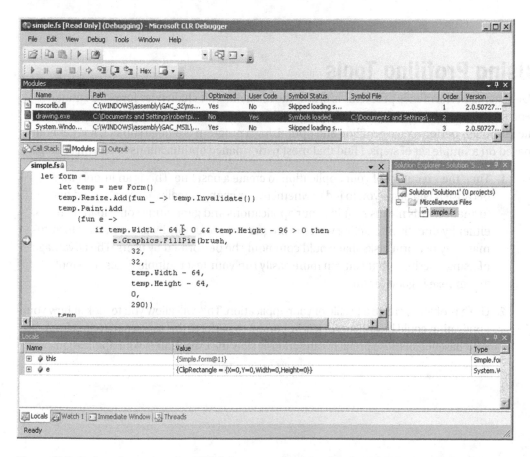

Figure 12-3. *Debugging using the GUI debugger available with the .NET Framework SDK*

Some sections of code can be difficult to debug because it is impossible to attach the debugger before they've executed. To allow these sections to be debugged more easily, .NET provides the `System.Diagnostics.Debugger` class. This has a useful method called `Launch()`. When this method is hit, it will generate a special type of exception that will cause Windows to show a dialog box offering the user the opportunity to attach a debugger. Once attached, the debugger will function normally, and you'll be able to step through the code as you'd expect.

■**Note** Another option for debugging on the Windows platform is WinDbg. This is a tool originally targeted at unmanaged code, but it has been extended to managed code, such as F# programs, via `SOS.dll`. WinDbg is quite a bit harder to use than your typical graphical debugger, but it has the advantage that it can be used to monitor software in production and thus investigate any production problems you have. You can find more information about how to set up WinDbg at `http://strangelights.com/FSharp/Foundations/default.aspx/FSharpFoundations.WinDbg`. Also, if you release your software and an exception is generated while a user is using it, the user will get the option to send an error report to Microsoft. You can register to receive these reports of your crashes at `http://msdn.microsoft.com/isv/resources/wer/`.

Using Profiling Tools

Debugging performance problems is one of the most difficult challenges for programmers. Fortunately, several tools exist to help you profile applications so you can see where problems lie. Although performance profiling and optimizing a program is a huge subject, it is generally based on a simple set of steps. I find that most performance optimizations follow these steps:

1. Time the execution of your application to create a baseline. This is an important step because it will allow you to judge whether your changes really have enhanced performance. This means running your applications and generating some load on them, either by directly interacting with the program or preferably by using a script to automatically perform tasks that would commonly be performed by users. The advantage of using a script is that you can more easily run your test multiple times. The tool `ntimer.exe` is good for this.

2. Use a profiler to create a profile of your application. This will allow you to look at how your application could be enhanced. It is important to perform this as a separate step from your baseline because profilers can seriously slow the execution of your application.

3. Form a hypothesis about what is causing your code to run slowly. This is the most difficult part of any performance investigation and generally involves a detailed analysis of the profile you generated.

4. Make changes to your code base, based on the conclusions you came to in the previous steps.

5. Rerun the baseline you took of your application. This will allow you to see whether your hypothesis is correct and whether you have enhanced the performance of your application.

6. If you have enhanced the performance of your code base, then you should commit the changes you made; otherwise, you should throw them away.

Typically, you'll repeat these steps until you are happy with the performance of your application. You'll now look at some tools that can help you profile your applications.

Ntimer

Although not actually a profiler, ntimer.exe is a nifty little tool that allows you to get the overall execution time for a program, which is useful for establishing a baseline for application performance. It's part of Windows 2003 Resource Kit Tools. Using ntimer.exe couldn't be simpler; just run ntimer followed by the name of the program you want to time and any command-line arguments you want to pass to it.

Perfmon and Performance Counters

Perfmon is a monitoring tool built into Windows, so it's readily available on every Windows machine. It allows you to examine performance counters that reveal information about almost every aspect of a machine. Select Control Panel ➤ Administrative Tools to open it (see Figure 12-4). The three counters that are loaded by default, Pages/sec (the number of pages swapped from disk each second), Avg. Disk Queue (the amount of information in the queue to be read or written to the disk), and % Processor Time (the amount of time the processor is actually in use), give you a good idea of the overall health of the machine. If any of these values are high, then the machine will probably seem slow and unresponsive.

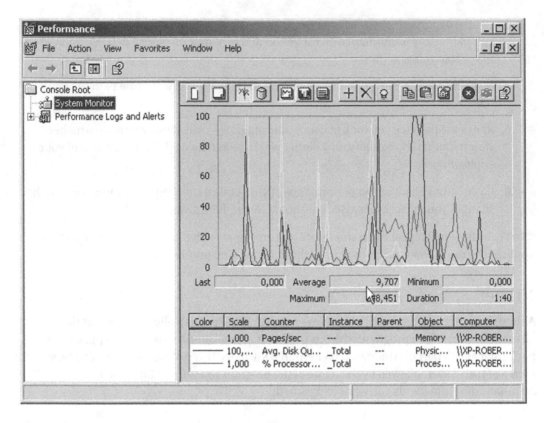

Figure 12-4. *Perfmon, a tool for monitoring performance*

If you want to examine other aspects of the machine's performance, you can add more counters by right-clicking the graph pane and choosing Add Counters. Since each piece of software installed on a machine can install its own counters, the number of counters varies from machine to machine, but a typical machine has at least 50 categories of counters (*performance objects*) and more than 100 counters. To help you navigate this maze of counters, Table 12-14 summarizes some of the most useful ones to the .NET programmer. It's important to remember when adding counters that most counters either can be the total for the machine or can be the total for a specific process; often it best to choose the one that is specific to the process you are trying to profile.

Table 12-14. *Useful Performance Counters and Their Meanings*

Performance Object	Counter	Description
Process	% Processor Time	This is the amount of processor time consumed by the process.
Process	Page Faults/sec	This is the number of page faults per second. If this number increases dramatically, this means the process does not have enough memory to operate effectively; you need to reduce your memory consumption.

Performance Object	Counter	Description
Process	Handle Count	This represents the number of files the process has open. If this number increases throughout the lifetime of an application, you are probably leaking file handles. In other words, you forgot to close a file stream by calling its `Dispose()` method.
Process	Private Bytes	This is the number of bytes used by the process that are not shared with other processes. If this figure continues to rise throughout the lifetime of an application, this typically means you have a memory leak.
.NET CLR Exceptions	# of Exceptions Thrown/sec	This measures the amount of .NET exceptions being thrown. If this number is high, then your application will perform poorly since exceptions are relatively expensive in .NET.
.NET CLR Jit	% Time in Jit	This tells how much of the CLR's time is spent just-in-time compiling the application. If this figure is too high, then you might consider using `ngen.exe` when you deploy your application. This will precompile the application, removing the need for the JIT compiler.
.NET CLR Memory	# Bytes in all Heaps	This is the amount of memory consumed by managed objects in your program. If this figure grows continually, then you might have a memory leak.
.NET CLR Memory	% Time in GC	This is the amount of time your application spends in garbage collection (GC). If this number is too high, then you might need to consider changing the way you use memory; typically you will be looking to reduce the number of objects you create. However, do not panic if the application spends a seemingly large amount of time in GC; typically, most applications, managed or unmanaged, spend a lot of time managing memory. If this figure is greater than 20 percent, then there might be cause for concern. However, only if the figure is consistently higher than 50 percent should you put some effort into trying to bring this number down.
.NET CLR Memory	Finalization Survivors	This is the number of objects that were not garbage collected because they required finalization. If this counter is high, it means that you are forgetting to call the `Dispose()` method on objects that implement the `IDisposable` interface, which will add unnecessary overhead to your application.

Although the counters in Table 12-2 will serve as a useful starting point when investigating any .NET performance problem, it's probably best not to limit yourself to these counters. It is usually best to try to find the counter that most directly relates to your problem.

■**Caution** Memory leaks can still occur in managed applications, typically when you still have references to objects that you are no longer using. For example, if your program places an object in a collection at the top level of a module and doesn't remove it when it has finished with it, then the memory associated with that object has effectively been leaked, since it's no longer in use and won't be reclaimed.

You can also use Perfmon to log performance counter values to a file. This can be useful when monitoring applications in production. Typically, you set up Perfmon to log counters you think will help you diagnose performance problems. Then if users complain about a sudden drop in application performance, you retrieve the logs to evaluate what caused the problem. Logging performance counters to a file is quite easy and intuitive; you just need to open the Performance Logs and Alerts node on the left side of Perfmon, then right-click the main pane, and finally choose New Log Settings, which allows you to choose the counters you want to log and when you want to log them. Again, for this logging to work correctly, you must start the Performance Logs and Alerts service, which is not started by default.

■**Note** You can read performance counter values within your code and create your own performance counters using the class System.Diagnostics.PerformanceCounter. You can find more information about how to do this at http://strangelights.com/FSharp/Foundations/default.aspx/ FSharpFoundations.PerfCounters.

NProf

NProf is a timing profiler. It measures the amount of time it takes to execute a method and displays this to the user as a percentage of the overall execution time. As a timing profiler, it is suitable for investigating problems where you believe a section of code is running too slowly. It is an open source utility available from http://www.sourceforge.net.

NProf, shown in Figure 12-5, is quite straightforward to use; it is the interpretation of the results that can be the tricky part. To start a profile, just select the executable you want to profile, and give its command-line arguments; alternatively, you can connect to an ASP.NET application. When you've chosen the application you want to profile, you can start profiling by pressing F5, and when the application finishes, NProf will list all the methods called during the application and statistics about them such as the number of times a method was called and the overall percentage of time spent in this method. There is also a window that allows you to see the callees of the method.

Once you've collected this information, you usually look at which methods take the highest overall percentage of execution time and consider how this can be reduced. Typically, you look at the callees to try to figure out whether any of them can be removed or replaced with calls to other methods that execute faster.

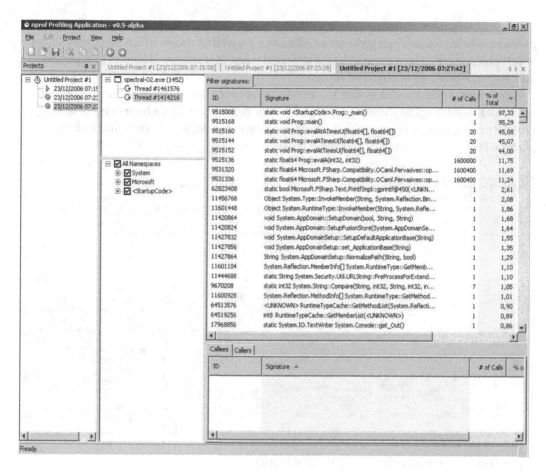

Figure 12-5. *The NProf profiler GUI*

It's also worth looking at the methods that have the highest number of calls. In this case, you typically look at the callers to try to figure out whether a method is being called when it's not necessary to call it.

Note At the time of this writing, two releases of NProf, 0.10 and 0.9.1, are available. Both are available from http://nprof.sourceforge.net. Release 0.10 runs considerably faster than 0.9.1, but the UI has been cut down to the bare minimum. I actually prefer the 0.9.1 version because I find it easier to use. I hope future releases will revert to the old UI while retaining the speed of the latest version.

CLR Profiler

Despite its name, the CLR Profiler is not a general-purpose profiler for the CLR. It is, in fact, a managed-memory profiler. If you see that your application has memory-related performance problems but have no idea what is causing them, then the CLR Profiler can help you get a better idea of what types of objects are taking up memory and when they get allocated.

The CLR Profiler can generate several different types of graph to help you visualize how memory is being used. It can generate an *allocation graph* that shows which methods created which object types, a histogram of all the allocated types, histograms of objects by ages and address, and timelines of object allocation.

Perhaps the most useful feature is the ability to generate a histogram of the types in use on the managed heap, as shown in Figure 12-6. This allows you to get a better idea of which types are consuming memory. With this knowledge, you can review the code and look for places where you can remove instances of types.

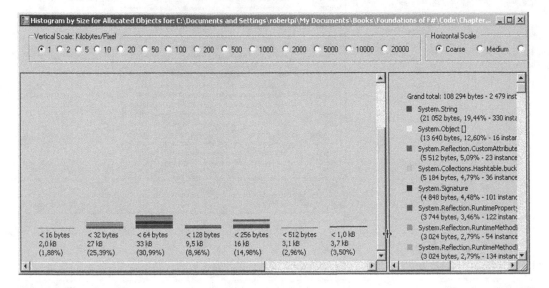

Figure 12-6. *A histogram generated by the CLR Profiler*

CLR Profiler also has a command-line mode where it logs its results to a file. This is useful because you can use it as part of an automated testing process to check that each build doesn't have any regression errors.

Note This tool is freely available for download from `http://www.microsoft.com/downloads/details.aspx?familyid=a362781c-3870-43be-8926-862b40aa0cd0&displaylang=en`.

Summary

In this chapter, you surveyed a number of development tools that help make the lives of the F# users easier. Some tools, such as `fsi.exe` (F# interactive), are very flexible, and you'll probably use them every time you code in F#; others you'll use less frequently to track down tricky bugs. In the next chapter, you'll look at compatibility and advanced interoperation.

CHAPTER 13

■ ■ ■

Compatibility and Advanced Interoperation

In this chapter, you will look at everything you need to make F# interoperate well with other languages, not just within the .NET Framework but also using unmanaged code from F# and using F# from unmanaged code.

■**Caution** Throughout this book, I have made every effort to make sure the only language you need to understand is F#. However, in this chapter, it will help if you know a little C#, C++, or .NET Common IL, although I've kept the code in these languages to the minimum necessary.

Calling F# Libraries from C#

You can create two kinds of libraries in F#: libraries that are designed to be used from F# only and libraries that are designed to be used from any .NET language. This is because F# utilizes the .NET type system in a rich and powerful way, so some types can look a little unusual to other .NET languages; however, these types will always look like they should when viewed from F#.

So, although you could use any library written in F# from any .NET language, you need to follow a few rules if you want to make the library as friendly as possible. Here is how I summarize these rules:

- Always use a signature .fsi file to hide implementation details and document the API expected by clients.

- Avoid public functions that return tuples.

- If you want to expose a function that takes another function as a value, expose the value as a delegate.

- Do not use union types in the API, but if you absolutely must use these types, add members to make them easier to use.

- Avoid returning F# lists, and use the array System.Collections.Generic.IEnumerable or System.Collections.Generic.List instead.

- When possible, place type definitions in a namespace, and place only value definitions within a module.

- Be careful with the signatures you define on classes and interfaces; a small change in the syntax can make a big difference.

I will illustrate these points with examples in the following sections.

Returning Tuples

First I'll talk about why you should avoid tuples; if you return a tuple from your function, you will force the user to reference fslib.dll. Also, the code needed to use the tuple just doesn't look that great from C#. Consider the following example where you define the function hourAndMinute that returns the hour and minute from a DateTime structure:

```
#light
module Strangelights.DemoModule
open System

let hourAndMinute (time : DateTime) = time.Hour, time.Minute
```

To call this from C#, you will need to follow the next example. Although this isn't too ugly, it would be better if the function had been split in two, one to return the hour and one to return the minute.

```
static void HourMinute()
{
    Tuple<int, int> t = DemoModule.hourAndMinute(DateTime.Now);
    Console.WriteLine("Hour {0} Minute {1}", t.Item1, t.Item2);
}
```

The results of this example, when compiled and executed, are as follows:

```
Hour 16 Minute 1
```

Exposing Functions That Take Functions As Parameters

If you want to expose functions that take other functions as parameters, the best way to do this is using delegates. Consider the following example that defines one function that exposes a function and one that exposes this as a delegate:

```
#light
open System
open System.Collections.Generic

let filterStringList f (l : List<string>) = l |> Seq.filter f
```

```
let filterStringListDelegate
    (del : Predicate<string>)
    (l : List<string>) =
        let f x = del.Invoke(x)
        new List<string>(l |> Seq.filter f)
```

Although the `filterStringList` is considerably shorter than `filterStringListDelegate`, the users of your library will appreciate the extra effort you've put in to expose the function as a delegate. When you look at using the functions from C#, it's pretty clear why. The following example demonstrates calling `filterStringList`; to call your function, you need to create a delegate and then use the `FuncConvert` class to convert it into a `FastFunc`, which is the type F# uses to represent function values. As well as being pretty annoying for the user of your library, this also requires a dependency on `fslib.dll` that the user probably didn't want.

```csharp
static void MapOne()
{
    List<string> l = new List<string>(
        new string[] { "Stefany", "Oussama",
            "Sebastien", "Frederik" });
    Converter<string, bool> pred =
        delegate (string s) { return s.StartsWith("S");};
    FastFunc<string, bool> ff =
        FuncConvert.ToFastFunc<string, bool>(pred);
    IEnumerable<string> ie =
        DemoModule.filterStringList(ff, l);
    foreach (string s in ie)
    {
        Console.WriteLine(s);
    }
}
```

The results of this example, when compiled and executed, are as follows:

```
Stefany
Sebastien
```

Now, compare and contrast this to calling the `filterStringListDelegate` function, shown in the following example. Because you used a delegate, you can use the C# anonymous delegate feature and embed the delegate directly into the function call, reducing the amount of work the library user has to do and removing the compile-time dependency on `fslib.dll`.

```csharp
static void MapTwo(
{
    List<string> l = new List<string>(
        new string[] { "Aurelie", "Fabrice",
            "Ibrahima", "Lionel" });
    List<string> l2 =
        DemoModule.filterStringListDelegate(
            delegate(string s) { return s.StartsWith("A"); }, l);
```

```
foreach (string s in l2)
{
    Console.WriteLine(s);
}
}
```

The results of this example, when compiled and executed, are as follows:

```
Aurelie
```

Using Union Types

You can use union types from C#, but because C# has no real concept of a union type, they do not look very pretty when used in C# code. In this section, you will examine how you can use them in C# and how you as a library designer can decide whether your library will expose them (though personally I recommend avoiding exposing them in cross-language scenarios).

For the first example, you will define the simple union type Quantity, which consists of two constructors, one containing an integer and the other a floating-point number. You also provide the function getRandomQuantity() to initialize a new instance of Quantity.

```
#light
open System

type Quantity =
| Discrete of int
| Continuous of float

let rand = new Random()

let getRandomQuantity() =
    match rand.Next(1) with
    | 0 -> Quantity.Discrete (rand.Next())
    | _ ->
        Quantity.Continuous
            (rand.NextDouble() * float_of_int (rand.Next()))
```

Although you provide getRandomQuantity() to create a new version of the Quantity type, the type itself provides static methods for creating new instances of the different constructors that make up the type. These static methods are available on all union types that are exposed by the assembly by default; you do not have to do anything special to get the compiler to create them. The following example shows how to use these methods from C#:

```
static void GetQuantityZero()
{
    DemoModule.Quantity d = DemoModule.Quantity.Discrete(12);
    DemoModule.Quantity c = DemoModule.Quantity.Continuous(12.0);
}
```

Now you know how to create union types from C#, so the next most important task is being able to determine the constructor to which a particular Quantity value belongs. You can do this in three ways; I cover the first two in the next two code examples, and I cover the third at the end of this section.

The first option is that you can switch on the value's Tag property. This property is just an integer, but the compiled version of the union type provides constants, always prefixed with tag_, to help you decode the meaning of the integer. So if you want to use the Tag property to find out what kind of Quantity you have, you would usually write a switch statement, as shown in the following example:

```
static void GetQuantityOne()
{
    DemoModule.Quantity q = DemoModule.getRandomQuantity();
    switch (q.Tag)
    {
        case DemoModule.Quantity.tag_Discrete:
            Console.WriteLine("Discrete value: {0}", q.Discrete1);
            break;
        case DemoModule.Quantity.tag_Continuous:
            Console.WriteLine("Continuous value: {0}", q.Continuous1);
            break;
    }
}
```

The results of this example, when compiled and executed, are as follows:

```
Discrete value: 65676
```

If you prefer, the compiled form of the union type also offers a series of methods, all prefixed with Is; this allows you to check whether a value belongs to a particular constructor within the union type. For example, on the Quantity union type, two methods, IsDiscrete() and IsContinuous(), allow you to check whether the Quantity is Discrete or Continuous. The following example demonstrates how to use them:

```
static void GetQuantityTwo()
{
    DemoModule.Quantity q = DemoModule.getRandomQuantity();
    if (q.IsDiscrete())
    {
        Console.WriteLine("Discrete value: {0}", q.Discrete1);
    }
    else if (q.IsContinuous())
    {
        Console.WriteLine("Continuous value: {0}", q.Continuous1);
    }
}
```

The results of this example, when compiled and executed, are as follows:

```
Discrete value: 2058
```

Neither option is particularly pleasing because the code required to perform the pattern matching is quite bulky. There is also a risk that the user could get it wrong and write something like the following example where they check whether a value is Discrete and then mistakenly use the Continuous1 property. This would lead to a NullReferenceException being thrown.

```
DemoModule.EasyQuantity q = DemoModule.getRandomEasyQuantity();
if (q.IsDiscrete())
{
    Console.WriteLine("Discrete value: {0}", q.Continuous1);
}
```

To give your libraries' users some protection against this, it is a good idea to add members to union types that perform the pattern matching for them. The following example revises the Quantity type to produce EasyQuantity, adding two members to transform the type into an integer or a floating-point number:

```
#light
open System

let rand = new Random()

type EasyQuantity =
| Discrete of int
| Continuous of float
    with
        member x.ToFloat() =
            match x with
            | Discrete x -> float_of_int x
            | Continuous x -> x
        member x.ToInt() =
            match x with
            | Discrete x -> x
            | Continuous x -> int_of_float x
    end

let getRandomEasyQuantity() =
    match rand.Next(1) with
    | 0 -> EasyQuantity.Discrete (rand.Next())
    | _ ->
        EasyQuantity.Continuous
            (rand.NextDouble() * float_of_int (rand.Next()))
```

This will allow the user of the library to transform the value into either an integer or a floating-point without having to worry about pattern matching, as shown in the following example:

```
static void GetQuantityThree()
{
    DemoModule.EasyQuantity q = DemoModule.getRandomEasyQuantity();
    Console.WriteLine("Value as a float: {0}", q.ToFloat());
}
```

Using F# Lists

It is entirely possible to use F# lists from C#, but I recommend avoiding this since a little work on
your part will make things seem more natural for C# programmers. For example, it is simple to
convert a list to an array using the List.to_array function, to a System.Collections.Generic.List
using the List.to_ResizeArray function, or to a System.Collections.Generic.IEnumerable using
the List.to_seq function. These types are generally a bit easier for C# programmers to work with,
especially System.Array and System.Collections.Generic.List, because these provide a lot more
member methods. You can do the conversion directly before the list is returned to the calling
client, making it entirely feasible to use the F# list type inside your F# code.

If you need to return an F# list directly, you can do so, as shown in the following example:

```
let getList() =
    [1; 2; 3]
```

To use this list in C#, you typically use a foreach loop:

```
static void GetList()
{
    Microsoft.FSharp.Collections.List<int> l = DemoModule.getList();
    foreach (int i in l)
    {
        Console.WriteLine(i);
    }
}
```

The results of this example, when compiled and executed, are as follows:

```
1
2
3
```

Defining Types in a Namespace

If you are defining types that will be used from other .NET languages, then you should place
them inside a namespace rather than inside a module. This is because modules are compiled
into what C# and other .NET languages consider to be a class, and any types defined within
the module become inner classes of that type. Although this does not present a huge problem
to C# users, the C# client code does look cleaner if a namespace is used rather than a module.
This is because in C# you can open namespaces using only the using statement, so if a type is
inside a module, it must always be prefixed with the module name when used from C#.

I'll now show you an example of doing this. The following example defines the class TheClass, which is defined inside a namespace. You also want to provide some functions that go with this class; these can't be placed directly inside a namespace because values cannot be defined inside a namespace. In this case, you define a module with a related name TheModule to hold the function values.

```
#light
namespace Strangelights
open System.Collections.Generic

type TheClass = class
    val mutable TheField : int
    new(i) = { TheField = i }
    member x.Increment() =
        x.TheField <- x.TheField + 1
    member x.Decrement() =
        x.TheField <- x.TheField - 1
end

module TheModule = begin
    let incList (l : List<TheClass>) =
        l |> Seq.iter (fun c -> c.Increment())
    let decList (l : List<TheClass>) =
        l |> Seq.iter (fun c -> c.Decrement())
end
```

Using the TheClass class in C# is now straightforward because you do not have to provide a prefix, and you can also get access to the related functions in TheModule easily:

```
static void UseTheClass()
{
    List<TheClass> l = new List<TheClass>();
    l.Add(new TheClass(5));
    l.Add(new TheClass(6));
    l.Add(new TheClass(7));
    TheModule.incList(l);
    foreach (TheClass c in l)
    {
        Console.WriteLine(c.TheField);
    }
}
```

Defining Classes and Interfaces

In F# there are two ways you can define parameters for functions and members of classes: the "curried" style where members can be partially applied and the "tuple" style where all members must be given at once. When defining classes, your C# clients will find it easier to use your classes if you use the tuple style.

Consider the following example in which you define a class in F#. Here one member has been defined in the curried style, called CurriedStyle, and the other has been defined in the tuple style, called TupleStyle.

```
type DemoClass = class
    val Z : int
    new(z) = { Z = z}
    member this.CurriedStyle x y = x + y + this.Z
    member this.TupleStyle (x, y) = x + y + this.Z
end
```

When viewed from C#, the member CurriedStyle has the following signature:

```
public FastFunc<int, int> CurriedStyle(int x)
```

whereas the TupleStyle will have the following signature:

```
public int TupleStyle(int x, int y);
```

So if you wanted to use both methods from C#, you would end up with code that looked as follows:

```
static void UseDemoClass()
{
    DemoClass c = new DemoClass(3);
    FastFunc<int, int> ff = c.CurriedStyle(4);
    int result = ff.Invoke(5);
    Console.WriteLine("Curried Style Result {0}", result);
    result = c.TupleStyle(4, 5);
    Console.WriteLine("Tuple Style Result {0}", result);
}
```

It is clear from this sample that users of your library will be much happier if you use the tuple style for the public members of your classes.

Specifying abstract members in interfaces and classes is slightly more complicated because you have a few more options. The following example demonstrates this:

```
type IDemoInterface = interface
    abstract CurriedStyle : int -> int -> int
    abstract OneArgStyle : (int * int) -> int
    abstract MultiArgStyle : int * int -> int
    abstract NamedArgStyle : x : int * y : int -> int
end
```

Note that the only difference between OneArgStyle and MultiArgStyle is that the latter is not surrounded by parentheses. This small difference in the F# definition has a big effect on the signature as seen from C#. With the former, you see the signature as this:

```
int OneArgStyle(Tuple<int, int>);
```

With the latter, you see the following signature:

```
int MultiArgStyle(int, int);
```

The latter is a good bit friendlier for the C# user. However, you can take it bit further and add names to each of your parameters. This won't change the signature the C# user will use when implementing the method, but it will change the names they see when using Visual Studio tools to implement the interface; furthermore, some other .NET languages treat argument names as significant. This may sound like a small difference, but it will make implementing your interface a lot easier, because the implementer will have a much better idea of what the parameters of the method actually mean.

The following example shows the C# code for implementing the interface IDemoInterface defined in the previous example. It makes it clear that C# users will be happier with interfaces containing methods specified using either MultiArgStyle or NamedArgStyle.

```
class DemoImplementation : IDemoInterface
{
    public FastFunc<int, int> CurriedStyle(int x)
    {
        Converter<int, int> d =
            delegate (int y) {return x + y;};
        return FuncConvert.ToFastFunc(d);
    }

    public int OneArgStyle(Tuple<int, int> t)
    {
        return t.Item1 + t.Item2;
    }

    public int MultiArgStyle(int x, int y)
    {
        return x + y;
    }

    public int NamedArgStyle(int x, int y)
    {
        return x + y;
    }
}
```

Using F# with the .NET Framework Versions 1 and 1.1

Using F# with the .NET Framework versions 1 and 1.1 is surprisingly straightforward, because all you need to do is use the compiler switch --cli-version, discussed in more detail in Chapter 12. However, there are some small differences in both the F# code that you can write and the resulting assembly that you need to be aware of, so if at all possible, I recommend using the .NET Framework 2.

Readers who are familiar with the differences between the .NET Framework versions 1, 1.1, and 2 may have expected that any code that uses type parameterization, or *generics* as it more commonly known, would not compile using the .NET Framework versions 1 and 1.1. However, this is not the case, because these differences can be compiled away by the F# compiler.

Consider the following simple example:

```
let doNothing x = x
```

The function doNothing is generic because the parameters are of any type, and you can guarantee that the returned value will be the same as the input parameter. If you check the function's signature, using the Visual Studio tooltips or the compiler's -i switch, you see the following:

```
val doNothing : 'a -> 'a
```

meaning that doNothing takes a parameter of type 'a and returns a value of type 'a where 'a is a type parameter. Unsurprisingly, in the .NET Framework 2, this compiles down to have the following signature in C#:

```
public static T doNothing<T>(T x)
```

However, when compiled under the .NET Framework version 1 or 1.1, the function will have the following signature:

```
public static object doNothing(object x)
```

This means if you are creating a library for use with the .NET Framework version 1 or 1.1, the users of your functions from other .NET languages will have to cast the object returned to its original type. They would not have to do this if using a version of the library compiled for the .NET Framework 2.

The other problem area is arrays, because these were pseudogeneric in the .NET Framework versions 1 and 1.1 and fully generic in the .NET Framework 2. For those of you not familiar with the .NET Framework version 1 or 1.1, *pseudogeneric* means that arrays in the .NET Framework version 1 or 1.1 could have a type parameter, but nothing else could. For example, the method GetFiles from the System.IO.Directory class has the following signature, meaning that it returns an array of type string:

```
public static string[] GetFiles(string path);
```

These pseudogeneric arrays are trouble for F# because its array type is fully generic. Effectively this means that if you are using "pure F#" (that is, not calling methods from libraries written in C#), then it is OK to use the F# Array module when using the .NET Framework version 1 or 1.1. You will notice that arrays will always appear as object arrays (Object[]) when viewed from other .NET languages, but they seamlessly keep their types when used from F# code. When calling methods that accept arrays, or return arrays, like the aforementioned GetFiles method, then you will need to use the CompatArray module located in the Microsoft.FSharp.Compatibility namespace.

This will all be clearer when you see an example. Consider the following F# code that creates an array and then maps it to create a new array:

```
#light
let ones = Array.create 1 3
let twos = ones |> Array.map (fun x -> x + 1)
```

This code will compile under the .NET Framework versions 1, 1.1, and 2; however, the signatures of these values when viewed from other .NET languages would be as follows:

```
public static object[] ones { get; }
public static object[] twos { get; }
```

If you are designing a library and interoperation is important to you, you could replace the calls to the array module with calls to the CompatArray module, and you get the signatures typed using pseudogeneric arrays, just as your clients from other .NET code would probably want and expect. This means under the .NET Framework versions 1 and 1.1, you should use the following code:

```
#light
open Microsoft.FSharp.Compatibility
let ones = CompatArray.create 1 3
let twos = ones |> CompatArray.map (fun x -> x + 1)
```

This would mean that your module would have the signatures as shown here when viewed from other .NET languages:

```
public static int[] ones { get; }
public static int[] twos { get; }
```

Similarly, when using the .NET Framework versions 1 and 1.1, calls to methods from assemblies not written in F#, including all assemblies in the BCL, will generally use pseudogeneric arrays. This means when using the .NET Framework versions 1 and 1.1, it's important to use the CompatArray module and not the Array module. For example, the following will compile without a problem in the .NET Framework 2, but in both 1 and 1.1, it will not compile.

```
#light
open System.IO
open Microsoft.FSharp.Compatibility
let paths = Directory.GetFiles(@"c:\")
let files = paths |> Array.map (fun path -> new FileInfo(path))
```

When compiled using the `--cli-version 1.1` switch, it will give the following error:

```
prog.fs(5,13): error: FS0001: Type mismatch. Expecting a
        string [] -> 'c
but given a
        'a array -> 'b array.
The type string [] does not match the type 'a array
```

This is easily corrected by replacing functions from the Array module with their equivalents in ComptArray, as shown in the following example:

```
#light
open System.IO
open Microsoft.FSharp.Compatibility
let paths = Directory.GetFiles(@"c:\")
let files = paths |> CompatArray.map (fun path -> new FileInfo(path))
```

Calling Using COM Objects

Most programmers who work with the Windows platform will be familiar with the Component Object Model (COM). To a certain extent the .NET Framework was meant to replace COM, but the system remains popular and is likely to be with us for some time. Many of the APIs in Windows are exposed as COM objects, and although more and more now have managed equivalents within the .NET Framework, there are still some without managed equivalents. Also, there are still some vendors that sell software that exposes its APIs via COM.

The .NET Framework was designed to interoperate well with COM, and calling COM components is generally quite straightforward. Calling COM components is always done through a managed wrapper that takes care of calling the unmanaged code for you. You can produce these wrappers using a tool called TlbImp.exe, the Type Library Importer, that ships with the .NET SDK.

Note You can find more information about the TlbImp.exe tool at the following site: http://msdn2.microsoft.com/en-us/library/tt0cf3sx(VS.80).aspx.

However, despite the existence of TlbImp.exe, if you find yourself in a situation where you need to use a COM component, first check whether the vendor provides a managed wrapper for it. This is quite common; for example, if you want to automatically manipulate programs from Microsoft Office 2003, then you need to use the COM APIs they provide, but there is no need to use TlbImp.exe to create a new wrapper, because Office already ships a series of managed wrappers contained in assemblies prefixed with Microsoft.Office.Interop.

However, sometimes it is necessary to use TlbImp.exe directly. Fortunately, this is very straightforward; normally all that is necessary is to pass TlbImp.exe the location of the .dll that contains the COM component, and the managed wrapper will be placed in the current directory. So if you wanted to create a managed wrapper for the Microsoft Speech API, you would use the following command line:

```
tlbimp "C:\Program Files\Common Files\Microsoft Shared\Speech\sapi.dll"
```

Note I find two command-line switches to be useful with TlbImp.exe. These are /out:, which controls the name and location of the resulting manage wrapper, and /keyfile:, which can provide a key to sign the output assembly.

The resulting .dll is a .NET assembly and can be used just like any .NET assembly—by referencing it via the fsc.exe command-line switch -r. A useful side effect of this is if the API is not well documented, you can use an assembly browser, such as Reflector discussed in Chapter 12, to find out more about the structure of the API.

After that, the worst thing I can say about using managed wrappers is you might find the structure of these assemblies a little unusual since the COM model dictates structure, and therefore they do not share the same naming conversions as most .NET assemblies. You will notice that all classes in the assembly are post-fixed with the word Class, and each one is provided with a separate interface; this is just a requirement of COM objects. The following example shows the wrapper for the Microsoft Speech API that you created in the previous example being used:

```
#light
open SpeechLib

let voice = new SpVoiceClass()
voice.Speak("Hello world", SpeechVoiceSpeakFlags.SVSFDefault)
```

Note More managed .NET APIs are becoming available all the time; the latest version of Office, Office 2007, ships with a fully managed .NET API, and Windows Vista includes a managed version of the Speech API. Although the basic calling of COM components is straightforward if you do a lot of COM-based programming in F#, you will soon find there are subtleties. You can find more information about COM programming at http://strangelights.com/FSharp/Foundations/default.aspx/FSharpFoundations.COM.

Using P/Invoke

P/Invoke, or *platform invoke* to give its full name, is used to call unmanaged flat APIs implemented in DLLs and is called using the C or C++ calling convention. The most famous example of this is the Win32 API, a vast library that exposes all the functionality built into Windows.

To call a flat unmanaged API, you must first define the function you want to call; you can do this in two parts. First you use the DllImport attribute from the System.Runtime.InteropServices namespace, which allows you to define which .dll contains the function you want to import, along with some other optional attributes. Then, you use the keyword extern, followed by the signature of the function to be called in the C style, meaning you give the return type, the F# type, the name of the function, and finally the types and names of the parameters surrounded by parentheses. The resulting function can then be called as if it were an external .NET method.

The following example shows how to import the Windows function MessageBeep and then call it:

```
#light
open System.Runtime.InteropServices

[<DllImport("User32.dll")>]
extern bool MessageBeep(uint32 beepType)

MessageBeep(0ul) |> ignore
```

The following code shows how to use P/Invoke when the target function expects a pointer. You need to note several points about setting up the pointer. When defining the function, you need to put an asterisk (*) after the type name to show that you are passing a pointer. You need to define a mutable identifier before the function call to represent the area of memory that is pointed to; this may not be global, in the top level, but it must be part of a function definition. This is why you define the function main, so the identifier status can be part of the definition of this. Finally, you must use the address of operator (&&) to ensure the pointer is passed to the function rather than the value itself.

```
#light
open System.Runtime.InteropServices

[<DllImport("Advapi32.dll")>]
extern bool FileEncryptionStatus(string filename, uint32* status)

let main() =
    let mutable status = 0ul
    FileEncryptionStatus(@"C:\test.txt", && status) |> ignore
    print_any status

main()
```

The results of this example, when compiled and executed (assuming you have a file at the root of your C: drive called test.txt that is encrypted), are as follows:

```
1ul
```

> **Note** P/Invoke can be one of the trickiest things you can do in .NET because of the need to marshal data between the managed and unmanaged worlds, often requiring you to define structures that represent the data to be marshaled. You can find more information about marshaling and other aspects of P/Invoke at `http://strangelights.com/FSharp/Foundations/default.aspx/FSharpFoundations.PInvoke`.

The `DllImport` attribute has some useful functions that you can set to control how the unmanaged function is called; I summarize them in Table 13-1.

Table 13-1. *Useful Attributes on the* `DllImport` *Attribute*

Attribute Name	Description
CharSet	This defines the character set to be used when marshaling string data; it can be `CharSet.Auto`, `CharSet.Ansi`, or `CharSet.Unicode`.
EntryPoint	This allows you to set the name of the function to be called. If no name is given, then it defaults to the name of the function as defined after the extern keyword.
SetLastError	This is a Boolean value that allows you to specify whether any error that occurs should be marshaled and therefore available by calling the `Marshell.GetLastWin32Error()` method.

> **Note** As with COM components, the number of flat unmanaged APIs that have no .NET equivalent is decreasing all the time; always check whether a managed equivalent of the function you are calling is available, which will generally save you lots of time.

Using Inline IL

Inline IL allows you to define your function's body directly in intermediate language (IL), the language into which F# is compiled. This was mainly added to the language to implement certain low operators and functions such as addition and box and not. It is rare that you will need to use this feature because the F# libraries `fslib.dll` and `mllib.dll` already expose all of the functionality built into IL that you are likely to need. However, for those rare occasions where you need to do something that you can't do in F# but you can in IL, it's nice to know you have the option of inline IL.

Caution To use inline IL effectively, you really need to have a good understanding of IL. Some of the passages in this section will not make sense if you do not have at least a basic knowledge of IL. You can find resources to help you learn IL at `http://strangelights.com/FSharp/Foundations/default.aspx/FSharpFoundations.IL`.

Using inline IL is simple; you just place the IL instructions you would like between parentheses with pound signs, as in (# #). The IL instructions are placed inside a string and use the standard notation that can be compiled with `ilasm.exe`. This must be correctly formed IL, or you will get a compiler error. You can then pass parameters to your IL instruction; they are pushed onto the IL evaluation stack. You must also use the standard colon notation to tell the compiler what the return type will be; this is placed inside the parentheses. You will also need to be explicit about the types of the parameters since the compiler has no way of inferring their types.

You'll now look at an example of using inline IL. Imagine for whatever reason that you do not want to use the add and subtract operators defined in the F# base library `fslib.dll`; say you want to replace them with your own functions. So, you define two functions, add and sub, whose bodies are defined using IL:

```
#light
let add (x:int) (y:int) = (# "add" x y : int #)
let sub (x:int) (y:int) = (# "sub" x y : int #)

let x = add 1 1
let y = sub 4 2

printf "x: %i y: %i" x y
```

The results of this example, when compiled and executed, are as follows:

```
x: 2 y: 2
```

The programmer should be careful when using this technique because it is trivial to write a program that does not make any sense, and the compiler is unable to warn you about this. Consider the following program where you revise your previous example to replace the "add" instruction with a "ret" instruction, which means "return a value" and makes no sense in this context. This example will compile without error or warning; on execution, you will get an error.

```
#light
let add (x:int) (y:int) = (# "ret" x y : int #)

let x = add 1 1
```

The results of this example, when compiled and executed, are as follows:

```
Unhandled Exception: System.InvalidProgramException: Common Language Runtime
detected an invalid program.
   at Error.add(Int32 x, Int32 y)
```

Note One tool distributed with .NET SDK can help you detect these kinds of errors. The tool is called `peverify.exe`, and you can find more information about `peverify.exe` at `http://msdn2.microsoft.com/en-us/library/62bwd2yd(vs.80).aspx`.

Using F# from Native Code via COM

Although it is more likely that you will want to call native code from F# code, sometimes you might want to call F# library functions from native code. For example, suppose you have a large application written in C++, and perhaps you are happy for the user interface to remain in C++ but want to migrate some logic that performs complicated mathematical calculations to F# for easier maintenance. In this case, you would want to call F# from native code. The easiest way to do this is to use the tools provided with .NET to create a COM wrapper for your F# assembly; you can then use the COM runtime to call the F# functions from C++.

Caution Using COM in C++ is a huge topic, and it is advisable that any programmer wanting to call F# in this way is already experienced in C++/COM. If you need more information about this topic, you can find some starting points at `http://strangelights.com/FSharp/Foundations/default.aspx/FSharpFoundations.CPPCOM`.

To expose functions through COM, you need to develop them in a certain way. First you must define an interface that will specify the contract for your functions, the members of the interface must be written using named arguments (see the section "Calling F# Libraries from C#" earlier in the chapter), and the interface itself must be marked with the `System.Runtime.InteropServices.Guid` attribute. Then you must provide a class that implements the interface; this too must be marked with the `System.Runtime.InteropServices.Guid` attribute and also `System.Runtime.InteropServices.ClassInterface`, and you should always pass the `ClassInterfaceType.None` enumeration member to the `ClassInterface` attribute constructor to say that no interface should be automatically generated.

I'll now show an example of doing this; suppose you want to expose two functions called Add and Sub to your unmanaged client. So, create an interface IMath in the namespace Strangelights, and then create a class Math to implement this interface. You then need to ensure that both the class and the interface are marked with the appropriate attributes. The resulting code is as follows:

```
namespace Strangelights
open System
open System.Runtime.InteropServices


[<Guid("6180B9DF-2BA7-4a9f-8B67-AD43D4EE0563")>]
type IMath = interface
    abstract Add : x: int * y: int -> int
    abstract Sub : x: int * y: int -> int
end


[<Guid("B040B134-734B-4a57-8B46-9090B41F0D62");
ClassInterface(ClassInterfaceType.None)>]
type Math = class
    new () = {}
    interface IMath with
        member this.Add(x, y) = x + y
        member this.Sub(x, y) = x - y
    end
end
```

The functions Add and Sub are of course simple, so there is no problem implementing them directly in the body of the Math class. If you needed to break them down into other helper functions outside the class, then this would not have been a problem; it is fine to implement your class members in any way you see fit. You simply need to provide the interface and the class so the COM runtime has an entry point into your code.

Now comes arguably the most complicated part of the process—registering the assembly so the COM runtime can find it. To do this, you need to use a tool called RegAsm.exe. Suppose you compiled the previous sample code into a .NET .dll called ComLibrary.dll; then you would need to call RegAsm.exe twice using the following command lines:

```
regasm comlibrary.dll /tlb:comlibrary.tlb
regasm comlibrary.dll
```

The first time is to create a type library file, a .tlb file, which you can use in your C++ project to develop against. The second registers the assembly itself so the COM runtime can find it. You will also need to perform these two steps on any machine to which you deploy your assembly.

The C++ to call the Add function appears after the next list; the development environment and how you set up the C++ compiler will also play a large part in getting this code to compile. In this case, I created a Visual Studio project, choosing a console application template, and activated ATL. Notice the following about this source code:

- The #import command tells the compiler to import your type library; you may need to use the full path to its location. The compiler will also automatically generate a header file, in this case comlibrary.tlh, located in the debug or release directory. This is useful because it lets you know the functions and identifiers that are available as a result of your type library.

- You then need to initialize the COM runtime; you do this by calling the CoInitialize function.

- You then need to declare a pointer to the IMath interface you created; you do this via the code comlibrary::IMathPtr pDotNetCOMPtr;. Note how the namespace comes from the library name rather than the .NET namespace.

- Next you need to create an instance of your Math class; you achieve this by calling the CreateInstance, method passing it the GUID of the Math class. Fortunately, there is a constant defined for this purpose.

- If this was successful, you can call the Add function; note how the result of the function is actually an HRESULT, a value that will tell you whether the call was successful. The actual result of the function is passed out via an out parameter.

Here's the code:

```cpp
#include "stdafx.h"
#import "ComLibrary.tlb" named_guids raw_interfaces_only

int _tmain(int argc, _TCHAR* argv[])
{
    CoInitialize(NULL);
    comlibrary::IMathPtr pDotNetCOMPtr;

    HRESULT hRes = pDotNetCOMPtr.CreateInstance(comlibrary::CLSID_Math);
    if (hRes == S_OK)
    {
        long res = 0L;
        hRes = pDotNetCOMPtr->Add(1, 2, &res);
        if (hRes == S_OK)
        {
            printf("The result was: %ld", res);
        }

        pDotNetCOMPtr.Release();
    }

    CoUninitialize ();
    return 0;
}
```

The results of this example, when compiled and executed, are as follows:

```
The result was: 3
```

When you execute the resulting executable, you must ensure that `ComLibrary.dll` is in the same directory as the executable, or the COM runtime will not be able to find it. If you intend that the library be used by several clients, then I strongly recommend that you sign the assembly and place it in the GAC; this will allow all clients to be able to find it without having to keep a copy in the directory with them.

■**Note** Another option for calling F# code from unmanaged code is by the custom hosting of the CLR. This is even more complicated than calling F# methods via COM; however, it can give you fine-grained control over the behavior of the CLR. If you want to investigate this option, please see `http://strangelights.com/FSharp/Foundations/default.aspx/FSharpFoundations.CLRHosting`.

Summary

In this chapter, you saw some advanced techniques in F# for compatibility and interoperation. Although these techniques are definitely some of the most difficult to master, they also add a huge degree of flexibility to your F# programming.

Index

You Need the Companion eBook

Your purchase of this book entitles you to buy the companion PDF-version eBook for only $10. Take the weightless companion with you anywhere.

We believe this Apress title will prove so indispensable that you'll want to carry it with you everywhere, which is why we are offering the companion eBook (in PDF format) for $10 to customers who purchase this book now. Convenient and fully searchable, the PDF version of any content-rich, page-heavy Apress book makes a valuable addition to your programming library. You can easily find and copy code—or perform examples by quickly toggling between instructions and the application. Even simultaneously tackling a donut, diet soda, and complex code becomes simplified with hands-free eBooks!

Once you purchase your book, getting the $10 companion eBook is simple:

❶ Visit **www.apress.com/promo/tendollars/**.

❷ Complete a basic registration form to receive a randomly generated question about this title.

❸ Answer the question correctly in 60 seconds, and you will receive a promotional code to redeem for the $10.00 eBook.

2855 Telegraph Avenue • Suite 600 • Berkeley, CA 94705

eBookshop

THE EXPERT'S VOICE™

Offer valid through 11/28/07.

Printed in the United States
By Bookmasters